ANCIENT
America

Praise for *Ancient America*

"The magnificent archaeological sites left by America's native peoples are wondrous enough without the myths and exaggerations that often contaminate popular discussions about them. There is no one better than archaeologist and writer Kenneth Feder at debunking the misconceptions and stereotypes and then showing in reader-friendly prose what's real and true. The fifty sites in this welcome and lively new book reveal an extraordinary legacy of intelligent and capable ancient peoples and cultures. Let Feder be your personable guide and host."

—**Kendrick Frazier, editor of *Skeptical Inquirer*,
author of *People of Chaco: A Canyon and Its Culture***

"Kenneth Feder is one of those rare scholars who can make seemingly esoteric concepts accessible and enjoyable to a general audience. And now he has written a travel guide, but it is unlike any I've read—not just a list of places to visit but a guided tour of ancient America and its peoples that is both educational and fun. Think 'Carl Sagan meets Bill Bryson.'"

—**Michael Alan Park, Central Connecticut State University**

"*Ancient America* takes readers on a journey to prehistoric American archaeological sites, some well-known and others little-known, each significant in its own way. Feder's style is sometimes whimsical but always informative, and he relates his own personal experiences at each site. He encourages the reader to add these sites to their travels and to learn more about the amazing accomplishments of the diverse cultures that once inhabited ancient America."

—**William R. Iseminger, Cahokia Mounds State Historic Site**

"Feder leads us on a cross-country virtual tour of some of the most accessible archaeological sites in the United States spanning 13,000 years and invites us to see them for ourselves to appreciate the diversity, adaptability, and creativity of America's original inhabitants. Start with this book as your guide and you will experience all of that."

—**Andrew Sawyer, SunWatch Indian Village/Archaeological Park**

ANCIENT
America

FIFTY ARCHAEOLOGICAL SITES TO SEE FOR YOURSELF

KENNETH L. FEDER

ROWMAN & LITTLEFIELD
Lanham • Boulder • New York • London

This one is for Jenn
How about fifty more sites?

Published by Rowman & Littlefield
An imprint of The Rowman & Littlefield Publishing Group, Inc.
4501 Forbes Boulevard, Suite 200, Lanham, Maryland 20706
www.rowman.com

6 Tinworth Street, London SE11 5AL, United Kingdom

British Library Cataloguing in Publication Information Available

Library of Congress Cataloging-in-Publication Data
Names: Feder, Kenneth L., author.
Title: Ancient America : fifty archaeological sites to see for yourself / Kenneth L. Feder.
Description: Lanham, Maryland : Rowman & Littlefield, a wholly owned subsidiary of The Rowman & Littlefield Publishing Group, 2017. | Includes bibliographical references and index.
Identifiers: LCCN 2016038670 (print) | LCCN 2016042249 (ebook) | ISBN 9781442263123 (cloth : alk. paper) | ISBN 9781442263130 (electronic) | ISBN 9781538127315 (paperback)
Subjects: LCSH: Indians of North America—Antiquities—Guidebooks. | United States—Antiquities—Guidebooks.
Classification: LCC E77.9 .F43 2017 (print) | LCC E77.9 (ebook) | DDC 973.1—dc23
LC record available at https://lccn.loc.gov/2016038670

Printed in the United States of America

Contents

Cliff Dwellings, Great Houses, and Stone Towers...................101

Rock Art 145

Acknowledgments

I guess the Grateful Dead had it right when they sang: "Lately it occurs to me, what a long strange trip it's been." That's been true for me both literally and figuratively. Long and strange, to be sure. But more important, it's also been exciting and glorious. And now there's a book. I couldn't be happier.

As you are probably aware, books always are collaborative efforts. A large group of people contribute, though their names don't end up on the front cover. But without the help of all of those folks, this book would never have come to life.

First, many colleagues helped by actually bringing me to some of the sites enshrined on my list of fifty. Brad Lepper of the Ohio Historical Society was instrumental as my archaeological tour guide to the sites in Ohio. Brad is the best colleague anyone could hope for; on this and many other projects, he has been an amazing source of information, assistance, and inspiration. Brad also hooked me up with Andy Sawyer at SunWatch Indian Village, and the folks there simply could not have been nicer; Sun-Watch is a great place to learn about America's past. Also in Ohio, thanks to Katie Rippl for guiding me through Fort Ancient and to Keith Bengston at Serpent Mound. I also must thank Rick Perkins, my personal guide at Mound City. Bill Iseminger at Cahokia is a brilliant archaeologist, as well as a talented writer and artist. He has always been extremely generous to me, and this project has been no exception.

Don't hate me, but I was able to avoid the red tape usually required to visit Little Petroglyph Canyon in California. I have Naval Air Weapons Station base archaeologist Mike Baskerville to thank for that. I got the personal tour, and I can't thank Mike enough.

Desi and Ken Ekstein were helpful and generous with directions to additional sites and also for Desi's spectacular drone photographs of the Blythe Intaglios. Our meeting at Blythe was pure serendipity, and I am so grateful for what they contributed. Thanks also are due to Lyn Hood and Steve Horton, who were incredibly helpful at the Three Rivers Petroglyph Site. They have served as the site's "recreation hosts" (yup, that's their official title), living at the site in their recreational vehicle. What a cool job! I'm jealous.

No list of acknowledgments would be complete without expressing my sincerest thanks to Harris Hardy for his moving and heartfelt discourse on the significance of Canyon de Chelly. For Harris the canyon isn't a site, it's home; I can't imagine a better way of learning about the place than having him as my guide. Greg Lameman was our river guide on the San Juan from Bluff to Medicine Hat. He went out of his way to bring us to the rock art. And thanks to Greg, I didn't fall out of the raft and drown at "8-Foot Rapids." I genuinely appreciate that!

Though the Volcanic Table Lands sites that BLM archaeologist Greg Haverstock introduced me to in Southern California are not among my fifty, they certainly form the nucleus of "fifty more sites you can see for yourself." He went above and beyond, taking the better part of a day to drive us around. Of course he should thank me for giving him an excuse to get out of the office on a beautiful June day. You're welcome, Greg! Greg also introduced me to rock art researcher David Lee, and I am grateful to him for our extremely interesting conversation about the meaning of the art and the importance of its protection and preservation. David gave me a lot to think about. Tom Sanders at the Jefferson Petroglyph Site in Minnesota devoted several hours of his time to guide me through that rock art site, even though it was seasonally closed when I was there. It was fascinating to visit a site so different from those I had encountered in the Southwest.

Susan Pease is the Dean of Arts and Sciences at my institution, Central Connecticut University. She has been remarkably supportive of all my various projects over the years, including the work that led to this book. My deepest thanks, Susan; your help has been greatly appreciated. (Okay, now that I've given you a shout-out, can I have some more funding for travel? Pretty please.)

As you read this book, you'll figure out that my fifty sites project was a quintessential "labor of love." And how wonderful to get to share that labor with the people at Rowman & Littlefield. You could not wipe the smile off my face after my initial telephone conversation with R&L editor Leanne Silverman. After discussing my project for more than an hour and a half, Leanne said, "Well, Kenny, you've probably figured out that I have been talking to you for this long because I'm really interested in publishing this book." She's been a joy to work with. But she's not alone in deserving thanks here; Leanne has minions! A million thanks (that's 20,000 for each of my fifty sites) to assistant editor Carli Hansen, who managed to keep the many parts of the juggling act that was this project in the air at the same time; Karie Simpson, who was tremendously helpful with issues related to the figures; Jehanne Schweitzer, senior production editor extraordinaire, who was incredibly helpful in the copyediting and keeping me on task, not always an easy thing to do; and Andrea Kendrick, the assistant editor at the beginning of the project. I genuinely appreciate a copy edit in which my voice can still be heard and people who know my work can say, "That's Kenny's writing alright. And his grammar certainly is improving." A great big thanks to Paulette Baker for accomplishing that monumental task.

I think my kids, Josh and Jacob, figured out in a hurry that all those family "vacations" weren't really vacations at all but research trips. At least that's what I told them to say if they were ever called on to testify before the IRS. Wait; should I be saying this in print? Whatever! In truth, I can't imagine anything better than involving my kids in my archaeological odyssey. You should too (I mean you should involve your kids, not mine). I thank them for their patience, unique insights, and active participation.

And then there's Jenn, who joined me midway through my archaeological odyssey—and midway through my life. Jenn has an almost supernatural ability to find petroglyph and pictograph panels. I guess I should be particularly pleased that she is enamored of ancient things, as I increasingly fit into that category. Love you, Jenny-bean.

A lot of people deserve my deep and fundamental appreciation for making this book possible. Those are the folks who had the foresight to recognize that archaeological sites are important, interesting, valuable, significant, and worthy of protection and preservation. I include in that list Teddy Roosevelt; the National Park Service; the Bureau of Land Management; state, county, and town site stewards; as well private families who have made it their duty to preserve the past for the future. Without their efforts, the fifty sites honored in this book might not exist.

Finally—and I know this will sound lame in a world where irony often trumps sincerity—I must give credit where credit is due: America's first peoples. It was, after all, their labor, imagination, creativity, artistry, and genius that created the places I take you to in this book. And it is to those people I give my ultimate "thank you."

Enough! Now it's your turn. Go hike, climb, explore, study, learn, and revel in America's remarkable past. I hope you enjoy your odysseys through time as much as I have enjoyed mine.

Introduction

Ancient America's hidden history revealed!!! Okay. I admit to feeling a little disingenuous opening with that headline. *Technically* it is accurate, but the hyperbole is readily apparent given the overabundance of exclamation points.

This book does indeed reveal "ancient America's hidden history," but not in the way that it's "revealed" in far too many television documentaries, cable series, websites, and popular books about our country's past. These programs, sites, and publications are replete with stories of ancient aliens, paranormal Sasquatches, lost continents, and wandering Templar Knights. In truth, many of these sources don't reveal America's hidden history; they just make it up.

I will not be exposing here the secret truth about extraterrestrials visiting North America in antiquity. I can confidently report that, despite the claims made on a certain cable TV series, ancient aliens did not land in North America and inspire rock art depictions of space-suited extraterrestrials. But that doesn't make the rock art I will be sharing with you any less beautiful, interesting, or worthy of attention (Figure 1). The artwork is truly amazing, but don't take my word for it. Go see it for yourself.

*Figure 1. This 700-year-old petroglyph does not represent the face of an extraterrestrial. Instead, it is an example of the kind of remarkable artistic expression you can see at the **Three Rivers Petroglyph Site (Site 38)** in southern New Mexico.*

*Figure 2. Monks Mound at **Cahokia (Site 9)** is an example of the monumental earthworks produced by Native Americans.*

Also, I won't be talking about Atlantis. Despite the claims of Ignatius Donnelly, the nineteenth-century popularizer of Plato's allegory of a lost continent, the mound-building cultures of the American Midwest and Southeast were not inspired by Atlanteans escaping the cataclysmic destruction of their homeland. It's a dead certainty that American Indians built the mounds, and that's far more interesting than fantasies of lost Atlantis. Best of all, the mounds are still there for us to visit and experience for ourselves (Figure 2). In this book, I hope to inspire you to do exactly that.

There is indeed a hidden history of America's first peoples, and helping you discover it is one of my goals. That history hasn't been hidden intentionally. There's no occult conspiracy on the part of the Smithsonian, NASA, the Illuminati, the Rotary Club, or even professional archaeologists like me. No, the "hidden history" I'm referring to is the result of general ignorance and historical amnesia. It's also due, I sheepishly admit, to a failure on the part of archaeologists—myself included—to get the word out about the fascinating true stories of American antiquity.

The Truth about America's First Peoples

Most people are unaware of, and will likely be very surprised by, the high level of engineering, architectural, and artistic sophistication reflected in the fifty archaeological sites and places profiled here. Regardless of all those discussions in your high school social studies class, and even though you mostly paid attention in your introductory college course in anthropology, the term "American Indian" or, if you prefer, "Native American," likely conjures up images of movie or television stereotypes. Indians live in tepees. They're horseback-riding nomads. They wear feathered headdresses, hunt buffalo, and scalp settlers; and when they're done scalping those settlers, they smoke peace pipes with the survivors.

Maybe, especially if you live in the Northeast, the image with which you're most familiar depicts American Indians living in wigwams, planting a lot of corn, and being the suckers who shared that corn with the Pilgrims just before those colonists returned the favor by giving them smallpox.

But here's the deal. Some American Indians were nomadic, but not all. Some lived in tepees, but not all. Many relied on corn for subsistence, but not all. Some now run spectacularly successful casinos, but not all. Okay, they do all make fry bread, but can you blame them? It's just so delicious. But back to my point. The sixteenth-, seventeenth-, eighteenth-, and nineteenth-century European explorers and settlers of North America encountered a variety of cultures as broad as that seen anywhere in the world. Explorers and settlers in the Midwest and Southeast wrote about their encounters with vast empires of pyramid-building farmers whose quite sedentary population centers were flanked by miles of cornfields and whose societies were ruled by powerful kings. European writers described peaceful farmers in the American Southwest living in enormous, finely constructed and elaborate adobe and stone apartment complexes. Other writers in the Southwest recorded the presence of beautiful buildings ensconced in seemingly inaccessible cliff niches, leaving the impression of breathtaking castles suspended in midair. Others remarked on the awe-inspiring natural galleries where, by etching into or painting onto rock surfaces, ancient artists shared their spiritual world by creating tens of thousands of depictions of a broad array of complex geometric forms, naturalistic animals, and spirit beings. The remains of many of these monuments, sites, and works of art still exist—and you can visit them.

Giving Credit Where Credit Is Due

Some European explorers were so impressed by the remains and ruins they saw in the canyons, floodplains, cliff faces, and prairies of North America they denied that the ancestors of the living native peoples they encountered could have been responsible. For example, Montezuma Castle in Arizona wasn't built by followers of the Aztec king who bore that name. That label was bestowed by Europeans who were of the opinion that only a great and sophisticated culture, like that of the Aztecs, could have constructed such an impressive and remarkable building. The Europeans were half right. The builders were bearers of a great and sophisticated culture, but not that of the Aztecs. The responsible party was a tribe of Native Americans, ancestors of the modern Hopi Indians. Go see the place for yourself; I'll tell you how in this book.

The same holds true for the northern New Mexico site that was given the name "Aztec," again in the false belief that the monumental structure found there, with its beautiful and elaborate stone masonry, must have been built by a highly accomplished civilization. It was, but here again the site's name incorrectly implied that this civilization was not that of local Indians but instead originated in Mexico. Toltec Mounds in Arkansas is another impressive American Indian site, this one with monumentally scaled earthworks that were, literally, great pyramids produced in soil. The site is named for a Mexican civilization, the Toltecs, who predated the Aztecs. These sites were named in a way that denied their connection to the native peoples of the United States. Again, you can and should see these places for yourself.

One of the purposes of this book is to encourage you to visit as many as you can of fifty of the most amazing archaeological sites located in the United States (Figure 3). In the pages to follow, I'll explain the importance of these particular sites, and also provide practical information to facilitate your journey through time.

The hidden history we'll explore in this book is one that is "hidden in plain sight." It is a history that you can examine and see for yourself. The research I conducted for this involved a personal archaeological odyssey. Along the way, I visited each of the fifty sites presented here. You won't need to leave your easy chair to appreciate these places, but I hope I can inspire you to conduct your own archaeological odysseys to gain a personal appreciation for America's amazing ancient past.

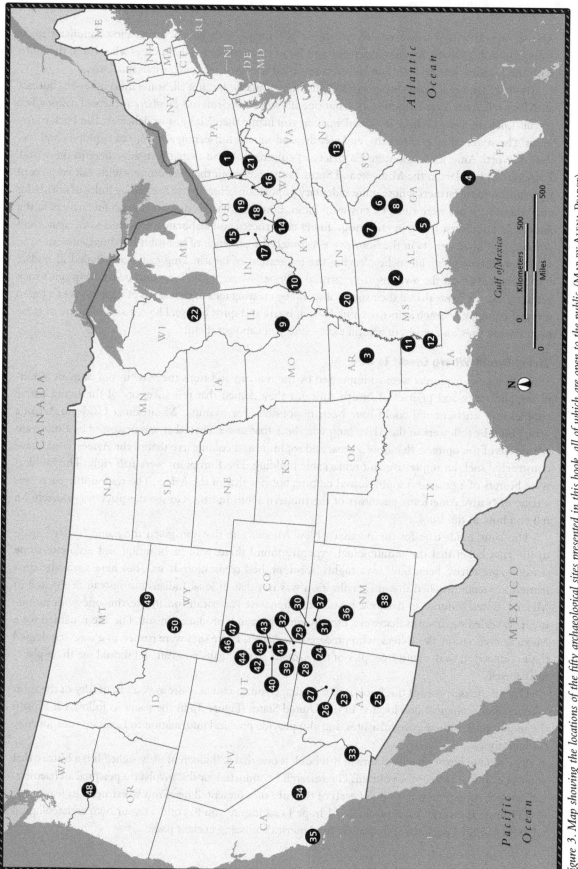

Figure 3. Map showing the locations of the fifty archaeological sites presented in this book, all of which are open to the public. (MAP BY ALENA PEARCE)

Why Visit the Past?

In his work *The Go-Between*, English novelist L. P. Hartley phrased it this way: "The past is a foreign country; they do things differently there." It's a nice bit of phrasing, and in a sense it's an important goal of every archaeologist to serve as a tour guide for non-archaeologists who wish to visit the "foreign country" that is the past.

A virtual visit through the pages of a book (like this one) is interesting and instructive, but if you can, plan an actual visit to the places where ancient people lived. Our species has been around for a vast stretch of time, and we humans have found amazingly varied ways to adapt to the spaces and places in which we have lived. Our modern human condition has evolved from the lives lived by past peoples; using the archaeological record to explore the diversity of those peoples who have gone before can provide important insights into who we are today. And there's no better way of doing that than seeing the sites for yourself.

Think about it; open the newspaper on any given day and you will read stories of global warming—or cooling; of recessions and depressions; of resource depletion, ethnic violence, and warfare. The archaeological record shows that ancient members of the human family have been there and done that. Warfare, environmental degradation, climate change, technological change, resource depletion, drought, and poverty are not new challenges facing our species. When you visit the sites presented in this book, you will be directly confronted by evidence of conflict, of the impacts of short-term environmental disasters like droughts and long-term processes of climate change, as well as the devastating effects of economic collapse. The past is indeed "a foreign country," one that's important to visit for the insights it may provide on these and many other issues vexing modern humanity.

If all that sounds way too depressing, not the kinds of things you want to be reminded of when taking the kids on vacation, fair enough. Rest assured that the places I am encouraging you to visit are also just incredibly cool—monuments to the unexpected abilities of people who, from our lofty perch in the twenty-first century, we too often view as simple or primitive.

Okay, so where would you go to visit the past? Ordinarily, the word "archaeology" conjures thoughts of the exotic cultures of ancient Egypt (vast pyramid complexes; the Great Sphinx!), Mexico (Maya temples!), or Greece (the Parthenon!), and with good reason. These are incredible monuments, the intriguing shadows cast by past cultures. But you don't need to go quite so far away to visit the past. And you won't need a passport. The fifty sites featured in this book are not in exotic or foreign locales but instead can be found along America's byways and in its parks and backyards.

In our own country we have an amazing past populated by the remnants of the communities of our nation's first inhabitants. Ancient bison hunters and first farmers, builders of earthen pyramids and adobe cliff houses, stone calendar makers, cave painters, and makers of giant animal images in earth and stone; all lived here, in America, and left behind in great profusion evidence of their artistic and technological genius. The archaeological record of North America is intensely fascinating and worthy of respect, attention, and preservation (Figure 4). It's also worthy of a personal visit by you.

In the Pages to Follow . . .

The sites profiled here certainly do not represent an all-inclusive digest of archaeological sites open to the public across the United States. Nor do these fifty sites constitute an exhaustive representation of the many fascinating sites spread around this country. In winnowing that vast collection to fifty profiles, I chose what I felt were the fifty most important and visually interesting sites. These sites will leave any visitor with a uniquely personal perspective of the remarkable histories and spectacular accomplishments of the first Americans. This is my recommended list of "the fifty ancient sites in the United States you should see before you die." Fairly or not, many states (including my own, Connecticut) have no

Figure 4. Archaeological sites are precious resources for learning about the lives of past peoples.

sites in my listing. It's not that there aren't important sites in these states—there are; but none made it into my top fifty according to the criteria I employed. To be included in my listing, a site had to be iconic in some sense, representative of a specific period in American antiquity, and emblematic of a particular ancient culture or region. There is some personal favoritism here; my list of fifty is unlikely to be exactly the same as a list of "fifty top sites" from another archaeologist. Almost all of my fifty have been officially recognized as significant. Many are listed on the federally administered National Register of Historic Places, an honor roll of important historical sites; some have been designated as National Historic Landmarks; and four have even been recognized as World Heritage Sites, a listing that includes Stonehenge and the Giza pyramids.

My fifty sites also share another essential characteristic: They all are open to the public. This is to encourage, even inspire, you to see some of these wonderful places for yourself—to engage in your own archaeological odyssey. My hope is for you to visit the past, travel through time, surround yourself with antiquity, expose your kids or grandkids to America's archaeological heritage, be surprised, learn lots, and, most important, have a great trip.

How to Use This Book

Before we begin exploring specific locations, some basic background about America's ancient past will help you understand and appreciate the fascinating places listed here. In the next section, Ancient America, I'll paint a quick picture of the climate and geography of North America over the last several thousand years. We'll also discuss the diverse peoples who first settled—and whose descendants continue to populate—this continent. This section also provides narrative background about the different genres of sites included in the book: First Peoples; Mound Builders; Cliff Dwellings, Great Houses, and Stone Towers; and Rock Art—the vast outdoor, ancient art museums filled with "galleries" of pictographs (painted images), petroglyphs (pictures etched, incised, and pecked into rock surfaces), and geoglyphs (ground drawings on a massive scale). The remainder of the book explores the fifty archaeological sites I encourage you to see for yourself, grouped according to genre.

Site profiles in each of these four groupings are presented alphabetically by state and further broken down into separate types. You will quickly realize that the different genres roughly correspond to geographic areas of the continental United States. I'll begin with First Peoples, a category with a single site where you can visit a rockshelter lived in by a group of the first humans to settle North America more than 13,000 years ago (**Site 1, Meadowcroft Rockshelter**). There are many sites in the United States where the remains of those First Peoples have been studied, but very few are open to the public, and fewer still allow you to see the actual remnants of the archaeological excavation.

From there we'll travel across the East, Midwest, and Southeast, where the most prominent remains consist primarily of mounds, mounds, and more mounds. In the Southwest the defining features are cliff dwellings, great houses, and stone towers. Rock art sites are also clustered predominantly in the Southwest, although there are stunning sites stretching into the Rocky Mountains and closer to the Pacific Ocean. At the beginning of each grouping of sites, you will find a map identifying the location of specific sites relative to one another.

At the beginning of each site profile, I offer a narrative of my own experience visiting the site, based on a **Journal Entry** I kept during my visits to the past. These reflect my personal reactions to the remarkable sites produced by America's first peoples.

This entry is followed by a straightforward description of **What You Will See:** the incredibly cool art or mounds or cliff dwellings or freestanding structures you will encounter in your journey through time.

Next I answer the question **Why Is [Site Name] Important?** Part of my process of compiling a list of fifty ancient sites included a consideration of their incredible beauty and even mystery—their "wow factor." However, I am a college professor, and I'd also like you to appreciate these sites for what they teach us about the intellectual, artistic, and spiritual lives of the ancient peoples who produced them. My fifty sites aren't just uniquely beautiful and impressive; they are also uniquely informative about the lives of the first Americans and help us understand America's past.

Each site profile closes with an overview of the practical details you'll need to know as you plan your visit. This includes:

1. **Site Type.** I label each site by the primary features it offers the archaeological time traveler. The Mound Builders genre includes Burial Mounds, Enclosure Mounds, Platform Mounds, Effigy Mounds, and Villages. The Cliff Dwellings, Great Houses, and Stone Towers genre features those edifices. Finally, the Rock Art genre includes Petroglyphs, Pictographs, and Geoglyphs. Some sites possess characteristics of more than one of these type labels.

2. **Wow Factor.** I've also put together a rubric (one to five stars) for scoring some subjective elements, such as the site's "wow factor." My scorings are entirely subjective of course, but I think they are a pretty good guess at how beautiful, impressive, even astonishing you will find the sites to be. If I placed the site in this book, you can be sure I was pretty wowed by it, so every site has a pretty high score.

3. **Museum.** Here I let you know about any on-site museums.

4. **Ease of Road Access.** If a site gets five stars, it means that the route is entirely paved and you can drive there in your low-clearance, two-wheel-drive family sedan. Fewer stars imply a rougher road, and I let you know if it's best to use a four-wheel-drive vehicle for safe access (true in only a couple of cases).

5. **Ease of Hike.** I like a good hike, but when I look at trail guides and see "strenuous," "difficult," "climbing," or "lots of exposure" (meaning steep drop-offs along the trail), I get a little nervous, so I wanted to give you my subjective impression of the difficulty of the hikes. If you're an experienced hiker, all fifty sites are easy to get to. If you hate hiking, sites with fewer stars might not be best for you. Trust me; while hiking back up and out of **Site 40, Horseshoe Canyon**, people were passing me by while I was trying to catch my breath. I survived, and the site certainly was worth the trek, but I figured you might like to be warned about some of the longer, steeper hikes or the ones with significant exposure to heights.

6. **Natural Beauty of Surroundings.** When you are hiking to or through an incredible archaeological site, you're often going to be in the midst of a stunning natural landscape. Again, my scoring here is subjective, but it should give you a good idea of the site's general surroundings.

7. **Kid Friendly** rankings are based on opportunities for running around and the potential for interactivity. If your kids are fine with just looking at amazing sights/sites, all the places in this book will be five stars for them. But some of the hikes may be a little easier than others for little ones; others offer more distractions for kids in general.

8. **Food.** It's always smart to bring along a cooler with drinks and snacks, but some sites, especially those with museums, offer limited food choices.

9. **How to Get There.** I provide an address for use with your GPS and/or narrative directions for finding the site.

10. **Hours of Operation.** I tell you when the site is open to visitors, but always check the website I've provided for changes.

11. **Cost.** There is no cost to visit many of the fifty sites on my list. For sites located in national parks, you can purchase an annual "America the Beautiful" pass. That pass covers up to four adults in the

same vehicle—and may save you money over the course of your trip. For a nominal fee, people age 62 and older can get a Senior Pass which provides a lifetime of entry to sites administered by the National Park Service. The pass also allows you to bring up to three additional adults when you visit. It is an amazing bargain. Outside the national park system, cost may vary by the age of visitors; some offer discounts, and prices may change by the time you read this book. While none of them are terribly expensive—these sites aren't theme parks—your best bet is to check the relevant website for current prices.

12. **Best Season to Visit.** My recommendations are based primarily on weather, but also on crowds.

13. **Website.** Where available, I've provided the official website for the archaeological site. If there isn't one, I provide a useful source for additional pre-travel research.

14. **Designation:** This includes the designation of the site—as a national monument, a state park, Bureau of Land Management property, etc. Also listed here is whether a site is a National Landmark, World Heritage Site, or similar designation.

Finally, when I refer to a site profiled elsewhere in the book, its name will appear in **bold** and will include the site number according to the table of contents (for example, **Site 9, Cahokia Mounds State Historic Site**).

Ancient America

H ere's a very, very brief summary of North American prehistory, providing some general anthropological and historical context for the sites we'll be visiting in this book. Think of this as the equivalent of "Shakespeare in 5 Minutes."

Who Are the American Indians?

To begin, all American Indians are related biologically, culturally, and historically, but they are not all identical peoples bearing exactly the same culture. It's like Europe: The people who live there are all Europeans, but they are also French, Italian, Spanish, British, Swedish, German, Polish, and so forth. There is plenty of cultural diversity among the native peoples of Europe—different languages, religions, foods, art, traditions, architecture—just as there is plenty of cultural diversity among the native peoples of North America.

Though each Native American group is unique, all are descended from the same stock: people who migrated to the New World from Asia at the end of the Pleistocene epoch. Despite the name commonly applied to the period, "the Ice Age," the Pleistocene wasn't just about ice, snow, and cold. Beginning 1.8 million years ago, it was a complex climatic period punctuated by bouts of very cold temperatures with widespread ice coverage, but interspersed by times of ice retreat and temperatures as warm as the present. Paleoclimatologists (the job title for people who study ancient climates) generally believe that the Pleistocene ended about 10,000 years ago. Some suggest that we may still be the Pleistocene—just a quiet, warmer period. How human-induced climate change will affect these natural cycles is anybody's guess. My advice: Don't throw away your snow shoes just yet.

Just as it does today, water during the Pleistocene evaporated from the world's oceans and fell as frozen precipitation—snow and ice—in cold regions. Unlike the present, however, during cold stages of the Pleistocene that frozen stuff didn't melt off seasonally. Imagine a really bad winter. Imagine your lawn and the roads on which you regularly commute covered in snow. Imagine that none of it melts in spring or even in summer; it just sticks around, with more ice and more snow being added all the time. Now imagine that happening, almost unabated, for literally thousands of years. (Fun, right? Well, maybe if you're into skiing or snowmobiling . . .) This process created extensive, mile-high, long-lived bodies of ice called glaciers, especially in northern latitudes and higher elevations (Figure 5). Because that ice didn't melt and return to the oceans, those oceans became somewhat depleted of water and sea levels dropped worldwide, sometimes dramatically. In fact, during glacial peaks, some lasting for millennia, those levels went down by as much as 400 feet, and broad swaths of land previously underwater became exposed.

One of these newly exposed territories was a very broad "land bridge," as much as 1,000 miles wide from north to south, connecting the Old and New Worlds between present-day Siberia in northeast Asia and Alaska in northwest North America (Figure 6). That swath of land is called the Bering Land Bridge or just Beringia (named for eighteenth-century Russian explorer Vitus Bering). Bottom line: During peaks of Pleistocene cold cycles, the world was a very different place than it is today.

Figure 5. The modern glaciers that envelope Greenland provide a model for what much of the northern half of North America looked like during the Pleistocene, or Ice Age.

We know that there were people living in eastern Siberia by about 40,000 years ago. We also know that the period between 40,000 and 12,000 years ago can be characterized as a glacial maximum. That means that soon after people had moved into the far northeastern margins of Asia, the Bering Land Bridge was exposed and likely presented a tempting new territory into which they could expand their population. Merely by following the herds of animals they depended on for food, these Asians slowly entered into what was, truly, a new world. They became the first Americans.

First Peoples

Archaeological evidence shows that the earliest human migration into the New World from the Old occurred certainly more than 13,000 and perhaps as much as 20,000 or possibly even 30,000 years ago (**Site 1, Meadowcroft Rockshelter**, classified in this book as a First Peoples site). The genetic study of Native Americans conforms very well to the archaeology; they were northeast Asians, and they arrived more than 13,000 years ago.

The earliest inhabitants of the New World were drawn here initially as a result of the incredibly rich Ice Age environment that characterized much of the North American continent. Teeming herds of large game animals including bison, woolly mammoth, mastodon, caribou, and horse dominated the landscape and were hunted by the early settlers, who are called Paleo-Indians. The Paleo-Indians lived in relatively small, nomadic hunting bands spread out across the landscape of North America.

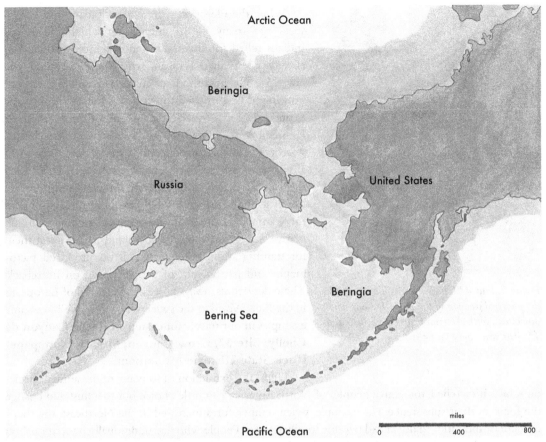

*Figure 6. During the height of the Pleistocene, worldwide sea level was depressed by as much as 400 feet, exposing broad swaths of land currently underwater. This led to the creation of a 1,000-mile-wide (north to south) land bridge connecting northeast Asia and northwest North America. (*Map by Jennifer Davis*)*

The stone tips of their spears are found in great profusion in virtually every one of our states. These stone points are extremely sharp, finely made, and symmetrical and are manufactured of natural materials including volcanic glass (obsidian) and stones like flint, chalcedony, and jasper. Further, they are characterized by a North American invention—a broad channel called a "flute" (like the concave designs seen on fluted columns) chipped into both faces of the point. Found nowhere else in the world, including the homeland of their Asian ancestors, these flaked channels are presumed to have aided in hafting the stone points onto wooden shafts and, perhaps, in facilitating the flow of blood from the wound of an animal pierced by one of them. The oldest of the fluted points are called Clovis (after a site in New Mexico where they were first found) and date to more than 13,000 years ago. They tend to be long, shaped like a willow leaf, with the flutes traveling from the base to about one-third to one-half their lengths (Figure 7). Clovis points tend to be found in association with the remains of woolly mammoths and mastodons, so it is assumed that these animals were the preferred game of these people. The other type of fluted point is named Folsom (after a site in which they were first found, also in New Mexico). Folsom points are a bit more recent than Clovis, dating to sometime after 11,500 years ago. They tend to be shorter than Clovis, and their flutes travel nearly the entire length of both faces. Folsom points tend to be found in association with the remains of bison rather than extinct elephants. Folsom points likely were made by the descendants of those who made Clovis and reflect a change in the animals the people hunted.

Figure 7. Fluted "Clovis" points like these were the preferred weapon of the Paleo-Indians who inhabited North America between 13,000 and 11,500 years ago. (THINKSTOCK)

When the Pleistocene drew to a close around 10,000 years ago, many of the animals on which the Paleo-Indians relied for their subsistence became extinct. You already knew that; I mean, when's the last time you saw a woolly mammoth or mastodon walking around? You might be surprised to learn that horses also became extinct in North America at the end of the Pleistocene. Remember the discussion of Native American cultural stereotypes in the introduction? Not all American Indians were equestrians, but some certainly were. That wasn't the case, however, until Spanish explorers reintroduced horses to the continent in the sixteenth century. Some of those animals escaped into the wild and became feral, and Native Americans captured them and began using them for transportation. Some native artists produced pictographs and petroglyphs of people riding on horseback. These depictions always postdate the arrival of Europeans in the New World in the sixteenth century. We'll see some examples in our travels; for example, **Site 24, Canyon de Chelly; Site 37, Crow Canyon; Site 41, Newspaper Rock State Historic Monument.**

Upon the extinction of so many of the animal species on which they relied, the native peoples of North America had little choice but to adjust and change the focus of their subsistence. For example, when temperatures increased in the Northeast, the then-resident caribou moved north and became locally extinct. People who had traditionally hunted caribou needed to change their diets. Luckily, as the climate warmed, vegetation changed from the treeless tundra in which caribou thrive to, first, a coniferous forest and then, by about 8,000 years ago, a mixed deciduous forest much like the modern one, filled with oak, maple, hickory, and walnut. That forest supported large numbers of deer, and people began relying on this species for meat and hides. The human re-adaptation to the changing climate of post-Pleistocene America characterizes the cultural period following the Paleo-Indian, which archaeologists call the Archaic. The hallmark of the Archaic period is, in fact, the great diversity of cultural adaptations that evolved as groups living across North America adjusted to the newly established, post-Pleistocene environments (Figure 8).

The first peoples of the New World were the ancestors of the folks encountered by European visitors, explorers, and settlers, beginning with the Norse incursion about 1,000 years ago and again after the voyages of Christopher Columbus a little more than 500 years ago. The diversity of their adaptations and their ability to adjust their strategies for survival to the conditions presented in every imaginable habitat with which they were confronted in the New World is a testament to the genius of the first peoples of the Americas. These diverse cultures produced the diverse sites that are the focus of this book.

The Mound Builders

As they moved south from their entry point in Alaska at the end of the Pleistocene, some of the descendants of the first settlers of America eventually arrived in the regions we now know as the American Southeast and Midwest. As the Pleistocene waned, some of these newly settled areas became characterized by thick, broad, resource-rich woodlands filled with an abundance of wild foods including many species of animals, especially deer, as well as edible seeds, nuts, berries, and roots. These wild crops were so

Typical North American Chronology

Archaeologists think of the deep history of North America in terms of four major prehistoric cultural periods:

I.   **Paleo-Indian:** 13,500 to 9,000 years ago

II. **Archaic:** 9,000 to 3,000 years ago
     A. Early Archaic: 9,000 to 8,000 years ago
     B. Middle Archaic: 8,000 to 6,000 years ago
     C. Late Archaic: 6,000 to 4,000 years ago
     D. Terminal Archaic: 4,000 to 3,000 years ago

III. **Woodland:** 3,000 to 350 years ago
     A. Early Woodland: 3,000 to 2,000 years ago
     B. Middle Woodland: 2,000 to 1,000 years ago
     C. Late Woodland: 1,000 to 350 years ago

IV. **Contact:** This period dates to the first European exploration and settlement and varies throughout North America.

Figure 8.

abundant that, even without agriculture, there was plenty of food available and the human population increased. In some places the Archaic people didn't need to move around a lot to find resources, and with adequate planning and food storage, local villages could be inhabited year-round. This abundance of food and the near-permanence of villages allowed plenty of free time for people to engage in activities beyond what was necessary to put food on their tables. That kind of stability and habitat richness allowed for additional population growth.

Large rivers, among them waterways we now call the Ohio, Missouri, and Mississippi Rivers, provided natural, navigable avenues for the movement of people and raw materials, as well as finished goods. Trade flourished, and even raw materials available only from a great distance away—for example, shell from the Gulf Coast or copper from Michigan—moved along those rivers to the residents of present-day Ohio, Illinois, Indiana, and the rest of the Midwest and Southeast, who then used them to produce beautiful and impressive works of art.

In some particularly ecologically privileged locations, local population size increased dramatically and there was an uptick in what anthropologists call social complexity. With an increase in population came the need to coordinate and organize the lives of people living in increasingly dense, permanent settlements. Some people—perhaps folks who were already perceived as having powerful connections to the spirit world—became political decision makers and social leaders. Having authority over others, wealth appears to have become concentrated in their hands. Their houses grew larger, and they were able to monopolize rare, valuable, and sought-after raw materials. Their increasing wealth and social status was accompanied by the ability of these powerful people to command the labor of their followers. This is exactly what we see in the archaeological records of ancient Egypt, Mesopotamia, the Indus River Valley, and elsewhere.

In America we see the results of that developing power in the construction of monumentally scaled earthworks. For example, beginning more than 5,000 years ago at a place called Watson Brake in Louisiana (unfortunately this site won't be among the fifty I discuss here as it is not, as of this writing, open to the public), the native peoples of the New World began moving around large quantities of dirt, using it as a construction material to produce impressive mounds. Over the next 4,700 years or so, virtually right up until, and in some places past, the point of European exploration and colonization of the New World, various Native American societies developed and practiced their own mound-building traditions. We'll see several of those mounds in our travels.

In some cases, the burials of the evolving class of rulers grew in size and complexity as well. Large earth mounds began to mark the tombs of this emerging elite class. As did the pyramids of ancient Egypt, these burial mounds represent tangible symbols of the growing power and importance of the leaders of their societies, even in death. The burial mounds and the beautifully crafted works of art often found interred with the dead are the most obvious archaeological manifestations of the mound-building cultures called Adena, beginning about 2,800 years ago, and Hopewell, beginning about 2,200

GREAT MOUND AT MARIETTA, OHIO.

Figure 9. Nineteenth-century engraving of a conical burial mound—today called **Cemetery Mound (Site 16)**—*located in Ohio.*

years ago, and are among the coolest things we will see in our archaeological odyssey (Figure 9). Adena and Hopewell differ in some of the particulars of their artifact styles. Where the geographic extent of Adena is confined mostly to Ohio, Indiana, Kentucky, and West Virginia, Hopewell culture sites are found far more broadly, with their mounds and artifacts spread across the entire American Midwest. In terms of art, mound construction, trade, geographical extent, and reliance on agriculture, Hopewell is more elaborate and impressive than Adena. Most archaeologists view Adena at least in part as a precursor to Hopewell.

What happened next, beginning about 2,000 years ago, was a real game changer. There was a revolution in subsistence that resulted from two parallel processes. First, in an attempt to increase productivity and food yield of the wild crops on which they depended, local people in the Midwest and Southeast began tending those plants by preparing seed beds in spring; caring for seedlings; and weeding, watering, and protecting plants from marauding animals. By encouraging the growth of individual plants that, for example, sprouted first, grew most quickly, and produced the largest edible seeds or fruits, Native Americans initiated their own agricultural revolution through the process known as "artificial selection." These plants included well-known crops like the sunflower and lesser known ones like lamb's-quarters and pigweed. Agriculture increased the overall productivity of the region and allowed for the development of even larger human populations with even greater density. Agriculture was more efficient than foraging, and fewer people were needed to engage directly in subsistence pursuits. This freed up the time of increasing numbers to do other things: engage in trade, participate in warfare, produce artworks, and build even more monumentally scaled earthworks.

The second process resulted from a quantum leap in agricultural efficiency, made possible by the introduction of a crop that continues to be one of our planet's most significant food sources: maize.

Today the world's farmers grow more maize than they do wheat, rice, or potatoes. Originating in Central America more than 5,000 years ago, maize—known by most people as corn—entered into what is now the American Southwest by about 3,200 years ago and then the Midwest by about 1,700 years ago.

Maize is a crop rich in nutrients, including many of the amino acids necessary for life. Add beans and squash to maize and you have what some native groups called "the three sisters." The combination of these three crops was important for a healthy diet because beans and squash provide the amino acids that are missing in corn. A diet including all three crops provides a complete protein in a nonanimal package. Brilliant! Beyond this, maize is a hardy, resilient crop with very high yield potential, and it is genetically malleable. Varieties of corn can be grown across an enormous range of habitats. Maize's origins are in the tropics, but varieties can be grown successfully today as far north as Canada.

Especially after the movement of corn into North America, some societies experienced a great leap in their ability to feed more mouths on less acreage. At that point we see in the archaeological record evidence of increasing sedentism, villages of greater size, and a ramping up of social and economic inequality. In other words, some people became rich and power became concentrated in their hands, other people were poor, and some fell in the middle. In the maize-growing cultures that developed in the rich bottomlands of major river valleys in the American Midwest and mid-South, America saw the development of class societies, with the rich and powerful at the top and regular working people at the bottom. In this culture, now called Mississippian, most of the regular folks were farmers who were able to produce far more food than they needed to feed themselves and their families. Their agricultural surplus provided the food necessary to support the ruling group as well as classes of people who did not farm but might be specialists in artistic pursuits, including ceramics, the manufacture of stone tools, crafting works in shell, fabric production, and metallurgy.

Though they still constructed burial mounds for the interments of their leaders, with the support of rising populations and with increasing power and wealth concentrated in the hands of those few leaders, earthworks became even more monumental. Some were elevated platforms, on top of which were constructed the homes of the rulers of these societies. The elevated status of the leaders of these groups was symbolized by the elevated context of their homes on the tops of artificial, symmetrical mountains of earth, the platform mounds.

In most cases, individual mounds or clusters of such earthworks marked the locations of ceremonial or religious centers, with small resident populations of the ruling and priestly classes. A broad and dispersed series of hamlets and villages surrounded these ceremonial centers, where farmers lived, grew food, and gave their allegiance to and provided material support for the leaders and craftspeople living in them. In return they received the benefits of being members of a chiefdom or kingdom: military protection, perhaps an infrastructure that included roads, the protected movement of goods, and probably the promise of a place in the afterlife. In a few instances, **Site 9, Cahokia** is the clearest example, ceremonial centers evolved into population centers of a truly urban character. Cahokia was a Native American city with a large resident population that dominated a broad expanse of surrounding territories filled with smaller communities. It is about as far removed from the common stereotype of nomadic Indians as you can get. The residents of these communities likely viewed Cahokia as the capital of their nation and those who lived atop the platform mounds located there as their leaders. Cahokia is still an amazing place today, and we will visit it in our odyssey.

The Mound Builder Myth

The mounds, especially the ones I'm including in our fifty-site archaeological odyssey, are hard to miss, but don't feel bad if you've never heard of them. A lot of folks haven't. In fact, historian Roger Kennedy hadn't heard of them either. That's kind of shocking, since from 1979 to 1992 Kennedy was the director of the Smithsonian Institution's National Museum of American History. Yeah, that's *the* official, national history museum of the United States. Kennedy was a trained historian, a highly regarded researcher, and a brilliant writer. In an interview conducted in 2009 he admitted that until the 1990s he was wholly unaware of the Native American cultures that constructed a multiplicity of variously configured earthworks in the American Midwest and Southeast.

It's bad enough that, as I noted earlier, the names given to some ancient Native American sites by European explorers and settlers implied that groups other than Native Americans built them. An even more unfortunate version of this misappropriation of the archaeological record of North America involves an elaborate myth concocted by early European settlers: the existence of an entire lost race of mound builders—a race that bore no connection to American Indians. This mound builder myth claimed that a lost race—maybe they were Europeans, perhaps they were members of the Lost Tribes of Israel, or maybe they were Atlanteans after all—must have constructed the thousands of earthworks distributed across the ancient landscape of North America. The mounds were perceived by at least some of the Europeans who encountered them as being too large and too complex, as well as requiring too much concentrated and coordinated effort, to have been the work of American Indians. We recognize now that this is nonsense—arguably racist nonsense at that. Denying that American Indians could have been responsible for mound construction represents a sad chapter of American history.

Kinds of Mound Builder Sites

The earthworks of the various mound builder cultures are legion and diverse. We can divide the kinds of mounds or earthworks found in North America, examples of which we'll be visiting in our journey through time, into a number of separate categories:

Burial Mounds

Most American burial mounds are conical piles of earth with circular bases. They often are large—the tallest are nearly 70 feet high—and meticulously symmetrical (Figure 10). In many cases, the tombs of

*Figure 10. Nineteenth-century engraving of the Adena burial mound called the **Grave Creek Mound (Site 21)**, located on the western border of West Virginia.*

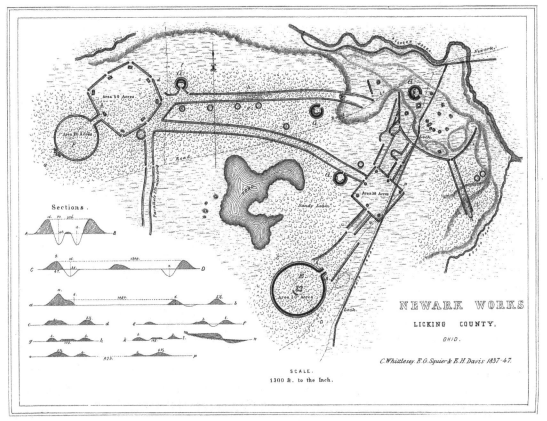

*Figure 11. Nineteenth-century surveyor's drawing of a series of mound enclosures, today elements of the **Newark Earthworks (Site 19)**. (WHITTLESEY, SQUIER, AND DAVIS 1848)*

people who likely were of tremendous importance in their societies have been found in the bottoms of these earthworks. Think of these mounds as a Native American version of Egyptian pyramids. They're generally smaller and built of dirt, not stone, but the fundamental concept is the same—a monumental tomb, the construction of which required the marshaling of significant resources and labor, intended as the final resting place of an important person, perhaps a leader or a priest. Sometimes additional interments were added after the mound was constructed by digging shallow pits into its side and placing the remains of the deceased, sometimes cremated, in the holes. Some large burial mounds aren't circular but are oval at their base, creating an elongated earthwork with a linear ridge at its apex. These oval mounds usually contain multiple burials, most of which were added after the mound itself was constructed. The Adena and Hopewell cultures mentioned earlier are perhaps best known for their construction of burial mounds (**Site 16, Cemetery Mound; Site 17, Miamisburg Mound; Site 18, Mound City, Hopewell Culture National Historical Park; Site 21, Grave Creek Mound**).

Enclosure Mounds

Enclosures are sizable spaces delineated and distinguished from the surrounding landscape by one or more earthworks (Figure 11). The individual earthworks in an enclosure most often are artificial ridges of dirt, generally broader on the bottom and narrower as you approach the top, and may be only a few feet high. A cross section of such a mound is in the shape of a parabola, and they are in essence the equivalent of earth berms or ridges. Some enclosures are circular, circumscribed by a mound built as a large ring. In some examples, four individual linear mounds were built at right angles to one another, intersecting at their ends to create a four-sided enclosure—a square or rectangle. Sometimes the enclosed

space presents a more complex geometric shape. One of the mound sites
in my list of fifty is composed of a
series of discontinuous linear earthworks that, together, delineate and
enclose an octagonal space of about
50 acres. Finally, the mounds marking
some enclosures are irregular in form,
following the edges of a natural, flat-
topped hill, for example.

The mound ridges marking the
enclosure sites do not appear to have
been defensive in nature. They could
not have supplied very much practical protection to those within the
enclosure from enemies attacking
them. It appears that the construction
of a mound or mounds to enclose a
space was intended to ritually separate an area deemed sacred—the area
within the enclosure—from the surrounding territory. This likely was the
case in a couple of our fifty sites (**Site
18, Mound City, Hopewell Culture
National Historical Park** and **Site 19,
Newark Earthworks,** both in Ohio).

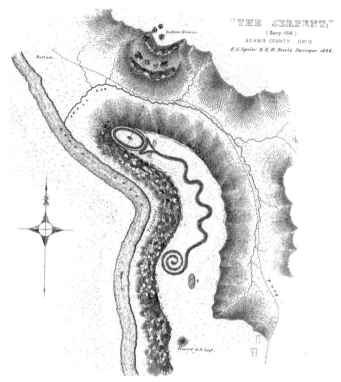

Figure 12. Nineteenth-century surveyor's drawing of an effigy mound called, obviously, **Serpent Mound (Site 14)** *in Ohio.* (SQUIER AND DAVIS 1848)

Effigy Mounds

An effigy mound is an often beautiful, sometimes monumental sculpture in which the artist's medium was earth or stone cobbles (Figure 12). Effigy mounds found in the United States include those in the shape of a coiled snake (**Site 14, Serpent Mound** in Ohio, certainly my favorite effigy earthwork), marching bears, various other small mammals, reptiles, and flying birds (**Site 6, Rock Eagle Effigy Mound**). It's very difficult to suss out the precise meaning of effigy mounds to the people who made them. Are they art, religion, or a bit of both? In any event, whatever they mean, effigy mounds are very cool.

Platform or Temple Mounds

These generally are the largest of the earthworks built by the mound builder cultures. (Figure 13 is a historical engraving depicting Monks Mound at **Site 9, Cahokia**.) Usually square or rectangular at their base—though they sometimes have a more complex footprint—the sides of these mounds were built at various angles from gentle to steep, sometimes with multiple tiers or levels. Many of the temple mounds are in the shape of truncated pyramids. Imagine a typical Egyptian pyramid with its top one-third to one-half missing, leaving a flat platform at its apex upon which a structure might be built. Each of the four faces of a platform mound, therefore, is in the shape of a trapezoid, not a triangle as in Egyptian pyramids. Archaeologists excavating the tops of platform mounds have often found the remains of often large, elaborate log or wattle and daub structures. Artifacts recovered in the remains of those structures suggest that the buildings atop the mounds were temples or palaces in which the society's rich and powerful lived. Historical accounts by Spanish explorers in the Southeast and French traders

Figure 13. Nineteenth-century engraving of a platform or temple mound, today called Monk's Mound, located at **Cahokia (Site 9)** *in Illinois.*

near the mouth of the Mississippi confirm that the ruler of the community, along with the ruler's family, lived in the buildings atop some of the platform mounds.

The largest of these monuments, Monks Mound, is named for the Trappist monks who lived nearby and farmed one of the terraces of the earth pyramid many years after the Indian site was abandoned. Monks Mound is located at the site today called **Cahokia (Site 9),** though we have no idea what its residents called their city; it had been abandoned by the time European explorers of the Midwest arrived there. Monks Mound is nearly 100 feet high, its base covers 14 acres, and it contains more than 21 million cubic feet of dirt. That's a lot of dirt; more to the point, that's a lot of work undertaken by an enormous number of people whose labor must have been very tightly organized to accomplish the task. The mound builder cultures possessed no beasts of burden; the earthworks were the product entirely of people power. Monks Mound is, by volume, the fifth-largest pyramid in the world. And it's not in Egypt or Mexico; it's in Illinois. The other Platform Mound sites included here are **Site 2, Moundville Archaeological Park; Site 3, Toltec Mounds; Site 4, Crystal River; Site 5, Kolomoki; Site 7, Etowah; Site 8, Ocmulgee; Site 10, Angel Mounds; Site 13, Town Creek Mound; Site 20, Pinson Mounds;** and **Site 22, Aztalan Mounds.**

Village Sites

Some of the mound sites we will visit in this book, especially those with platform mounds, were villages, some with substantial populations. But there also are thousands of communities spread across the

Midwest and Southeast where there are no platform, burial, or enclosure mounds, and therefore little to see beyond a modern, agricultural landscape. One wonderful exception to this is included in my fifty-site odyssey: **Site 15, SunWatch Indian Village** in Ohio. Though there are no earthworks there, replicas of the houses at SunWatch have been built directly in the footprints of their archaeological remains, providing a unique perspective of life among the ancient people of the Midwest. The other Platform Mound sites also were occupied villages, but I am including only a couple of other sites in the "village" category—**Site 11, Poverty Point** in Louisiana and **Site 12, Grand Village of the Natchez** in Mississippi—where there are mounds, but the primary reason for visiting them is the extensive village located at each.

Many mound sites can still be visited today. They're not hidden, but often preserved and celebrated as historic landmarks, national monuments, and state parks. They are impressive and truly monumental, representing an important part of American history. Sadly though, not many people know about these places. Equally sadly, not enough people visit them to witness firsthand the amazing achievements of America's first inhabitants.

Cliff Dwellings, Great Houses, and Stone Towers

We now travel west, where many people are at least passingly familiar with two of the modern Native American tribes living in the American Southwest: the Navajo and the Hopi. With a population of more than 300,000, the Navajo are, depending on the details of how a tribe defines its membership, either the first or second most populous tribe in the United States. The Cherokee are the other group in the top two in population size.

The modern Hopi and their close relatives (including the Zuni, Jemez, Tanoan, and other people living in communities in Arizona and New Mexico) are included in a more broadly defined group, the Pueblo Indians. The "Pueblo" name was conferred on them by Spanish explorers in the sixteenth century. *Pueblo* is Spanish for "town." Those explorers were struck by the beauty of the villages of the native peoples they encountered, consisting of finely made, multistory, adobe apartment complexes. While the Pueblo or Puebloan people have a much smaller population (estimated to be about 35,000), their roots in the American Southwest are far deeper than those of the Navajo.

In a sense, the modern Pueblo people can be at least indirectly traced to the first human settlers of the Southwest, who arrived more than 13,000 years ago. Based on archaeology, history, language, and genetics, the ancestors of the modern Navajo moved into the Southwest from the north only about 700 years ago. Most of the village sites presented in this book that are located in the American Southwest—including those exhibiting cliff dwellings (**Site 23, Montezuma Castle; Site 24, Canyon de Chelly; Site 26, Walnut Canyon; Site 28, Betatakin; Site 29, Mesa Verde**); great houses (**Site 24, Canyon de Chelly; Site 25, Casa Grande; Site 27, Wupatki; Site 30, Aztec; Site 31, Chaco Canyon**); and stone towers (**Site 32, Hovenweep**)—were the work of the direct and indirect ancestors of the modern Pueblo people.

Cultural Streams of the Ancient Southwest

Based on the diversity exhibited at sites in the Southwest, archaeologists have divided up ancient cultural groups there; those divisions are often largely based on pretty technical considerations. It's complicated. Certainly we see fundamental commonalities among the ancient peoples spread across the Southwest; for example, their construction of buildings using adobe and stone and their reliance on corn, beans, and squash in their diets. But we also see in the archaeology of the region that folks in different areas made different styles of pottery, employed different types of masonry in their architecture, and had somewhat differing diets. Are those differences sufficient to call them different cultures? Would they have defined themselves as different peoples? Unfortunately we can't go back in time and ask people living in different regions if they view the folks living on the other mesa, or on the other side of the mountain, river, or desert, as members of their group or as foreigners, as friends or as enemies. We can't even be certain they spoke the same language or spoke mutually intelligible dialects of the same language.

There's plenty of diversity in the cultural practices and beliefs of the modern Pueblo people who live in their twenty-one existing communities—the "pueblos" mentioned by sixteenth-century Spanish explorers. For example, some modern Pueblo groups trace their ancestry exclusively through the female line. If you're a kid, you belong to your mother's lineage, not your father's. But other Pueblo people trace their family ties through their fathers. You belong to your father's family and are not a member of your mother's. For a cultural anthropologist, that's a pretty big deal and an important difference.

The spoken language of the Pueblo people varies from place to place, but most—for example, among the various Hopi groups—speak dialects of the same language. Some modern Pueblo people, however (for example, the Zuni), speak a language unintelligible to other Puebloans. Again, that's a pretty significant difference.

With all that diversity among living people, it's not surprising that we see plenty of diversity in the archaeological record of the ancestors of those folks. Archaeologists have identified and defined a number of different "cultural streams" leading to the modern Pueblo cultures of the Southwest. These streams include Mogollon, Sinagua, Hohokam, and Ancestral Puebloan (Figure 14).

Each of these named archaeological cultures exhibited somewhat differing practices and lived in distinct though not necessarily exclusive geographical ranges. For example, the shapes, colors, and styles of the pottery they made are recognizably different. Their houses—in terms of size, the specifics of the masonry, their overall appearance, and even details of their entry doors—vary. The ways in which they memorialized and interred their dead, again, are different. The foods they emphasized in their diets and their reliance on rainfall or irrigation in support of their agriculture also differ across time and space. But in the end, it should be emphasized that the people who made the great houses and cliff dwellings and who produced many of the art sites we will be visiting across the face of the American Southwest were closely related, sharing far more in common than what distinguished them. Let me describe the most commonly identified archaeological cultures of the American Southwest.

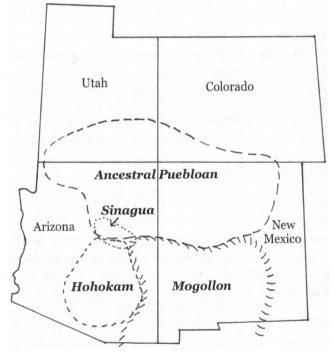

Figure 14. Geographical distribution of the primary archaeological cultures located in the American Southwest. (Map by Jennifer Davis)

Mogollon

Briefly, *Mogollon* refers to sites located primarily in the southern reaches of New Mexico, southern and eastern Arizona, and northern Mexico. The name comes from the Mogollon Mountains that are in the core of this group's geographic range. Those mountains were named for an eighteenth-century Spanish governor of New Spain.

Like all native peoples of the Southwest, early in their history the Mogollon were foragers of wild plants and animals, but by about AD 650 the Mogollon embraced farming as their primary mode of subsistence, focusing on the iconic Native American triumvirate of corn (maize), beans, and squash. Originally building and living in semi-subterranean "pit-houses," Mogollon people began constructing aboveground pueblos by about AD 1000 and cliff dwellings a couple hundred years later.

Perhaps the most distinctive of the Mogollon subgroups were the Mimbres people, best known for their singular and stunning ceramics with white backgrounds and festooned with striking, jet black depictions of animals, fish, and insects in a sharply geometric style. It's unique and incredibly cool stuff. And my one tattoo, a lizard, is based on a Mimbres motif. The rock art we'll see at **Site 38, Three Rivers Petroglyph Site** was produced by Mogollon people and reflects the overall look of Mimbres art.

Hohokam

Sites bearing the specific characteristics labeled *Hohokam* are found in southern and central Arizona; the modern city of Phoenix sits in about the middle of Hohokam territory. *Hohokam* is a Pima Indian word for "the people living in the Sonoran Desert." Flourishing between AD 1 and AD 1500, the Hohokam left behind a large number of sites signifying an extensive population with substantial "great houses," large, free-standing adobe apartment houses, like those at **Site 25, Casa Grande**. The Hohokam are distinguished as the ancient American Southwest culture most reliant on and successful at the construction of irrigation canals for farming—which, like the Mogollon, was based on the cultivation of corn, beans, and squash. The extensive network of well-engineered canals, which must have required a tremendous amount of coordinated labor, is the hallmark of the Hohokam.

Sinagua

Sinagua is Spanish for "without water." Sites designated as Sinagua are located in central and northern Arizona, ensconced in a small pocket north of the core area of the Hohokam. Sinagua sites are distinguished from the other defined archaeological cultures of the Southwest primarily on the basis of their pottery styles. We will visit the remnants of a number of their villages, including **Site 23, Montezuma Castle**; **Site 25, Walnut Canyon**; and **Site 27, Wupatki**. Some researchers actually include the Sinagua sites under the heading of Ancestral Puebloan; they are really quite similar.

Ancestral Puebloan

Ancestral Puebloan refers to sites located primarily around the Four Corners region, called that because four states—Arizona, New Mexico, Utah, and Colorado—meet there at right angles. It is fair to say that the construction both of great houses and cliff dwellings reached its zenith, in terms of both size and elaboration, among the people we now call Ancestral Puebloan. Among the Ancestral Puebloan sites listed in my fifty are **Site 28, Betatakin**; **Site 29, Mesa Verde**; **Site 30, Aztec**; **Site 31, Chaco Canyon**; and **Site 32, Hovenweep**, as well as the cliff dwellings and great houses located in **Site 24, Canyon de Chelly** (the art we will visit there is mostly Navajo).

By the way, "Ancestral Puebloan" has in the past been called "Anasazi," and many authors still use that name. The problem with *Anasazi* is that the word originated, not among the modern descendants of the people who actually built and lived in the sites we label with that term, but in the Navajo language. The meaning of *Anasazi* makes its use even more problematic. When European settlers of the American Southwest asked the Navajo about the identity of the builders of the abandoned cliff dwellings and great houses that abounded in the region, the Navajo referred to those builders as *ana'ai* (which means "alien," "enemy," or "foreigner") and *sazi* (which refers to a body that has entirely decomposed). In other words, the Navajo labeled the people who built the sites as, essentially, "People who weren't Navajos and whose bodies have decayed to dust." You can imagine that this Navajo term is not favored by the Pueblo people.

Ultimately, from your perspective as a time traveler, mastering the technical differences among the named archaeological cultures in the Southwest is not crucial; anyway, the names we impose on them today bear little relationship to what those people called themselves. Don't worry; I promise there won't be a test. What *is* important is our understanding that the spectacular sites we will visit all reflect the genius of Native America. In all of them we see evidence of their clear ability to carve out a life in a hot, dry environment that often presented very challenging and difficult conditions for agriculture. Their architecture was impressive, sophisticated, and beautiful and reflects the great skill of their masons. There is evidence that they were careful observers of the night sky and preserved their observations in art. They built a vast system of roads and participated in a far-flung network of trade and social interaction.

However you divide up their cultures, the agriculture, architecture, astronomical knowledge, trading networks, art, and technology of the ancestors of the various groups and subgroups of the modern Pueblo and Navajo people are amazing and impressive. And what's great about it all is that you can visit and personally experience places that reflect that genius.

Rock Art

How old is art? For how long have we human beings been depicting the real world around us, the visions seen in our dreams or in a trance, or simply the shapes and forms that inhabit our imaginations?

If you've ever taken an art history course in high school or college, you've almost certainly seen ancient depictions that are usually called the "first art." These would be the cave paintings of the European Upper Paleolithic dating to as much as 35,000 years ago. Indeed, the paintings our ancient human ancestors rendered on the walls of caves like Chauvet, Lascaux, and Altamira of animals including horse, rhinoceros, woolly mammoth, and elk are remarkable. But, it turns out, the magnificent tableaux produced by these Ice Age Europeans were not necessarily the earliest art. Archaeologists have now traced back equally old art to caves in Indonesia, where ancient people produced naturalistic paintings of local animals and even left imprints of their hands, the equivalent of an early signature and message: "We were here!" Even older abstract scribbles and doodles—incised lines in pieces of ochre, a soft mineral—have been found in southern Africa dating to more than 70,000 years ago. Other objects representing what amount to "paint pots" have been found in South Africa as well, and date to more than 100,000 years ago. Even more remarkable, a recent reanalysis of a shell dating to more than 1 million years ago on the island of Java revealed the presence of a series of engraved lines produced by a human ancestor with a brain capacity only about two-thirds that of a modern human being.

This astonishing evidence implies that art, however we define it, has extremely deep roots in the human lineage. It might even be argued that art isn't just something human beings do because we are capable of it; maybe the artistic representation of things we have seen, thought, and imagined is an imperative, something we *need* to do. Think about that when you consider all of those finger paintings, watercolor masterpieces, and pen-and-ink drawings that end up hung from magnets on refrigerators all across America. It's not just cute; it's a reflection of how modern human children are part of a continuum of the artistry that has defined our species.

The art you will see in our fifty-site journey represents a remarkable place on that continuum. Here you will see *petroglyphs*, images etched, incised, scratched, or pecked into rock faces by breaking through an external, often dark patina, and exposing the lighter rock beneath to produce an image. You will also see *pictographs*, images produced by the application of paint onto a rock surface. Occasionally the ancient artists of America combined those two techniques in the same art panel, adding flourishes of pigment to the incised image. Finally we'll visit a couple examples of *geoglyphs*, the manipulation of material on the ground—for example, by the arrangement of stones into a pattern—often on a monumental scale, to produce an image comprehensible only from above.

Styles of Rock Art

If you think back on your art history class, you'll probably remember (if only vaguely) a great profusion of artistic styles, schools, and movements that varied across time and space. There's realism, surrealism, impressionism, post-impressionism, romanticism, cubism, op-art, and on and on. Well, just as there is tremendous diversity of themes, styles, and approaches in the Western art tradition, so is there tremendous diversity in the art of Native America. If you are interested in an extremely detailed analysis of the many styles of rock art in the American Southwest, there is no better book to read than Polly Schaafsma's *Indian Rock Art of the Southwest*. For our purposes, I am going to list and describe some of the art styles we will most commonly encounter in our odyssey. Many of our fifty sites exhibit more than one art style, but I'll list some of the sites where each style is most common.

Fremont

Many of the Southwest rock art sites we'll see reflect a style of art called Fremont, named for the archaeological culture first defined from sites located along the Fremont River in north-central Utah where much of the style is concentrated. The Fremont people practiced a mixed economy—planting corn, beans, and squash and also hunting wild animals and gathering wild plants. Their sites generally date between 2,000 and 700 years ago. Fremont art is distinctive and recognizable. The most common animal depicted is the bighorn sheep. Fremont art also includes representations of deer, dogs, birds, lizards, snakes, spirals, human handprints, and *anthropomorphs*: images of humanlike beings standing on two legs. Fremont anthropomorphs usually have very broad shoulders, and their bodies taper to narrow waists; their body shapes are usually described as trapezoidal. In some versions the anthropomorphs lack arms or legs. Many Fremont anthropomorphs are wearing elaborate headdresses. Some of the slickest Fremont art we'll see is found at **Site 39, San Juan River**; **Site 44, Nine Mile Canyon**; **Site 46, McConkie Ranch**; and **McKee Springs in Site 47, Dinosaur National Monument.**

How old is the Fremont art? Rock art can be pretty hard to date directly. Radiocarbon dating works on things that were alive, not on rock. However, there is a radiocarbon date indirectly associated with Fremont art. The Pilling Figurines—eleven small sculptures found in Utah—in three dimensions bear a striking resemblance to the two-dimensional Fremont anthropomorph petroglyphs. Burned wood found at the same site has been dated to about 1,000 years ago. This date provides a good estimate for the age of at least some of the Fremont-style petroglyphs.

Jornada

All the Jornada style rock art in this book is found on black basalt boulders (basalt is a volcanic rock). The look is hard to define, but it's unique and recognizable. There are lots and lots of animals, including bighorn sheep, birds, fish, snakes, and insects. The bodies of the critters often are filled with intricate geometric designs. Jornada also features masks, rainbows, "cloud terraces" (square-stepped images), and mythical beings. The archetype of Jornada style rock art is found at **Site 38, Three Rivers Petroglyph Site** in southern New Mexico. The habitation site adjacent to the rocky crest where the art can be seen is dated to between AD 1000 and AD 1400, and that's a pretty good estimate for the age of the style. You'll also find lots of Jornada art at **Site 36, Petroglyph National Monument,** also in New Mexico.

Barrier Canyon

The Barrier Canyon style is characterized by extremely spooky pictographs of anthropomorphs. The images tend to be elongated; they look like human beings—well, spirit beings that look sort of human—that have been stretched. The stretchy thing is interesting, as after ingesting hallucinogens, fasting, or as a result of sleep deprivation, human beings often experience hallucinations in which everything seems to elongate. Perhaps such hallucinations were the inspiration for the Barrier Canyon art style. Barrier Canyon figures also tend to have very large, googly eyes and often lack arms or legs. The most recent dating of Barrier Canyon art places it in the range of 1,000 to 2,000 years ago. **Site 40, Horseshoe Canyon** (which used to be called Barrier Canyon, providing the name for the style) is the defining site. You'll also see Barrier Canyon pictographs at **Site 42, Buckhorn Wash;** Courthouse Wash in **Site 43, Moab;** and **Site 45, Sego Canyon.**

Coso

The art of the Coso Range in Southern California exhibits some stylistic similarities with what is called Interior Line Style art (seen at **Site 50, Dinwoody** in Wyoming). As in many of these art traditions, there are lots of animal depictions, many of which are bighorn sheep. There are also plenty of pronghorn antelope and deer, as well as lots of strange and otherwise uninterpretable geometric patterns etched into the rock. Coso art is also characterized by fantastical anthropomorphs and what appear to be pouches or bags that have been identified as "medicine bags," in which people would hold charms that were deemed to confer good luck and success on the bearer. The best place to see Coso art is at **Site 34, Little Petroglyph Canyon** in Southern California.

Dinwoody

The Dinwoody style characterizes a number of sites in the northern Great Plains and is actually a subset of a style called Interior Line Style. This tradition includes lots of anthropomorphs with rectangular bodies and large heads. There also are images of birds, and some of the anthropomorphs appear to have birdlike features, including wings. The more characteristic element of Interior Line Style rock art is the detailed, almost busy elements incised into the bodies of the depicted creatures. There are lots of straight and wavy lines, circles, and dots. **Site 50, Dinwoody Lake** in Wyoming is the source of the name of the style.

Northwest Coast

The art style of the Indians of the Northwest Coast in Oregon, Washington, western Canada, and Alaska is exemplified by their totem poles. It's a beautiful, recognizable, and unique style, with depictions of such animals as owls, beavers, wildcats, and whales. The rock art of the northwestern United States can be characterized as essentially a two-dimensional version of the art style of totem poles. The rock art at **Site 48, Horsethief Lake** in Washington's Columbia Hills State Park is a perfect example of this style.

Historic

The creation of rock art continued into the period of European migration to the New World. Perhaps the most obvious indicator of this is the themes and elements seen in the art. For example, depictions of horses, especially horses ridden by men holding guns, date to this historic period. Similarly, rock art showing cows, steam locomotives, and typical Euro-American houses reflect the native reaction to the presence of these new elements in their environment. **Site 37, Crow Canyon** in northern New Mexico, viewed by the Navajo as the place where they were created, has wonderful examples of their tribal rock art. **Site 41, Newspaper Rock** was used as a canvas for petroglyphs for centuries, if not millennia; there are some Fremont-looking bighorn sheep, but there also are some obviously recent historical markings of people on horseback. Similarly, the pictographs of **Site 24, Canyon de Chelly,** including local animals (the paintings of Antelope House), and the amazing painting on the rock wall near Standing Cow Ruin that shows a procession of men riding on horseback, holding guns, and surrounding a horseback rider wearing a cape exhibiting a Christian cross represent what is effectively a historical document of Navajo interaction with the Spanish invaders of their canyon. Also, the rock painting at **Site 35, Chumash Painted Cave** appears to be of recent historical vintage, perhaps no more than about 500 years old. The geoglyphs found at **Site 33, The Blythe Intaglios** may be associated with historical tribes in Southern California, and **Site 49, The Bighorn Medicine Wheel** also appears to be less than 1,000 years old.

Explaining the Art

Maybe one of the essential elements of art is that there is no single explanation for it. Is the rock art seen in our fifty-site jaunt through time religiously motivated? Some of it likely was. How else to explain the images of spirit beings at the Great Gallery in **Site 40, Horseshoe Canyon**? Was it intended as history? Is the Great Hunt Panel at **Site 44, Nine Mile Canyon** a record documenting a particularly successful hunt of bighorn sheep? Was it intended to entertain, even to make people laugh? I certainly laughed when I saw the depiction of the flute-playing sheep at Sand Island, included here as part of **Site 39, San Juan River** in Bluff, Utah. And why, oh why, do so many of the males depicted in rock art have gigantically long penises? And how will you explain those to your 4-year-old? I'm sorry; you're on your own there.

I am not going to attempt to explain the art here. Especially as a non-Native person, I feel uncomfortable imposing a view about the meaning of art that is steeped in the perspective of Western art traditions. But I will say this: The rock art you will see is amazing. It's beautiful, intriguing, astonishing, confounding, moving, and thought-provoking—in other words, it is art. And that explanation is more than enough.

Alright. We have now reached a point where it's time to move on, literally and figuratively, and begin our trek through time.

First Peoples and Mound Builders

Figure 15.

(MAP BY ALENA PEARCE)

Site 1   Meadowcroft Rockshelter

Avella, Pennsylvania

Journal Entry

September 20, 2014

When driving through the deeply green, lush, modern forest that characterizes western Pennsylvania, it is almost impossible to imagine the ancient alien world of Ice Age America. That world was characterized by mile-high fields of glacial ice whose margins were home to an astonishing menagerie of animals. There were enormous, furry elephants with 15-foot long tusks, ground sloths the size of elephants, saber-toothed cats with arching canine teeth more than a foot in length, and bison 50 percent larger than the already gigantically scaled American buffalo. When you look into the enormous alcove today called the Meadowcroft Rockshelter, you are looking at the living space of a group of human beings who called that alien world home. Meadowcroft is our most distant destination in time.

What You Will See

The site is part of the Meadowcroft Rockshelter and Historic Village, which is run by the Senator John Heinz History Center. Every time you have used Heinz ketchup on your burger and fries, you've helped fund the preservation of this site. Pour it on! Along with a small village of historic buildings (you can watch a blacksmith forging iron tools) and a re-creation of a sixteenth-century Indian community—when we were there, you could try your hand at throwing a spear at a model of a deer—there is the rockshelter.

Excavation of the rockshelter (it's more of an alcove in the rock than a true cave) was directed by archaeologist Dr. James Adovasio and is one of the most meticulously investigated sites in North America. Realizing the importance of this site in the study of the earliest human settlement of the New World, the excavation itself has been preserved. You can still see the dig units and stratigraphic profiles exposed by the excavators, each level still bearing its identification tag (Figure 16). Realizing early on the great potential significance of this site, the archaeologists kept extremely accurate track of where and in which layer each recovered artifact was found. By recovering organic material in each of those layers and then applying radiocarbon dating, an age could be assigned to each artifact. The oldest layer has been firmly dated to more than 13,000 years ago, and some of the oldest artifacts found at the site may be as much as 16,000 years old.

Visiting Meadowcroft is like visiting an active archaeological site. You can almost imagine that the archaeologists have taken a lunch break and will return any minute to continue their excavation. It's also like visiting a crime scene where criminologists have left their investigation in place. Adovasio and his crew were investigating not the scene of a crime but the scene of a life, one lived as much as 16,000 years ago. It's a remarkable place. When you visit, imagine those first Americans huddled under the roof of the shelter, creating a life in this new world as an enormous glacier covered the landscape mere miles to the north.

Why Is Meadowcroft Rockshelter Important?

Who first settled the New World? Where did those settlers came from? How did they get here? And when did they first arrive? These have long been key questions posed by scholars hoping to understand the origin and source of the native peoples of the Americas.

Figure 16. The excavation of Meadowcroft Rockshelter has been left as is. Here you can see the site as it was excavated by a team of archaeologists.

As long ago at the early 1600s, a Spanish missionary, José Acosta, shrewdly proposed that American Indians could have walked into the New World from northeast Asia across a land connection of some kind. Using the Bible as his guide, he maintained that since the animals of North and South America must be descendants of those saved on board Noah's Ark, and since the only way those animals could have reached the New World from the landing place of the Ark was by walking, there must be a land connection from the Old World to the New. Human beings, Acosta suggested, would have taken that same route to the New World. Since European explorers had not discovered a connection anywhere else, Acosta proposed that it must exist in the far north, on the west side of the new continent. And he was right.

Of course it would be convenient if we found the oldest human settlements in the New World close to that northwest entry point in Alaska and the Canadian Yukon, with sites progressively more recent as we moved away from that place, but that has not happened. In fact, most of the oldest sites in the New World have been found far from Alaska, in Texas (the Debra L. Friedkin site), Pennsylvania (Meadowcroft), and even Chile (Monte Verde) in South America.

Meadowcroft is an enormously significant site, a high-resolution, tightly focused snapshot of life among the earliest human settlers of the New World. The material remains at the site represent a window into America's ancient past; it shows us, for example, the nature of the stone tool technology of these early settlers and provides information about their subsistence in an inhospitable environment.

For that reason alone, it's a worthwhile stop on your journey through time. The preserved excavation and the shelter constructed around the entrance are quite impressive as well. It is also important to remember that these most ancient inhabitants of western Pennsylvania are the descendants of people more ancient still, whose trail back to their entry point via the Bering Land Bridge likely still presents us with archaeological evidence, not yet discovered, of the spread of human beings through the New World. The archaeological story of those truly "first Americans" remains to be found.

Site Type: First Peoples

Wow Factor: ✳✳✳ The wow factor here is based not so much on what the place looks like but on its significance.

Museum: There is a nice museum on-site. On occasion, the director of archaeology at Meadowcroft, Dr. James Adovasio, provides a tour of the site and lectures about his research. Check the website (below) for the schedule of his presentations.

Ease of Road Access: ✳✳✳✳✳

Ease of Hike: ✳✳✳✳ It's really not a difficult hike, but you do have to climb a bunch of steps.

Natural Beauty of Surroundings: ✳✳✳ The area is wooded and quite pretty.

Kid Friendly: ✳✳✳✳ The rockshelter itself is interesting, but kids will greatly enjoy the replica Indian village. When we were there, kids could use an atlatl to throw spears at a model of a deer.

Food: Bring your own.

How to Get There: It's about an hour southwest of Pittsburgh; 401 Meadowcroft Rd., Avella, Pennsylvania.

Hours of Operation: Saturday noon to 5 p.m.; Sunday 1 to 5 p.m.

Cost: See website.

Best Season to Visit: It can be very cold and snowy in winter in western Pennsylvania. Any other season might be a better bet.

Website: www.heinzhistorycenter.org/exhibits/meadowcroft-rockshelter

Designation: National Historic Landmark

Site 2 Moundville Archaeological Park

Moundville, Alabama

Journal Entry

August 15, 2008

It is incredibly impressive to stand in the expansive plaza at the Moundville archaeological site and look out on a dense concentration of twenty-six monumental, flat-topped pyramids of earth constructed in this one place by the people of the surrounding region. It is impossible not to try to imagine what it must have looked like in its heyday—a busy hub of activity as hundreds of laborers moved thousands of basket loads of dirt to create massive earth platforms for the homes of their chiefs and priests. It's impressive but also perplexing. What possessed all those people—mostly farmers who were otherwise pretty busy producing food for their families and their communities—to congregate at the place we call Moundville and devote so much of their time and energy to create all these elevated platforms for the homes of an elite class of people? Was that labor a form of tax, payment for the privilege of being a protected member of a society in which Moundville served as the spiritual, political, social, and economic capital? That's probably the case. But who were the elites, and how did they obtain the elevated status that earned them the elevated placement of their houses? That is unclear. Today, however, we can marvel at the beauty and symmetry of the mounds and appreciate the work that went into their construction. We also can marvel at the success of a society able to organize and command the labor of its citizens to create so many impressive monuments.

What You Will See

Moundville is a truly spectacular cluster of mounds, any one of which might be the large, primary mound at most other mound builder sites. Altogether, there are twenty-six large platforms of earth demarcating a plaza that covers about 20 acres (Figure 17). The site itself, as was the case for the other significant temple mound sites visited in my odyssey, was surrounded by a wall of wooden logs called a palisade. In this case, the palisade encloses the site on three sides of its rectangular footprint; the fourth side is demarcated by the Black Warrior River.

The largest truncated pyramid at the site, Mound B, stands about 58 feet high and is located at one end of the plaza. This appears to be the platform on which Moundville's ruler's house was built. A replica of that structure stands on top of the mound. It cannot be entered, and unfortunately both the modern wooden stairway and the reconstructed building were in pretty rough shape when I last visited the site in August 2008.

Why Is Moundville Important?

Moundville is an impressive site. The amount of soil that had to be moved to construct its mounds, the labor necessary to create the flat public space of the plaza, and the communal effort required to erect the palisade around the community shows the great ability of the mound builders to conscript, organize, and command large groups of laborers. Moundville wasn't built in a day, to paraphrase an old expression used to characterize the construction of ancient Rome.

Figure 17. Taken from the tallest of the lot, this photo provides a view of the spread of some of the twenty-six platform mounds across a flat, broad plaza at Moundville, Alabama.

In terms of size and hypothesized population, Moundville is second only to **Site 9, Cahokia.** In fact, Moundville's size, as the second-largest of the platform mound population and ceremonial centers, reflects the quantum difference of Cahokia's size: The residents of Moundville constructed 26 impressive mounds; the residents of Cahokia constructed more than 120. Nevertheless, Moundville was a large, bustling metropolis, like Cahokia the religious, economic, and social capital of a mound builder nation. Moundville's population is estimated to have been at least 1,000, with another 10,000 people living in surrounding villages owing allegiance to their larger neighbor.

A wealthy noble class was buried in splendor at Moundville, with well-made grave goods made from difficult-to-obtain materials like seashell and copper. Common folk were buried in simple graves without the beautiful objects that accompanied Moundville's rulers.

Moundville was occupied during a period similar to the other mound communities in our archaeological odyssey, from about AD 1000 to AD 1450, although for unknown reasons it appears to have suffered a serious decline in both population and importance after AD 1350. By the time Spanish explorers such as Hernando de Soto arrived in the 1540s, the community we today called Moundville was all but abandoned.

Site Type: Platform Mound

Wow Factor: **** The concentration of more than two dozen monumental mounds is very impressive.

Museum: The museum was being renovated during my visit to the site but has since reopened.

Ease of Road Access: *****

Ease of Hike: *****

Natural Beauty of Surroundings: ***

Kid Friendly: **** Lots of running-around room

Food: Bring your own.

How to Get There: Moundville is located just 14 miles south of Tuscaloosa, Alabama, and is accessible from I-20/59. Take exit 71A and go south on AL 69 for 13 miles to the park entrance.

Hours of Operation: The Moundville grounds are open daily 9:00 a.m. to dusk. The on-site Jones Museum is open daily 9 a.m. to 5 p.m.

Cost: See website.

Best Season to Visit: It's Alabama; summers are hot and humid.

Website: http://moundville.ua.edu

Designation: State park; National Historic Landmark

Site 3 Toltec Mounds Archaeological State Park

Scott, Arkansas

Journal Entry

April 18, 2012

Sometimes when walking around an ancient archaeological site during my odyssey, I thought to myself, *I would have liked living here.* Toltec Mounds was like that. It's quite simply a beautiful, peaceful place. The three primary and well-preserved mounds are impressive, quite lovely examples of what amounts to an ancient reengineering of the landscape. Also beautiful is the location of the site, adjacent to a water-filled meander scar, one of more than a dozen similar curved channels of water in the area that now are individual lakes but were in the past segments of the Arkansas River. Check out the region surrounding Toltec Mounds on Google Earth and you'll see them. Now looking like curved squiggles on the landscape, they are deserving of their common name, "oxbows," for their similarity in form to the U-shaped part of an ox's harness. Meander scars, or oxbows, are the footprints of active rivers, channels abandoned when powerful surges of flowing water literally reconfigured the flow of the river. As I walked around Toltec Mounds I thought about the people who had lived there. Certainly they had to deal with the ever-shifting channel of the Arkansas River. The soil must have been so rich for agriculture and their harvests so rewarding that the challenges they faced were worth the price they paid.

What You Will See

Toltec Mounds is a ceremonial center of the Mississippian culture dating from AD 600 to AD 1050. There originally were eighteen platform mounds at the site, located within a 100-acre enclosure demarcated by a rectangular ditch and ridge of earth nearly 10 feet tall on three sides and the banks of the oxbow lake on the fourth. Three of the mounds are pretty well preserved, and two of those are impressive (I.1). Mound A is nearly 50 feet high; Mound B is only a little smaller, about 40 feet. Both of those are platform mounds (Figure 18). The third preserved mound, Mound R, is a bit smaller. There are two established trails at the site. The Knapp Trail is paved, wheelchair-accessible, and about 0.8 mile round-trip. Follow it to see the three best preserved of the earthworks. The unpaved Plum Bayou Trail is 1.6 miles round-trip and provides a broader view of the site. The on-site museum is quite good, and a thoughtful and well-crafted short film provides some context for the site.

Why Is Toltec Mounds Important?

Toltec is a great site because it exhibits very clearly the characteristics of a Mississippian ceremonial center. When we in the West think of a great, ancient civilization, like that of the Sumerians in Mesopotamia (modern-day southern Iraq), the Egyptians, or the Aztecs or Maya, we think that dense populations of great urban settlements—simply, cities—are always part of the equation. The kind of place anthropologists generally label "ceremonial centers" is alien to many of our common assumptions about a civilization. And granted, **Site 9, Cahokia** in Illinois for sure and to a lesser extend **Site 2, Moundville** in Georgia were urban, with a dense concentration of people living in tightly packed neighborhoods. But most of the impressive mound builder sites were not great population centers.

Figure 18. The platform mounds at Toltec are very well maintained and beautifully symmetrical.

There is evidence of monumental construction in the form of impressive pyramids of earth. There is evidence of social stratification in the sumptuous burials of members of the elite classes. There also is evidence of finely crafted works of art, implying that at least some members of the community spent most, if not all, of their time producing these things for the rich folks to use in both life and in death. And there's plenty of evidence of vast and sophisticated trading networks for obtaining highly prized raw materials from their sources, often hundreds of miles distant. But many of the sites where we see this concentration of monuments, rich folks, and finely made objects, often crafted from exotic materials, do not exhibit evidence of very large populations. Instead these places of religious, social, political, and economic focus had small populations. These centers relied on a widely dispersed population of primarily farmers, who willingly provided their surplus food, their surplus labor (in building great monuments of soil for the elite classes), and perhaps even the lives of their children as warriors to the few but powerful inhabitants and keepers of the ceremonial centers.

The construction of the mounds and enclosing embankment at Toltec certainly took a tremendous amount of work, but there's very little archaeological evidence of people living at the site. Population estimates suggest that perhaps only about fifty people lived across this enormous and impressive site. The inhabitants almost certainly were the rulers and religious elite of a people, the majority of whom lived in farming villages spread across the region.

Site Type: Platform Mound

Wow Factor: **** Some of the individual mounds at Toltec are impressively large.

Museum: **** The museum is terrific. There are lots of beautiful artifacts on display that were found at the site.

Ease of Road Access: *****

Ease of Hike: **** The area where the mounds are located is pretty spread out, so you can walk a lot. Some of the main trails are paved and very flat.

Natural Beauty of Surroundings: ***** The beautiful, open parklike site abuts an old oxbow lake (Mound Pond).

Kid Friendly: **** Lots of room to explore

Food: Bring your own.

How to Get There: Toltec Mound State Park is located near Scott, Arkansas. From Little Rock take exit 7 off I-440; go 10 miles southeast on US 165 then travel 0.25 mile southwest on AR 386.

Hours of Operation: Grounds open daily dawn to dusk. Museum open Tuesday through Saturday 8 a.m. to 5 p.m.; Sunday 1 to 5 p.m.

Cost: Free. The museum offers guided tours for a nominal fee; check the website for schedules and costs.

Best Season to Visit: Arkansas is hot and humid in summer; no surprise there.

Website: www.arkansasstateparks.com/toltecmounds/

Designation: State park; National Historic Landmark

Site 4 Crystal River Archaeological State Park

Crystal River, Florida

Journal Entry

August 16, 2008

Ah, Florida—land of endless sunshine; oppressive, mind-numbing humidity; insects the size of small dogs; gigantic, exotic snakes that eat small dogs; a popular religion that involves some sort of a rodent deity; and early-bird specials where restaurateurs serve absurdly large meal portions for absurdly low prices, at a time absurdly too early for dinner. Oh, and they also have Crystal River Archaeological State Park.

Designated a national historic landmark, Crystal River is a large and impressive mound site with a major truncated pyramid of earth and shell and five subsidiary mounds. Crystal River is by far the most impressive of the mound sites in Florida. The people of Crystal River relied on the rich Gulf Coast habitat in which their village was located.

Figure 19. The primary mound at Crystal River, located on the west coast of Florida. The setting is beautiful and the mound well maintained.

Figure 20. One of the two upright stones found at Crystal River. Some interpret these objects as implying contact with the Maya, who regularly erected such stelae. You should be able to make out an inscription of a human head on the photograph on the left. The image on the right has an outline of the head drawn over the inscription. (JENNIFER DAVIS)

What You Will See

The Crystal River site has about the most beautiful setting of any of the mound sites we are visiting during our odyssey. It's located on the Gulf Coast of Florida, where the ocean is achingly blue and the sky is even bluer. As you walk around the site, you will see one very tall and impressive platform mound. Called First Temple Mound, it stands just shy of 30 feet high; you can climb a wooden stairway to its apex to get a nice view of the site and of the aquamarine water of Crystal River (Figure 19). Radiocarbon dating suggests that construction of this mound began in about AD 600. Population peaked in the area around AD 1000, and that likely marks the height of Crystal River's use as a ceremonial center for the Indians living along Florida's central Gulf Coast. As many as 1,000 people were buried at Crystal River. Many of the deceased were interred with finely made objects of ceramic and shell. Some were buried with copper jewelry including earrings; the copper to make this jewelry originated in Michigan, indicating the far-reaching nature of mound builder trade during this period.

Following the short trail around the site, you'll see five additional mounds, lots of Spanish moss, and, at least when I was there, some of the biggest grasshopper-looking things I've ever seen. They say that everything is bigger in Texas. No offense to Texans, but I doubt their bugs are bigger than those in Florida. I hope not, for the sake of Texans. Those suckers were huge. There's a nice on-site museum with artifacts excavated at the site and a 3-D scale model of the site.

Why Is Crystal River Important?

Crystal River Mound's location on the middle of Florida's west coast is significant in showing the vast geographic extent of mound builder societies. From the mountains of North Carolina to the prairies of

Oklahoma, from as far north as Wisconsin to as far south as Florida, up and down the major rivers of the American Midwest and Southeast and here at Crystal River along the Gulf Coast, Native Americans developed complex agricultural societies capable of producing monumental earthen pyramids, conducting long-distance trade, and supporting a powerful noble class.

Okay, you've heard me say that before about other mound builder sites. What makes Crystal River different and worth a visit beyond the obvious beauty of its Floridian Gulf Coast setting? It's the presence at the site of two upright stones, at least one of which has an incised image of a person (Figure 20). These artifacts are unique among mound builder sites and are reminiscent of the stelae of the Maya, the great civilization centered in eastern Mexico, Guatemala, and Honduras, and who, by the way, did NOT predict the end of the world for December 21, 2012. Apparent offerings of burned corn kernels and chert (a stone used to make tools) buried at the base of the Crystal River stones mirrors a similar practice seen at Maya stelae. Did Maya visitors cross the Gulf of Mexico and settle in Florida or at least inspire some of the cultural activities seen at Crystal River?

The level of contact, if any, between the native peoples of Mesoamerica and North America is a controversial issue in archaeology. There certainly was trade (especially for turquoise) between the native peoples of Mexico and the inhabitants of the American Southwest (where the turquoise resources were located). While the overall appearance of Maya sites—with their large, flat-topped pyramids bordering vast plazas—is generally reminiscent of at least some mound builder centers, there is no direct evidence for contact between the Maya and the mound builders. The upright slabs at Crystal River may be a clue concerning such contact, but only more research can answer this question. It's an interesting hypothesis and worth considering during your visit.

Site Type: Platform Mound

Wow Factor: *** The largest of the mounds is pretty impressive, but the biggest element of the wow factor is the setting of the site itself.

Museum: ****

Ease of Road Access: ****

Ease of Hike: ***

Natural Beauty of Surroundings: **** The surroundings are gorgeous, with lots of sailboats, seagulls, beautiful palm trees, and lizards.

Kid Friendly: **** Like I just said—lizards. Kids will love the place.

Food: Bring your own.

How to Get There: The site is located about 3 miles from the town of Crystal River, 2 miles north on US 19, 1 mile west on State Park Street, and left on Museum Pointe. Punch into your GPS: 3400 N. Museum Point, Crystal River, Florida.

Hours of Operation: Grounds open daily 8 a.m. to sundown. Museum open Monday and Thursday through Sunday 9 a.m. to 5 p.m. (closed Tuesday and Wednesday).

Cost: See website. You'll need correct change.

Best Season to Visit: It's Florida—hot and humid in summer.

Website: www.floridastateparks.org/crystalriverarchaeological/

Designation: State park; National Historic Landmark

Site 5   Kolomoki Mounds State Park

Blakely, Georgia

Journal Entry

August 15, 2008

Have you seen the bumper sticker "Mean People Suck"? As a general statement, I think we can all agree with that sentiment: Mean people really do suck. I include under that label folks who would break into a lovely little museum dedicated to memorializing the history of the native peoples of southwestern Georgia and then steal not just individual artifacts but also the opportunity for visitors to see, appreciate, and learn from those wonderful works of art and craft. This is exactly what occurred at Kolomoki Mounds State Park in 1974. Thieves broke into the on-site museum and absconded with 129 artifacts that had been excavated at the site. Artifacts are like books, especially in the case of a non-literate people who left behind no written account of their lives. Archaeologists can read tools, as well as works of art, and convey the stories these objects tell us in the here and now. The good news is that fifty-nine of those artifacts, those stories told by past people, have been recovered. The bad news is that seventy of them remain missing. That's seventy stories that may never be told again.

What You Will See

Kolomoki is a relatively small, but nevertheless impressive, mound site located in southwest Georgia. Two large mounds sit on either end of a broad plaza. The large platform mound is monumental and impressive,

Figure 21. The primary mound at Kolomoki, in Georgia.

Figure 22. A ceramic bird on display in the Kolomoki Mounds museum.

a 57-foot-high truncated pyramid with a rectangular footprint of 325 by 200 feet (Figure 21). To pile up enough earth to produce this mound, the makers would have needed to dig up, fill, carry, and pile up about 11 million one-gallon buckets of soil, a truly monumental undertaking. The other large earthwork is a pretty large conical mound. Six more smaller earthworks demarcate a small plaza. It's a very short, pleasant hike across the plaza from the main platform mound to the largest of the site's conical mounds. There's also a very nice museum on-site, built directly over and within the remains of a burial mound. So when you walk to the back of the museum, you're actually walking into the bowels of the burial chamber within the mound (weird!). Many of the burials have been left more or less as they were found, except that the skeletons are replicas. There are also some beautifully made ceramic vessels on display in the museum (Figure 22).

The site is situated within a state park with hiking, swimming, camping, fishing, boating, picnicking, and even minigolf. (I wonder what archaeologists in the future will make of minigolf courses.)

Why Is Kolomoki Important?

While Kolomoki isn't the largest or most impressive of the mound builder sites visited in our odyssey, it is nevertheless important, at least in part because it is one of the oldest. Radiocarbon dating shows that the site was occupied as early as AD 250, and the mounds were all built before its abandonment by AD 950. In other words, Kolomoki was already a ghost town by the time most of the other mound sites we're visiting in the Southeast were only getting started.

Kolomoki was a large community whose peak population exceeded 1,000, yet another example of a densely settled mound builder community in the American Southeast.

Site Type: Platform Mound, Burial Mound

Wow Factor: ** The largest of the Kolomoki Mounds is impressive.

Museum: The museum is built into and around a burial mound. When you walk into the museum, you are walking into the interior of the mound.

Ease of Road Access: *****

Ease of Hike: *****

Natural Beauty of Surroundings: ***

Kid Friendly: **

Food: Bring your own.

How to Get There: Kolomoki is located in southwest Georgia, in Kolomoki Mounds Historic Park; near Albany and 6 miles north of Blakely off US 27. Punch 205 Indian Mounds Rd., Blakely, Georgia, into your GPS.

Hours of Operation: Grounds open daily 7 a.m. to 10 p.m. Museum open daily 8 a.m. to 5 p.m.; closed on major holidays.

Cost: See website.

Best Season to Visit: It certainly is hot and humid here in summer, but since there's no long hike to take, a visit just about any time is fine.

Website: http://gastateparks.org/KolomokiMounds

Designation: State park; National Historic Landmark

Site 6 **Rock Eagle Effigy Mound**

Eatonton, Georgia

Journal Entry

August 23, 2008

As I stood in the tower built to afford visitors a bird's-eye view (a perfect use of that phrase) of Rock Eagle Effigy Mound, it was impossible not to imagine what it must have been like when it was being constructed. Stone cobbles of just the right size and color were hauled to the site by the basketful. Designers established the outline of a large bird of prey using pebbles or, maybe, drawing it in the soil with a stick. Perhaps some individuals climbed high up into the surrounding trees to direct those working below. From their perch, they were able to truly appreciate the competed work of public art. Though it is impossible to determine for certain its purpose to those who created it, as I viewed it from the tower, I thought about the bald eagles that occasionally fly over my house in northwestern Connecticut. They are breathtaking, and I am always moved by their majesty and by the freedom represented in their seemingly effortless flight. I think it is reasonable to perceive that the artists who produced Rock Eagle Effigy Mound were expressing their awe for the majesty and freedom represented by great birds of prey.

What You Will See

At the Rock Eagle Effigy Monument you'll have the opportunity to see one of only two rock mounds created in the shape of animals in the United States. (The other is located on Lake Oconee, also in Georgia. I haven't included that on in my list of fifty because it's not nearly as well maintained.) Rock Eagle is large, impressively beautiful, and well maintained. The effigy is huge, measuring a little more than 100 feet across its wingspan and about 120 feet from the top of its head to the base of its tail feathers (Figure 23). Its highest point, in the middle of the eagle, consists of a stone pile of primarily milky quartz cobbles about 10 feet high.

Luckily, you don't have to be a bird or a god (or a sky diver or ultralight pilot) to fully appreciate the entire image of the enormous eagle. An enclosed four-story-high stone tower, built during the Depression by the Civilian Conservation Corps, is located at the mound's base, right below the eagle's tail feathers. Even if you are a little freaked out by the prospect of climbing the open tower at **Site 14, Serpent Mound,** you'll be fine here; the Rock Eagle tower is very solid, and the viewing windows are small. From the top you'll be able to get a bird's-eye view of the, well, bird. Even from that vantage point, you'll need a wide-angle lens to photograph the entire thing.

Why Is Rock Eagle Effigy Mound Important?

What's not to like about a rock eagle with a more than 100-foot wingspan? Effigy mounds—animal shapes made of earth but also, rarely, constructed by piling up individual stones—afford a unique opportunity to view monumental works of Native American art, art that conceivably reflects the spiritual life

Figure 23. Rock Eagle Effigy Mound in Eatonton, Georgia.

of America's first inhabitants. Rock Eagle Effigy Mound is large and beautiful, and certainly worth a visit for those reasons.

Rock Eagle was partially excavated in the 1930s. Archaeologists found a human burial within the rocks that make up the mound. Effigy mounds can be difficult to date accurately, but Rock Eagle most likely was built sometime between 1000 BC and AD 1000.

Rock Eagle is beautiful, to be sure, and a variety of art we don't often hear about in that required art history course many of us sat through in college. It's neither a painting nor a sculpture; instead it's an arrangement, on a gigantic scale, of stones in the shape of an animal. Like **Site 14, Serpent Mound** in Ohio, and similar to **Site 33, Blythe Intaglios** in Blythe, California, Rock Eagle represents a broad category of monumental artworks produced by ancient peoples all over the world that can only be fully appreciated from a nonhuman perspective—that is, a vantage point from above, like that afforded only birds and, perhaps, the gods. Maybe you've heard of the ancient Nazca Lines of South America, ground drawings of a monumental spider, a monkey, birds, and fish. No, they weren't built or inspired by ancient astronauts who directed the primitive earthlings they encountered to make giant animal drawings. Seriously? But they likely were made to appeal to the gods who, as in so many cultures, were believed to reside in the sky. Hey, medieval churches in Europe were built in the form of giant crosses, their shape not viewable by the people who built and worshipped there, but seen by God on high. It's the same idea. Appreciate Rock Eagle for its beauty, its context, and its meaning—an ode by an ancient people to the spirit of the birds that possessed both great beauty and the ability to slip "the surly bonds of earth and dance[d] the skies on laughter-silvered wings" [RCAF Flight-Lieutenant John Gillespie Magee Jr. (1922–1941)].

Site Type: Effigy Mound

Wow Factor: ** The large-scale eagle made of piled rocks is pretty impressive.

Museum: None

Ease of Road Access: *** Access is by paved road; the signage is a little confusing, but you'll find it.

Ease of Hike: **** Like Serpent Mound, the walk to the effigy and the observation tower is easy. The stairs to the top of the enclosed tower (fear of heights shouldn't be a problem) is easy, but if your knees are achy, think twice.

Natural Beauty of Surroundings: ****

Kid Friendly: **

Food: Bring your own.

How to Get There: Rock Eagle Effigy Mound is located in a 1,500-acre park that is part of the University of Georgia campus in Eatonton, Georgia, less than an hour drive from Atlanta. The park is also used today as a 4-H center. The park is accessible from US 441, which you can get to from I-20. Turn onto Rock Eagle Road; follow it for 0.7 mile and then turn right onto the first road you encounter. From this road, turn left onto the first road on your left and follow it to the site parking lot.

Once we reached the park, we actually had a little trouble locating the mound, but if you persistently follow the signs, you'll be fine.

Hours of Operation: Grounds open year-round, dawn to dusk

Cost: Free

Best Season to Visit: Any time

Website: www.exploresouthernhistory.com/rockeagle.html

Designation: University of Georgia; National Register of Historic Places

Site 7   Etowah Indian Mounds State Historic Site

Etowah, Georgia

Journal Entry

August 14, 2009

We drove through North Carolina and into Georgia, arriving at Etowah Indian Mounds, a state historic park located in Cartersville, Georgia, in the early afternoon. Etowah is extremely well maintained and actually more impressive than I remembered from my first visit in summer 1982. There are three major surviving mounds. One is huge, shaped somewhat like Monks Mound at **Site 9, Cahokia.** A little less than two-thirds the height of Monks, it is still truly monumental. The two somewhat smaller, square-based mounds are especially well maintained, and all three mounds have wooden-log steps leading to their tops.

There's a museum on-site with an array of spectacular works of ancient art found at Etowah, including sculptures of a man and a woman (each kneeling and about 3 feet high). There also are a number of beautifully carved shell gorgets—amulets a couple of inches across showing humans, perhaps priests, dressed in bird costumes and carrying weapons. They're really quite lovely.

What You Will See

Etowah is one of the most significant mound builder sites in the American Southeast. There are three major temple mounds, the volume of which is second in size only to Monks Mound at Cahokia.

Figure 24. Two of the three primary mounds at Etowah in Georgia.

Figure 25. The artifacts on display in the Etowah museum are spectacular. Here are two not quite life-size, painted marble sculptures of a kneeling women (left) and a cross-legged man (right).

Radiocarbon dating indicates the site was built about AD 950. The site has been beautifully maintained by the state of Georgia as part of a state park. It only takes a couple of hours to leisurely walk the park and climb the stairs to the tops of each of the three platform mounds.

Etowah clearly was an important southeastern mound builder population and ceremonial center. Dating to AD 950, just before European contact in the early sixteenth century, Etowah presents, in total, about a half dozen mounds, three of which are substantial in size. The largest, Mound A, is huge; the platform at its apex is more than 60 feet above the plaza below (Figure 24 and I.2).

Along with an encompassing log wall or palisade, you'll see remnants of another kind of defensive feature at Etowah: a 10-foot-deep ditch around the entire 54-acre site that when filled with water would have served effectively as a moat. Anyone trying to attack the site would have to climb down into and then up the walls of the moat while Etowah's defenders could have rained arrows down on them from their position inside bastions that were part of the palisade. Not a pleasant proposition.

Along with the very well-maintained grounds and mounds, the museum at Etowah is just fantastic. The artisans at Etowah were top-notch, producing splendid works of art in clay, stone, and shell. The two sculptures of kneeling people—a man and a woman—are not only beautiful but also provide us with a snapshot of what Etowah's inhabitants looked like, including their clothing, makeup, hairstyles, and jewelry (Figure 25).

My favorite artifacts displayed in the Etowah museum are the gorgets, likely used as pendants suspended around the neck of their wearer. The Etowah gorgets are made of round pieces of shell. Using

Figure 26. The is one of two shell amulets called gorgets on display. Simply gorgeous.

stone tools to produce the designs, the artisans cut out some sections of the shell and etched lines into those portions they left intact (Figure 26, I.3). Then they smeared a black pigment onto the surface and finally wiped it off, with the pigment adhering to the interior of the etched lines. The two gorgets recovered at the site and on display depict what appear to be either human/raptor hybrids or warriors wearing an eagle or hawk costume. There appears to be a mask with a hooked beak and top feathers, taloned feet, and either actual wings or a cloak made to look like wings. How do we know the artists were depicting warriors? Both of the raptor-men are wielding bad-ass weapons that look like viciously barbed boomerangs. These are incredibly cool-looking works of art and, like so much of art, both modern and ancient, provide a window into the spiritual minds of the artists who produced them.

Why Is Etowah Important?

Etowah is a terrific example of a large, impressive mound builder ceremonial center. In all likelihood, its population was relatively small—not nearly as large as Cahokia's, which was truly urban in character—but great chiefs and priests lived at the site. So while Cahokia was unique—a truly singular outlier in terms of its overall spatial footprint, its population, the number of earthworks, its economic wealth, its domination of trading networks, the social standing of its elite class, and the geographic extent of its political power—it was not the only large, powerful "nation" in the American Midwest, mid-South, and Southeast. Etowah might be characterized as the Boston to Cahokia's New York City.

Recently archaeologists have been applying space-age technology at Etowah to determine its buried secrets without actually moving any earth. The remains of a large rectangular foundation were found on top of Mound A. This likely was the house of Etowah's chief or ruler. Though Etowah appears to have been abandoned by the time Spanish explorer Hernando de Soto passed through the Southeast, he did discuss the location of the chief's house in occupied villages he encountered, placing them at the apex of the tallest, flat-topped artificial mountain of earth.

Site Type: Platform Mound

Wow Factor: *** The three primary mounds at Etowah are massive, beautifully symmetrical, and very well maintained.

Museum: **** The museum has amazing displays of beautiful artifacts recovered at Etowah. The sculptures of seated and cross-legged women are very impressive, and the engraved shell gorgets (amulets) are stunning.

Ease of Road Access: *****

Ease of Hike: ****

Natural Beauty of Surroundings: ****

Kid Friendly: ****

Food: Bring your own.

How to Get There: Etowah Indian Mounds State Historic Site is located on Indian Mounds Road in Cartersville, Georgia, easily accessible from I-75 (exit 288). The nearest large city is Marietta. Punch 813 Indian Mounds Rd. SW, Cartersville, Georgia, into your GPS for exact directions from wherever you are.

Hours of Operation: Grounds open Wednesday through Saturday 9 a.m. to 5 p.m.; Sunday 2 to 5 p.m. Closed Monday and major holidays. Call (770) 387-3747 for last-minute schedule changes.

Cost: See website.

Best Season to Visit: Georgia. Summer. Hot. Other seasons might be more comfortable.

Website: http://gastateparks.org/EtowahMounds

Designation: State park; National Historic Landmark

Site 8 Ocmulgee National Monument

Macon, Georgia

Journal Entry

August 24, 2008

After a visit to my parents down in Delray Beach on Florida's east coast, it was back to touring. In a roundabout route we returned to central Georgia, near the city of Macon, where we stopped at **Ocmulgee Mounds.** Sure, you are right to question the sanity of a Northerner who elects to leave the air-conditioned comfort of his car to walk around a mound site in Georgia in August. If someone living in, say, the Canadian Yukon wanted to experience for the first time the evil twins, heat and humidity, central Georgia in August would be a good choice. Nevertheless, Ocmulgee is a very impressive, though not very well-known, temple mound site. I wonder if part of the problem is the name; it's hard to spell, a mystery to pronounce. Anyway, it's an interesting and impressive site, and the museum building is gorgeous—built in the Art Moderne style, white with all rounded corners.

What You Will See

Ocmulgee National Monument is an extensive site with seven mounds and a feature not seen at the other mound sites visited in our odyssey: a reconstructed earth lodge (Figure 27). Far larger than any

Figure 27. Reconstructed "earth lodge" at Ocmulgee Mounds. Yes, you can walk inside it.

Figure 28. View of a sample of the truncated, pyramidal mounds of Ocmulgee.

of the other earthworks at the site, Great Temple Mound looms above a great open plaza. This giant platform of earth is 55 feet high, and a wooden stairway leads to its top. From the apex of the Great Temple mound, you'll be able to see Lesser Temple Mound; Funeral Mound, in which more than one hundred burials of important individuals interred with impressive grave goods have been found; and the other, smaller earthworks at the site (Figure 28).

Don't miss the reconstructed earth lodge, a turf-covered structure. The original turf and supporting logs have been replaced, but the clay floor is original and dates back about 1,000 years. The reconstructed earth lodge does not appear to have been a residence but, instead, a ceremonial building more than 40 feet in diameter. None of the artifacts of daily life were found in its excavation, so it's unlikely that anyone lived there. It's a very impressive building, and you can walk inside and imagine being there during ceremonies a thousand years ago.

There's also a terrific on-site museum with a very extensive collection of impressive works of art excavated at the site. About 2,000 of the 2.5 million artifacts recovered during the 1934–1941 excavation of the site are on display.

Ocmulgee has been designated a national historic landmark. Naturalist William Bartram (1739–1823) visited Ocmulgee in 1774 and commented on its ancient grandeur:

> *"On the heights of these low grounds are yet visible monuments, or traces, of an ancient town, such as artificial mounts or terraces, squares and banks, encircling considerable areas. Their old fields and planting land extend up and down the river, fifteen or twenty miles from this site. If we are to give credit to the account the Creeks give of themselves, this place is remarkable for being the first town or settlement, when they sat down (as they term it) or established themselves, after their emigration from the west. . . ."*

Even as late as 1774, Bartram could recognize the old agricultural fields that had been cleared for planting by people who were, broadly speaking, the residents of greater Ocmulgee. In all likelihood, the 15- or 20-mile distance from Ocmulgee to which Bartram referred reflects the extent of the territory surrounding the ceremonial center, where smaller farming villages were located. The residents of these farming villages considered themselves to be part of the nation ruled over by the Ocmulgee elite class. It was the labor of these common people that produced the earthworks, and it was the agricultural surplus produced by these farmers and supplied to the elites—think taxes or tithes—that supported the lives and activities of that upper class.

Why Is Ocmulgee Important?

Like the other mound sites included in our tour, Ocmulgee is important as a reflection of the ability of ancient Native Americans to produce large and sophisticated earthworks, as well as their practice of living in large, urban-like communities with a complex socioeconomic structure. Whoops! There goes that university-speak again; sorry. How about this: Occupied between AD 900 and AD 1100, Ocmulgee is important because it helps tear down stereotypes too many of us harbor about Native American culture. The reconstructed earth lodge and the extensive museum display make Ocmulgee a valuable stop on your archaeological odyssey.

Ocmulgee is also important as an example of the growth of public archaeology during the Depression. Archaeological research was included among the work projects supported by the federal government to produce jobs for the unemployed. Trained archaeologists were given jobs directing sometimes large-scale excavation projects, and untrained workers were given jobs as diggers. During the eight years the site was part of this federal project, more than 800 people were engaged in excavating the site, making this the largest archaeological project ever conducted in the United States.

Site Type: Platform Mound
Wow Factor: **** The site covers an enormous expanse, and a few of the mounds are monumentally scaled.
Museum: The reconstructed earth lodge you can walk into is fantastic.
Ease of Road Access: *****
Ease of Hike: ****
Natural Beauty of Surroundings: ****
Kid Friendly: ****
Food: Bring your own.
How to Get There: Ocmulgee is located on the eastern edge of Macon, Georgia. The site is accessible from I-75. Take the exit for I-16 east and then either the first or second exit off I-16 to US 80 east. The park is 1 mile from that exit. Punch 1207 Emery Highway, Macon, Georgia, into your GPS.
Hours of Operation: Grounds open daily 9 a.m. to 5 p.m. Closed Christmas Day and New Year's Day.
Cost: Free except during the Ocmulgee Indian Celebration (third week of September) and Lantern Light Tours (in May). See website for those events.
Best Season to Visit: It's in Georgia, so of course it's going to be hot and humid in summer. Fall and spring are beautiful.
Website: www.nps.gov/ocmu/index.htm
Designation: National Monument

Site 9 Cahokia Mounds State Historic Site

Collinsville, Illinois

Journal Entry

Spring 2008

I first became aware of Cahokia as the only undergraduate student enrolled in a graduate course at my university. Everyone in the course had to choose an early "civilization" on which to write a research paper, and part of the requirement was to present a coherent, thirty-minute lecture on the ancient culture we had selected for our term paper. Most students took the obvious route, choosing Egypt of the pharaohs, Mesopotamia, the Aztecs, etc. In what I thought was a rather clever move, I went a different way, choosing a less-obvious culture, intentionally one the professor admitted he knew very little about: the mound builders of North America. Of course I knew nothing about them either and was pretty stressed when it came time for the oral presentation.

Ironically, perhaps precisely because I was a nervous but motivated undergrad in a grad course, I was more than prepared with my now too cute seeming 3 x 5 note cards. It all was a fabulous success—well, I passed the course—and inspired a lifelong fascination with the most spectacular of the mound builder sites, Cahokia.

That is why as soon as I got the chance to visit St. Louis in the mid-1970s, I immediately asked the hotel clerk how to get to Cahokia. He didn't have a clue what I was talking about, so I attempted to clarify: "You know," I explained, "the big Indian site." At this the clerk leaned in to whisper to me, a person he must have assumed was a completely deluded Easterner, "No, no. There haven't been any Indians around here for many years."

Cahokia has been one of the best-kept secrets in American history; even locals can be uncertain of its existence. Let's put an end to that uncertainty here and now. I've been to Cahokia several times. Now it's your turn.

What You Will See

Leave behind any stereotypes you may harbor of "primitive" tepee-dwelling, buffalo-hunting Native American nomads living a hand-to-mouth existence and in a perpetual state of war.

The temple mound societies of the American Midwest and Southeast were nothing like that. The fully agricultural people of the American Indian temple mound building culture built enormous monuments of earth. They were ruled by great leaders who were buried in sumptuous splendor; in a few cases they lived in large, dense, urban-like settlements. Mound builder society had more in common with Egypt of the Pharaohs than Hollywood stereotypes of the nomadic Indian. The temple mound builders were a Native American *civilization*. Cahokia is the most impressive of the mound builder sites on our archaeological odyssey.

If any ancient Native American site can be called a "city" it would be Cahokia (I.4). Even conservative estimates gauge its population between AD 1050 and AD 1200 to have been several thousand, and 10,000 or even 20,000 are not unreasonable estimates. Cahokia was effectively the capital of a geographically extensive American Indian empire whose reach was felt hundreds of miles away. Raw

Figure 29. Monks Mound at Cahokia is the largest earthwork in North America.

materials from across the American Midwest made their way to Cahokia, and works produced by Cahokia's artisans in stone, clay, shell, and copper are found hundreds of miles from the site. Cahokia is a terrific place and should be high on everyone's list of sites to visit.

Cahokia is a truly remarkable place. Plan to spend several hours there. There are about seventy surviving mounds, including Monks Mound, the largest monument built by Native Americans north of Mexico (Figure 29, I.5). Monks Mound is a flat-topped pyramid built in at least three levels. Its base covers about 14 acres, and 21 million cubic feet of dirt make up its mass. That immense volume makes Monks Mound the fifth-largest pyramid in the world; the only bigger pyramids are in Egypt and Central America. A stairway leads to the top, where you will stand about 100 feet above the plaza below. The climb will get your heart pumping, but it is well worth it. From the summit of Monks Mound you will be able to look down on a plaza surrounded by a few smaller, though still impressive, mounds. You'll also be able to see St. Louis, framed by its Gateway Arch.

Off to the side of Monks Mound there's a reconstructed section of a small part of the palisade that

Figure 30. This beautiful sculpture of a mother nursing an infant is an example of the skill of Cahokia's artists. You can see it at the splendid on-site museum.

Figure 31. Reconstruction of the primary Mound 72 burial at Cahokia. The man depicted here was a great ruler whose interment reflects the enormous power he must have wielded in life.

surrounded the central part of the city. An easy hiking trail takes you around the site, and you can walk by many of the larger, more impressive earthworks.

The on-site museum at Cahokia is extraordinarily impressive, with a large 3-D map of the site, huge painted murals presenting artistic depictions of the community at its peak, beautiful works of art (Figure 30), and a life-size walk-through diorama showing a residential part of the Cahokia community. You will also see a replica of the burial in Mound 72, where a man, probably an important ruler, was buried in a cape of 20,000 shell beads along with a thousand finely made stone arrow points and dozens of human sacrifices, including more than fifty young women (Figure 31).

Why Is Cahokia Important?

Cahokia was a Native American city occupied between AD 700 and AD 1400 and at its urban-like peak between AD 1050 and AD 1200. It was essentially the capital of an empire, with dozens of smaller ceremonial centers and hundreds upon hundreds of farming villages whose inhabitants owed their social, political, economic, and religious allegiance to the elites who lived at Cahokia itself. An enormous workforce produced monumental earthworks in this capital city; as many as 120 mounds were built at Cahokia. A palisade containing 20,000 logs enclosed the 200 acres that represented the heart of the community. The rich bottomland of the Mississippi River Valley provided the fertile soil in which Cahokia's farmers grew corn, squash, and other seed-bearing crops. Raw materials including pure copper, seashells, mica, and flint from sources across the entire extent of the American Midwest and Southeast poured into Cahokia, where its artisans manufactured fine works of art, some of which ended up in the graves of Cahokia's leaders. Some of those finely crafted works were traded to smaller communities located across the Midwest.

Cahokia is an important place to visit, and an especially important place to take your kids. Even in the twenty-first century, too many of us harbor Hollywood clichés of Native Americans. Wholly unlike Hollywood stereotypes, the people of Cahokia were participants in an urban Native American civilization called Mississippian.

Cahokia has been designated a National Historic Landmark and is one of only eight cultural sites in the United States that have been designated World Heritage Sites by the United Nations. That puts Cahokia in the company of sites like the Pyramids of Giza, Stonehenge, and the Roman Colosseum.

Site Type: Platform Mound (village, but really a city)

Wow Factor: ***** The site is astonishing. There are lots of mounds, and many are truly monumental. Monks Mound is especially "wow"-worthy. Cahokia is an amazing place.

Museum: ***** The museum at Cahokia sets the standard for archaeology museums. It's fantastic and enormously informative, with a very impressive village reconstruction.

Ease of Road Access: *****

Ease of Hike: **** Cahokia is huge, and you'll walk a lot to see the site in its entirety. The stair climb to the top of Monks Mound will get your heart pumping, but the amazing view is more than worth the effort.

Natural Beauty of Surroundings: ****

Kid Friendly: ***** Between the vast area for kids to run around and explore and the museum with lots of kid-oriented exhibits, even little ones should have a blast.

Food: Vending machines in the museum offer snacks and drinks.

How to Get There: Cahokia is located on Collinsville Road in Collinsville, Illinois, close to the Missouri border and a less than 20-minute drive from much of downtown St. Louis. The site is readily accessible from I-55/70 and I-255 in western Illinois.

Hours of Operation: The grounds are open daily from dawn until dusk. The museum is open Wednesday through Sunday 9 a.m. to 5 p.m. That may change, so check the website for current hours.

Cost: Free, but donations are recommended (see website). Shell out a few bucks. It's worth it!

Best Season to Visit: Any time

Website: http://cahokiamounds.org

Designation: State Historic Site; National Historic Landmark; World Heritage Site

Site 10 Angel Mounds State Historic Site

Evansville, Indiana

Journal Entry

April 22, 2008

Driving across the Wabash from Illinois to Indiana, it is clear you've entered another world, a world of danger and daring. After all, the speed limit on the highway in Indiana was 70 miles per hour, a full 5 miles per hour higher than on the Illinois side. Driving along the rolling plains of southern Indiana, I began wondering about that phrase: "rolling plains." They were plain alright, but they sure as hell didn't roll all that much. They were flat, so flat that one might begin to question the whole "the world is a sphere" thing. And across its eternal flatness were scattered slowly drilling oil wells. Oil in Indiana; who knew?

We finally arrived at Angel Mounds near Evansville and found a very nice on-site museum. A little worn on the outside, the building is cleverly shaped like two adjacent truncated pyramidal mounds. The interior displays present a series of walk-through dioramas with life-size mannequins depicting activities carried out by the residents of the village. These are very well done and convey a nice sense of the nature of village life in this impressive temple mound builder village. At its peak, Angel Mounds had a population of maybe 1,000 people, and several large earth mounds, one especially large, surrounded an extensive plaza. That mound is a combination flat platform of earth topped by a conical mound at one end. Angel Mounds is not Cahokia, but it's certainly worth the trip.

What You Will See

Though **Site 9, Cahokia** is, hands down, the largest and most impressive of the mound builder sites, there are a number of secondary but nevertheless impressive sites scattered across the American

Figure 32. The primary earthwork at Angel Mounds in southern Indiana is a monumental sculpture in soil.

Figure 33. A reconstruction of part of the palisade, or log wall, at Angel Mounds.

Midwest and Southeast that you can visit during an archaeological odyssey. Angel Mounds is one of those sites. Located hard fast against the Ohio River, along the border between southern Indiana and Kentucky, Angel was an important community spread across an area of about 100 acres.

As is the case in many of the large ceremonial and population centers that are secondary to Cahokia, there is a single substantial mound at the site (Figure 32). Instead of a simple, truncated pyramid, the main mound at Angel consists of a broad platform, with a higher conical mound on one of its edges.

There is a reconstructed part of the palisade. It's a little too perfect—you can see a much more authentic looking city wall at **Site 13, Town Creek Mound** (North Carolina)—but it gives you a bit of an idea of what the formidable wall enclosing the central part of the site may have looked like (Figure 33). There's also a reconstructed circular structure, located where the site's inhabitants built what amounts to a mortuary where bodies were prepared for burial.

Why Is Angel Mounds Important?

Angel Mounds was occupied between about AD 1100 and AD 1450. Like Cahokia and so many of the other large mound builder sites, Angel likely was a population and ceremonial center—a place with a concentration of leaders, priests, artisans, and merchants who participated in the business of running the society. Surrounding the main part of the site was a dispersed population of farmers, the peasants whose food surpluses likely supported the work—the religious ceremonies, art production, and the economic and political activities—conducted by the important people who lived in the area enclosed by the palisade. It has been estimated that Angel's sphere of influence, the area that the rulers of Angel viewed as their territory and inhabited by its citizens, had a diameter of 75 miles. In essence then, Angel was a mini-Cahokia—a large, primary settlement where the most powerful people lived. And like Cahokia,

Angel was surrounded by a large and dispersed series of agricultural hamlets whose residents saw Angel as the capital of their nation.

Were Angel and Cahokia enemies or allies, or was Angel part of Cahokia's "empire," a second-tier community that viewed Cahokia as its capital? It's difficult to know for sure. In the days before electronic communication, motor vehicles, or even animal-powered transportation, the political, economic, and social connections between settlements would have been more difficult to maintain and the control by a more dominant city over a smaller, less powerful community more problematic. Via today's interstate road system, Cahokia and Angel are 175 miles apart and a nearly 3-hour car ride. Certainly the residents of Cahokia and Angel knew of each other's existence and the people at Angel recognized the dominance of the Cahokians. But the precise nature of their relationship is unknown.

What happened to Angel in AD 1450? No one is certain why it was abandoned, but it is quite possible that the region simply could not support a very dense population. Possibly the residents of Angel ran out of firewood—a large, dense population of people can deforest an area pretty quickly—and their agricultural practices may have depleted the soil, causing people to abandon the town and disperse across the countryside. Without other methods of heating their homes and without ways of artificially increasing agricultural productivity, a large, dense community may no longer have been viable. There's no evidence of warfare or revolution, just simple abandonment. It does present us with an interesting example of what might happen when a human group gets too large for the local environment to support it.

Site Type: Platform Mound
Wow Factor: *** Small by Cahokia standards, Angel is still quite impressive, and the reconstructed part of the palisade is pretty cool.
Museum: ****
Ease of Road Access: *****
Ease of Hike: ****
Natural Beauty of Surroundings: ***
Kid Friendly: *** Lots of room to run and explore. The museum will appeal to older kids.
Food: Bring your own.
How to Get There: Angel Mounds is located near Evansville and Newburgh, Indiana, and readily accessible from I-164.
Hours of Operation: Museum open Tuesday through Saturday 9 a.m. to 5 p.m.; Sunday 1 to 5 p.m. Closed Monday. Parking lot gates are locked at other times, making trail access difficult when the museum isn't open.
Cost: See website.
Best Season to Visit: Year-round, although hot and humid in summer and cold in winter.
Website: www.indianamuseum.org/explore/angel-mounds
Designation: State Historic Site; National Historic Landmark

Site 11   Poverty Point National Monument

Epps, Louisiana

Journal Entry

December 27, 2008

Well, okay. I'm actually going to contradict my own criteria for site inclusion in our odyssey and include Poverty Point, even though, at least from a visual perspective, it's not a very impressive site. There's not, at least in its current appearance, a very high "wow factor." At one time the National Park Service maintained a tall watchtower that provided visitors with a bird's-eye view of the site, but safety and maintenance issues led to it being taken down. I imagine that without a viewing tower at **Site 14, Serpent Mound** in Ohio or **Site 6, Rock Eagle Effigy Mound** in Georgia, most viewers would not be terribly impressed either. You really do need a bird's-eye view of those as well as Poverty Point to appreciate the beauty of the two effigy mounds and the enormous size and scope of Poverty Point. Most of the site consists of low-lying parallel mounds, most of which are covered with trees. As a result, the site itself looks more like a nice park than a major archaeological site. The site covers an extensive area, and a paved park road allows you to drive between each site waypoint. At least one impressively tall mound can be climbed, and many beautiful artifacts are housed in the on-site museum. But the real reason to visit Poverty Point is its historic significance.

What You Will See

The earthworks at Poverty Point consist of a series of low, linear mounds in the shape of a half-circle that covers the west, north, and south quadrants of the site. In aerial photographs and maps, the earthworks give the impression of a giant amphitheater facing to the east (Figure 34). The

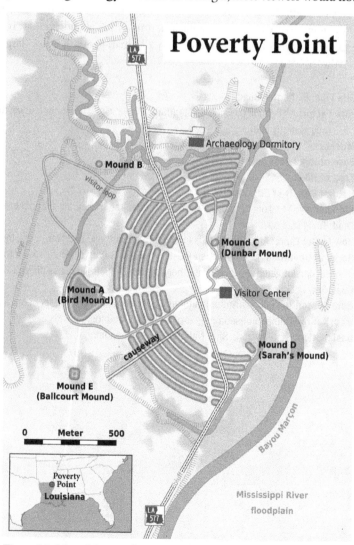

Figure 34. Map of the complex semicircle of segmented earthworks of Poverty Point. (MAXIMILLIAN DÖRRBECKER, WIKIMEDIA COMMONS)

Figure 35. Mound A, also known as Bird Mound because its footprint resembles an enormous, winged bird, is the largest mound at Poverty Point in Louisiana. Since my visit, the trees on Mound A have been removed, affording a better view of the earthwork.

mounds end at the site's eastern boundary, a narrow body of water called Bayou Macon. Though they are a bit subtle, when you visit the site you'll be able to see some of the six segmented ridges of earth. Each ridge segment is about 80 feet long and 5 feet high. Archaeological evidence indicates that the ridges were built up to serve as platforms on which residents built their homes. Though it may be hard to see because of vegetation and the lack of a tower for viewing the big picture, these artificial concentric ridges were a massive construction project, adding up to 6 miles of earth incorporating 53 million cubic feet of dirt into the earthworks at the site. Though the site's overall configuration cannot readily be seen on the ground, there are a couple of easily recognizable larger and impressive mounds on the site. The main platform mound at the site (Mound A) is impressively tall, towering about 70 feet above its base. It appears to have been constructed in the shape of a giant bird (Figure 35). A stairway leads up to the top.

An on-site museum explains the significance of the place and contains an exhibit of some of the finer artworks found there. Check out the beautiful pottery, stone spear points, lovely drilled stone beads, ceramic figurines, and other decorated clay objects, including some that look just like dice! My personal favorite piece of art recovered at Poverty Point is a truly stunning work: a precious little owl carved in red stone and likely worn as a pendant.

Why Is Poverty Point Important?

An important part of Poverty Point's significance rests in its age; it was occupied initially more than 3,200 years ago and exhibits significant and monumental earthwork construction soon after its occupation. The dating of the site puts its occupation at far before the burial mounds of Ohio and certainly before the platform temple mounds of the Midwest and Southeast. And, yes, its dating puts the initiation of monumental mound construction at before the Aztecs, the Maya, or the Inca. Poverty Point shows how, even at an early stage in its development, Native American mound builder societies were able to accomplish tremendous feats of earthmoving.

Long-distance trade also characterized Poverty Point. The raw material of many of the stone spear points you'll see in the museum originated in the Ozark and Ouachita Mountains and in the valleys of the Ohio and Tennessee Rivers. Steatite, a soft stone used by the residents of Poverty Point in the production of small sculptures, was obtained from northern Alabama and Georgia. The pure copper made into artifacts at the site comes from Michigan.

Okay, so Poverty Point reflects an impressive level of communal labor to produce earthworks. And there's evidence of long-distance trade. There's plenty of evidence for that in many of our fifty sites. What makes Poverty Point unique in this regard concerns the subsistence base of its residents. Ordinarily, societies that produce monumental structures are able to do so because they have a lot of surplus time on their hands. In an agricultural economy, farmers have the potential ability to produce far more food than they need to feed their families, enough food in fact to support classes of people not involved in farming. This includes artisans, soldiers, merchants, priests, rulers, and workers who can build monuments upon the order of those rulers.

Poverty Point is different. The people at Poverty Point were not farmers but were instead hunters of wild animals and gatherers of wild plant foods. Reliance on wild foods by a people who build great communal monuments is rare. At Poverty Point it is an indication of the incredible natural productivity of the site's location along the banks of Bayou Macon in the Lower Mississippi Valley.

Along with being a National Historic Landmark, Poverty Point has been designated a World Heritage Site. The US archaeological sites named as World Heritage Sites by the United Nations for their archaeological significance are **Site 9, Cahokia; Site 11, Poverty Point; Site 29, Mesa Verde;** and **Site 31, Chaco Canyon.** It should be no surprise that all four are included in our fifty-site odyssey.

Site Type: Village, Platform Mound

Wow Factor: * Poverty Point is an impressive site, but there no longer is a tower from which the visitor can get a bird's-eye view of the octagonal rows of mounded earth.

Museum: **** Exhibits contain a great array of artifacts recovered at the site.

Ease of Road Access: *****

Ease of Hike: *****

Natural Beauty of Surroundings: ****

Kid Friendly: ***

Food: Bring your own.

How to Get There: Poverty Point is located in the town of Epps in north-central Louisiana. The site is readily accessible from I-20. Take the Delhi exit, go north on LA 17, east on LA 134, and then north on LA 577.

Hours of Operation: Open daily 9 a.m. to 5 p.m. Closed Thanksgiving, Christmas, and New Year's Day.

Cost: See website.

Best Season to Visit: If you enjoy heat and humidity, Louisiana is your place in summer. Otherwise, try spring or fall.

Website: www.crt.state.la.us/louisiana-state-parks/historic-sites/poverty-point-state-historic-site/index

Designation: National Monument; World Heritage Site

Site 12 **Grand Village of the Natchez**

Natchez, Mississippi

Journal Entry

December 26, 2008
When you think of archaeology, the image in your mind is likely that of great antiquity, of a strange and alien people from a very long time ago. In this cliché, the only evidence we have of their lives is the hardware they made and then either lost or discarded. But Grand Village of the Natchez doesn't conform to that stereotype. The town isn't the equivalent of, for example, an ancient, pre-Neolithic community in the Middle East, where the material record is all we have to contribute to our understanding of the past. The place we today call the Grand Village of the Natchez was a bustling, thriving community as late as the eighteenth century, and it is a place where we have a historically recorded first encounter between a living, breathing mound building society—a tribe called the Natchez—and European explorers and traders. We know about this society, certainly as a result of the archaeology that has been conducted there but also because interlopers with writing saw it and recorded their descriptions and reactions. Unfortunately these descriptions and reactions were recorded in French. For too many years English-speaking thinkers and writers ignored those records, blithely speculating about the existence of a mysterious, non-Indian mound builder society while, all along, the mystery's solution lay in the recorded descriptions of French (and elsewhere, Spanish) trappers, explorers, missionaries, and settlers.

What You Will See

The Grand Village of the Natchez was occupied between about AD 700 and AD 1730. When you visit the site, you'll see three impressive temple mounds, today labeled A, B, and C but historically called

Figure 36. The primary mound at Grand Village of the Natchez in Natchez, Mississippi.

Abandoned Mound, Temple Mound, and Sun Mound (Figure 36). There is also a nicely replicated conical dwelling you can enter that gives you a nice idea of what a Natchez dwelling looked like in the early eighteenth century (I.6). There also is a terrific on-site museum where you can see some of the more impressive artifacts recovered at the site during archaeological excavations in 1930, 1962, and 1972. About 20 miles away is Emerald Mound, another Natchez Indian platform mound site. It's worth seeing if you're in the area.

Why Is Grand Village of the Natchez Important?

When Europeans began expanding into the American Midwest, explorers and settlers encountered the remains of what clearly had been a sophisticated culture, a culture that included what were, at the time of European contact, abandoned towns marked by massive earthworks including enormous flat-topped pyramids, artfully flaked stone tools, beautiful ceramics, and impressive burials filled with well-made objects. As mentioned early in this book, many Euro-Americans wrongly believed that Indians and their ancestors would have been incapable of producing the monumental mounds and splendid works of art found by archaeologists and believed instead that a mysterious culture from Europe, Africa, or Asia had populated the Americas in past millennia. Maybe it had been ancient Egyptian or Chinese migrants; perhaps it was the Welsh led by Prince Madoc. Or maybe it had been members of one of the Lost Tribes of Israel—anyone but the ancestors of the native peoples of the Midwest or Southeast. No, it couldn't have been Indians.

The Grand Village of the Natchez is particularly significant because it shows clearly that there were no mysterious, foreign mound builders but that American Indians had been responsible after all. Leading an expeditionary force of 800 men, the French explorer Antoine-Simon Le Page du Pratz traveled from France to Louisiana in 1718. He lived in a town near Natchez, Mississippi, from 1718 to 1728. During that time, du Pratz learned the local Indian language and as a result was able to describe native culture not simply though his own eyes but also from the perspective of the Indians themselves. More than just a journalist, du Pratz was in a real sense an anthropologist. He was an eyewitness to Indians living in the Grand Village of the Natchez, which he described as a large, densely occupied, urban-like community with a great ruler they called the Great Sun who lived in a temple located atop a large pyramidal mound of earth, the one archaeologists have labeled Mound B. Du Pratz said the big mound was about 100 feet around at its base—and it is. According to du Pratz, Mound A, or the Sun Mound, was the platform for a ceremonial temple inside of which burned an eternal flame. This temple also served as a charnel house, where the bodies of members of the elite were prepared for burial upon their deaths. Eyewitness accounts describe the human sacrifice of retainers and relatives upon the death of the Great Sun in 1728.

The site is also important as an object lesson of what happened when the native peoples of the New World became involved in the politics of competing settler groups. Hoping to maintain trade with both French and English settlers, the Natchez ended up getting drawn into wars with both European groups. The French were particularly nasty and sold more than 300 of the Natchez into slavery in the West Indies.

The Grand Village of the Natchez is especially important in that it presents an object lesson in how history helped solve an archaeological mystery.

Site Type: Village, Platform Mound

Wow Factor: ** The mounds are small compared to some other sites, but it's pretty cool that this site was visited by European explorers and settlers when it was actively the capital of the Natchez Indians.

Museum: **

Ease of Road Access: *****

Ease of Hike: ****

Natural Beauty of Surroundings: ****

Kid Friendly: ****

Food: Bring your own.

How to Get There: Grand Village of the Natchez is located at 400 Jefferson Davis Blvd. in Natchez, Mississippi.

Hours of Operation: Open Monday through Saturday 9 a.m. to 5 p.m.; Sunday 1:30 to 5 p.m.

Cost: Free

Best Season to Visit: It's in Mississippi. Prepare to sweat like crazy in summer. Spring, fall, or winter might be a better time to visit.

Website: www.nps.gov/nr/travel/mounds/gra.htm

Designation: State park; National Historic Landmark

Site 13 Town Creek Indian Mound State Historic Site

Mount Gilead, North Carolina

Journal Entry

August 14, 2008

It took us two days of driving from Connecticut in the southeastern leg of my odyssey, but we finally arrived at **Town Creek Mound,** a medium-size but very impressive mound site located near the town of Mount Gilead, North Carolina. Built a thousand years ago, Town Creek was a ceremonial center with a single small temple mound surrounded by a large plaza and the archaeological remains of hundreds of burials. The state has done a terrific job of keeping up the site, and there is a pretty well-done reconstruction of the temple located on top of the extant mound as well as the surrounding palisade. The palisade is particularly impressive and surrounds virtually the entire site. The setting and the site itself are beautiful, and there's a very worthwhile museum. Town Creek Mound was the first site formally excavated by archaeologists in North Carolina. It has been designated a National Historic Landmark.

What You Will See

At the Town Creek Mound site you will see the archaeological remnants of an impressive village occupied between AD 1150 and AD 1400. The primary mound is in terrific condition, with a ramp that

Figure 37. The main mound at Town Creek Mound in North Carolina. The reconstructed structure on its top was built in the footprint of its archaeological remains. You can climb the mound and walk into the building.

Figure 38. Town Creek Mound provided the best reconstruction of a palisade I saw in my archaeological odyssey.

allows you to walk to the top. On the top is a replicated temple that you are free to enter. They've done a terrific job of reproducing the temple; the ceiling and room, consisting of a superstructure of thin, long logs overlain by thatch, is a work of art (Figure 37).

There are a number of other replicated features at Town Creek. Along with the temple on top of the big platform mound, the palisade that surrounded the community has been partially rebuilt, giving you a good idea of what the enclosed village looked like a thousand years ago (Figure 38). Most of the reconstruction consists of just upright logs sunken into the ground and rising more than 10 feet above the surface. Part of the palisade has been more completely reconstructed, with horizontal cross pieces of branches and saplings woven into the vertical elements. These parts of the wall have then been finished with a coating or material to make a more or less smooth wall on both the interior and exterior. Originally this coating might have been mud, which would have required nearly constant work to maintain. I'm not sure what material was used in making the replica wall, but it's not mud. Based on the post-molds discovered during the site's excavation, archaeologists noted the presence of a number of bastions along the palisade. These represent small add-ons jutting to the outside of the enclosed area where, in all likelihood, warriors would have been posted as lookouts, providing them platforms from which they might defend the village from possible attackers.

A typical house has also been replicated, where you can see the nature of Town Creek residential architecture. Some parts of the house walls have been left unfinished, enabling a close look at the process of wattle-and-daub construction much like the palisade. There is also a reconstructed burial building. There's a very nice on-site museum, but what's really great about this site are the tour guides. When I visited, one of them (John) took us around the site, and you couldn't ask for a better informed or more enthusiastic guide.

Why Is Town Creek Important?

Located in North Carolina, Town Creek Mound reflects the vast geographic extent of the temple mound building culture of native America, one of the best-kept secrets of American history. Mound builder sites are found across the American Midwest and Southeast; there is even a mound builder outpost in Wisconsin (see **Site 22, Aztalan** later in this section). Admit it; most of you have probably not heard of mound-building Indians living in densely populated, urban-like settlements. Abandon stereotypes you might have harbored about Native American culture and visit Town Creek, where a large, complex community produced monumental structures like the primary temple mound and the palisade.

Town Creek Mound is a nice example of a small but significant ceremonial center of the temple mound building cultures. Town Creek was not a large city with a big population. It was instead the community in which lived the religious, social, and political elites—the big shots, the 1 percenters. Based on the archaeology conducted on and off at the site (some professional; some, unfortunately, little more than pillaging and pot hunting), as well as historical information supplied by local Indians, a broad area around the location of Town Creek was inhabited by a large number of agricultural villages whose inhabitants viewed the people living at the large site as their rulers and priests. Perhaps yearly, the members of the Town Creek nation would have congregated there for practical reasons—fixing the palisade, for example—but also for ceremonial reasons including feasting and religious ceremonies. People in the surrounding region might also have come together at Town Creek for the funerals of the people deemed important enough to be buried at their capital. To date, the remains of 563 people have been found buried at Town Creek, including small children and babies.

Site Type: Platform Mound

Wow Factor: *** The primary mound is beautiful, and the reconstructed house at its apex is cool. The reconstructed part of the palisade around the site, replete with bastions, is far and away the best I have seen and gives you a very good idea of what those city walls looked like at mound builder villages across the Southwest and Midwest.

Museum: ****

Ease of Road Access: *****

Ease of Hike: *****

Natural Beauty of Surroundings: ****

Kid Friendly: **** Plenty of territory for kids to explore. And kids will enjoy entering the reconstructed house atop of the main mound.

Food: Bring your own.

How to Get There: Town Creek Mound is located in Montgomery County, North Carolina, about 5.5 miles from the town of Mount Gilead on, predictably, Town Creek Mound Road. The closest cities are Greensboro and Charlotte (about 1.5 hours away) and Raleigh and Durham (about a 2-hour drive).

Hours of Operation: Open Tuesday through Saturday 9 a.m. to 5 p.m.; Sunday 1 to 5 p.m. Closed Monday and major holidays.

Cost: Free, but donations are accepted.

Best Season to Visit: Hot and humid in summer

Website: www.nchistoricsites.org/town/town.htm

Designation: State Historic Site; National Historic Landmark

Site 14 **Serpent Mound**

Peebles, Ohio

Journal Entry

April 20, 2014

As an archaeologist with a PhD, I am probably not supposed to say this, but you need to go to Serpent Mound for no other reason than it is just so incredibly cool. The earthwork is an effigy mound of sculpted earth more than 1,350 feet long in the sinuous, meandering shape of a coiled serpent resting on a peninsular, steep-sided ridge (Figure 39). The tail end spirals in on itself and resembles that of a rattlesnake. At its other end, the mouth is gaping and open, about to eat what appears to be an earth mound in the shape of an egg. We climbed to the top of the viewing tower for a bird's-eye view of the monumental snake. Just incredible. The tower is open, without walls, so if you have a fear of heights you might be a bit uncomfortable. But work through it; it's not that bad and well worth the trip up for the perspective it affords. During my most recent visit, an adorable and brave little girl of about eight or nine climbed to the top by herself while her scaredy-cat father (a very tough looking dude with lots of tattoos) stayed on the ground. Don't be that dad!

Figure 39. Serpent Mound in southern Ohio. This is the impressive view you get from the top of the observation tower.

Figure 40. Aerial photograph of Serpent Mound (GOOGLE EARTH)

Serpent Mound is an impressive work of sculptural art likely imbued with sacred power by the people who built it. It is an amazing thing to see and ponder (Figure 40).

What You Will See

Serpent Mound likely dates to the period after AD 1000; recent radiocarbon dating of organic material found inside the mound produced a date of AD 1040. This is long after the Hopewell Culture, whose people had built the burial mounds at, for example, **Site 18, Mound City**, were gone. Serpent Mound dates to a later people, the bearers of the Fort Ancient Culture.

A paved pathway takes you along both sides of the serpent. Definitely walk the path for the view it provides of the snake's head and coiled tail. There are lots of sign-posted alignment markers at the site. It appears that the positioning of the coils of the great serpent wasn't random; the loops were aligned to important points on the horizon, which marked the moon's monthly dance across the sky. This was a way for the makers of Serpent Mound to keep track of important days during the year. In other words, Serpent Mound was a sort of lunar calendar.

On a visit to the site back in 2009, I met with the site caretaker, Keith Bengston. Keith mentioned that New Agers had recently been drawn to the site, especially at the solstices, the first day of summer (and the day of the year with the most daylight hours) and the first day of winter (the day with the fewest daylight hours). Further, some New Agers apparently have decided that the mound's shape is not that of a snake but a sperm. This has led to some people sneaking into the state park after hours and having sex on top of the mound. Freud would have had a field day with people who have sex on top of a sculpture of a giant snake. Poor Keith was tasked with the job of cleaning up. Uh, gross.

I don't know about New Age perspectives about Serpent Mound, but it certainly is a special place that resonates with the intelligence and spirituality of its builders. When I was last there, it was a breezy day, with the wind producing very eerie sounds as it blasted through the trees growing along the edge of the ridgetop on which the effigy was built. It seemed a very appropriate "special effect."

There is a small museum at the site, but the displays have not been updated for quite some time, and budget cuts have curtailed the hours during which it is open. Don't worry too much about it; the mound is what you go there to see.

Why Is Serpent Mound Important?

Serpent Mound is one of a large number of earthworks in America known as "effigy mounds." As described earlier, these were monumentally scaled sculptures of earth in the shape of various animals including snakes, turtles, birds, and bears, among others. Serpent Mound is the best known because of its enormous size, location on a topographic eminence, state of preservation, and incredible and mysterious beauty. Recent analysis of the alignment of the serpent indicates that, along with the coils aligning with the moon, the head points toward the setting sun at the summer solstice, much in the way that Stonehenge, in the south of England, lines up with the day that marks the beginning of summer in the Northern Hemisphere.

Serpent Mound provides an important look inside the minds of ancient people who recognized the beauty and mysterious power of the snake and memorialized it on a grand scale.

Site Type: Effigy Mound

Wow Factor: **** It's a giant snake sculpted in earth. That's very cool.

Museum: There is a very small on-site museum. I've been to Serpent Mound a few times, and the museum has never been open.

Ease of Road Access: *****

Ease of Hike: ***** The hike around the snake is very easy; it's a pretty flat, paved pathway. Climbing to the top of the observation tower might be a challenge to anyone with bad knees but is otherwise no great challenge.

Natural Beauty of Surroundings: ***

Kid Friendly: ** It's a giant snake. Kids will think that's pretty cool.

Food: Bring your own.

How to Get There: Serpent Mound is located just off OH 73, 6 miles north of OH 32 and 20 miles south of Bainbridge in Adams County.

Hours of Operation: Open daily 9 a.m. to dusk

Cost: Free if you're a member of the Ohio Historical Society or the Arc of Appalachia Preserve System. See website for nonmember rates.

Best Season to Visit: Any time

Website: www.ohiohistory.org/museums-and-historic-sites/museum--historic-sites-by-name/serpent-mound

Designation: State park; National Historic Landmark

Site 15   SunWatch Indian Village

Dayton, Ohio

Journal Entry

April 23, 2009

Have you ever visited one of the many outdoor "living history museums" scattered across the United States? Here in New England we have two of the finest: Old Sturbridge Village and Plimoth Plantation, both in Massachusetts. Plimoth (the modern museum has retained the original spelling) is modeled of course on the historic village established by the Pilgrims in 1620. The modern version consists of a single lane along which the "residents" have constructed replicas typical of the early seventeenth-century houses in the historical village. There are gardens, an armory and meeting house, small pastures, and a palisade surrounding the village. If you walk outside of town, you'll find a small Indian village with a couple of wigwams ostensibly inhabited by members of the Wampanoag tribe going about their daily business. One of the most interesting approaches at Plimoth is the fiction maintained by the "residents"

Figure 41. Reconstructed house at SunWatch Indian Village in Ohio.

Figure 42. The interior of one of the houses reconstructed at SunWatch Indian Village.

that it is 1620 and you are visiting the actual seventeenth-century village. Those residents aren't just random people. They take on the personae of the people who actually lived there nearly 400 years ago. Not docents or museum guides, instead you will encounter William Bradford, John and Priscilla Alden, and many other residents of the original Plimoth. These historical reenactors are very good at maintaining that fiction and rarely break character. I once had an interesting conversation with one of the inhabitants. After telling me he had come from England to live in the New World, the man asked where I had traveled from. Without thinking, I told him "Connecticut." His response: "I know where that is, but it ain't been discovered yet."

Old Sturbridge Village has a more traditional approach to an outdoor historical museum. The houses, barns, offices, blacksmith shop, pottery shed, and mill buildings are for the most part authentic old buildings moved to OSV to create what amounts to a fictional nineteenth-century community. The employees are all actual docents with name tags and make no attempt to convince you they really are time-travelers from the past.

I bring up these examples because SunWatch Indian Village is another interesting approach to the outdoor history museum concept. SunWatch is a re-created 800-year-old Native American village, with houses, gardens, a plaza, and a palisade. The unique element of SunWatch is that it has been built on the actual footprint of the archaeological site whose excavation has allowed the accurate re-creation of the Native American village you can walk through today. It's a very cool approach and a very cool place.

Figure 43. The SunWatch museum's three-dimensional model of the village.

What You Will See

SunWatch is an 800-year-old village located along the Great Miami River. Based on its excavation, it was determined that SunWatch was a palisaded village with a handful of rectangular houses spread out across approximately 3 acres. Its population is estimated to have been about 250, and the community lasted only about twenty years. Based on the presence of a number of distinct ceramic styles, it has been interpreted that separate woman-based kinship groups called matrilineages, each with its own distinct pottery style, lived in the village. Burials were found within the palisade walls.

You will be able to walk around the 3-acre village and view and enter four reconstructed houses (Figure 41). From inside you'll see the beautifully constructed roofs, interior walls, and partitions (Figure 42). Part of the palisade has been rebuilt, and structures not yet rebuilt are marked by wooden posts in the exact locations where they were found archaeologically.

There is a very nice on-site museum filled with artifacts actually found at the site. Some of the artwork produced by the ancient village's residents is quite impressive. There's also a re-creation of a dog burial excavated at the site; the dog's human companions buried him in the same manner they might lay to rest a beloved family member. There's a nice twelve-minute film about the site, some dioramas, a simulated dig, and plenty of artifacts.

Visually the site itself isn't terribly impressive; there aren't any monumental mounds, for example. But maybe that's the point. SunWatch is an ordinary village that provides us with an extraordinary up-close and personal opportunity to see how regular people lived in western Ohio 800 years ago (Figure 43). That's pretty great.

Why Is SunWatch Indian Village Important?

There are plenty of archaeological sites open to visitors but very few indeed where researchers have actually reconstructed the ancient community itself right there at the site. Most of the sites described in this book require quite a lot of imagination to paint a picture of the ancient community's appearance. At SunWatch, you'll need little more than open eyes and a good pair of walking shoes.

Another element to the importance of SunWatch is the fact that many elements of the place are effectively ongoing experiments in ancient technologies related to construction, cooking, planting, and tool making. Replicative experiments have long made an important contribution to archaeological analysis. There may be no better way to understand the processes by which ancient peoples provided the necessities of life than to attempt to replicate those processes in the here and the now. There is certainly no better way to gain an appreciation for the skills possessed by ancient peoples than to try to learn those skills yourself through a process of trial and error. How long did it take to make a stone arrow point, and how difficult was it to do so? Try it for yourself. How much shelter did an ancient SunWatch village house afford its residents? Are the replicas built today dry during driving rainstorms? How warm is a replica village house in the middle of a difficult and cold winter? How productive were the agricultural fields maintained by the residents of SunWatch? How productive are our modern replicas? Experimental archaeology can help answer these kinds of questions and provide direct insights into the lives and livelihoods of ancient peoples. As an ongoing experiment in the culture of an ancient people, SunWatch Indian Village may be making its most important contribution to our knowledge of the human past.

Site Type: Village

Wow Factor: ** The "wow" here resides not in any particular feature of the site but in the fact that the reconstructed buildings and palisade have been placed in the actual footprint of the remains of the original village site.

Museum: **** The SunWatch museum has amazing artifacts on display, all of which were recovered at the site. The reconstructed dog burial is touching.

Ease of Road Access: *****

Ease of Hike: *****

Natural Beauty of Surroundings: ***

Kid Friendly: ***** Kids will love being able to go inside the reconstructed houses. I have been to SunWatch a couple of times, and there are always replicative activities going on outside, including tending the Indian gardens and building and maintaining houses and the palisade.

Food: Bring your own.

How to Get There: SunWatch is located off I-75, a few minutes south of downtown Dayton in western Ohio. Take exit 51 off I-75 and go west on Edwin C. Moses Boulevard, which becomes Nicholas Road after you cross the Dryden Road/South Broadway Street intersection. Cross South Broadway and turn left onto West River Road. SunWatch is 1 mile south on West River Road.

Hours of Operation: Open Tuesday through Saturday 9 a.m. to 5 p.m.; Sunday noon to 5 p.m. Closed on Monday.

Cost: See website.

Best Season to Visit: Any time

Website: www.sunwatch.org

Designation: Private; National Historic Landmark

Site 16 Cemetery Mound

Marietta, Ohio

Journal Entry

April 19, 2014

> *Death is a debt, to nature due,*
> *Which I have paid, and so must you.*

—Epitaph commonly encountered on gravestones in New England, dating to the eighteenth and nineteenth centuries

Death is the great equalizer, isn't it? Our religion, our ethnicity, our gender—all the characteristics we use to define our true selves—pale in the face of the certainty of our own mortality. There's no more visceral reminder of this than what is experienced when walking through an old graveyard. Stop and read the epitaphs on the stones. Among them you will find the brief and often poignant biographies of people long gone.

My visit to a cemetery in Marietta, Ohio, during a recent leg of my archaeological odyssey was filled with such reminders of lives long since passed. As we walked among the gravestones, the people buried beneath our feet were no longer merely anonymous historical figures but real people, whose loved ones grieved their deaths as they laid them to rest in this place of silent and serene beauty. For example, there was George Smith, who was born in England, lived in Troy, New York, and died unexpectedly in 1832 at the age of 54 while on a visit to Marietta. Then there were the two very young sons of Thomas and Sarah Flagg, placed under a single stone though they died more than ten years apart. Luther was barely two months old when he died in 1837; his brother, Uranius, was only a year and a half upon his death ten years later. As a parent myself, I can scarcely imagine the despair experienced by those boys' parents.

Why did we stop at a nineteenth-century graveyard in our archaeological odyssey? We did so because in its midst is a towering monument to death and mortality made by a people from another time. That monument is today called Cemetery Mound, a 30-foot-high sepulcher built by Ohio's native people some 2,000 years before the establishment of the nineteenth-century cemetery that now surrounds it.

What You Will See

Cemetery Mound (historically called the "Conus") is not the largest burial mound we will see in our fifty-site odyssey, but its context in the middle of a graveyard may be the most compelling (Figure 44). The graveyard is called, appropriately, Mound Cemetery and is surrounded by a middle-class neighborhood of single-family homes in an old industrial city in eastern Ohio. Imagine living in a bustling city on a street abutting a cemetery within which is an enormous, 2,000-year-old burial mound visible from your front porch. I think that would be pretty cool, actually, but that's just me. We parked in front of one of those houses, crossed the street, and spent nearly 2 hours walking the grounds, reading gravestones, climbing the mound (there are stairs), and immersing ourselves in the lives and deaths of the denizens of nineteenth-century Marietta. I am one of those strange people who find old cemeteries enormously interesting, so Mound Cemetery was a twofer for me: an ancient burial mound and a bunch of old gravestones (I.7).

Figure 44. Peering through the gates at Mound Cemetery, you can see the prehistoric earthwork surrounded by nineteenth-century gravestones.

At about 30 feet, Cemetery Mound is a bit less than half the height of **Site 17, Miamisburg** (Ohio) or **Site 21, Grave Creek** (West Virginia), other conical mounds included in my odyssey. It is, nevertheless, quite impressive. With a diameter of 150 feet at its base, its construction required digging, moving, and piling up more than 175,000 cubic feet of earth. That's a lot of dirt. Additionally, the builders of the mound excavated a shallow trench, completely encircling it. The soil from that trench was piled along its exterior, creating a circular ridge also circumscribing the primary earthwork. The mound and encircling trench and ridge together give the appearance of a quite beautiful and monumental sculpture made of soil, the kind of public artwork you might encounter in an elaborate garden or on a college campus. The burial mound appears to be affiliated with the Adena Culture and is at least 2,000 years old, though additional earthworks in the area likely were produced by the later Hopewell Culture. Very little archaeological research has been conducted at the site. There's no Mound Cemetery museum, so you won't be able to see artifacts recovered there. Nevertheless, it is a beautiful and singular place and certainly worth a visit.

The Conus was originally part of an elaborate series of earthworks in the area, including a square enclosure of 27 acres demarcated by linear mounds and another rectangular enclosure of 50 acres, inside of which were three small platform mounds. Two of the platform mounds still exist. One has the local library built on top; the other is the centerpiece of a town park.

The Marietta earthworks mark what may have been the first attempt in the United States to determine the age of an archaeological site by using tree rings. In 1788 a local reverend, Manasseh Cutler, counted more than 400 annual growth rings in the oldest trees being cut down from the tops of Marietta's mounds and suggested that those earthworks must, therefore, be at least 400 years old. Obviously the trees couldn't have started growing on the mounds until those mounds had been constructed. That was pretty sophisticated thinking for the time.

Why Is Cemetery Mound Important?

The town of Marietta, Ohio, was founded in 1788 following the establishment by the federal government of a region called "the Northwest Territories." Yup; in the eighteenth century, Ohio was considered to be the American northwestern frontier. Go figure. There was a bit of a land rush by folks living in New England for the wide open spaces of Ohio. In fact, some of Marietta's original settlers were Revolutionary War veterans from southern New England.

After a brief sounding of the mound by these first settlers and the realization that it contained at least one human interment, the remarkable for the time decision was made to preserve the site and, at the same time, establish a cemetery in the area surrounding it. That decision has produced quite a remarkable scene; today, hundreds of beautiful and sometimes elaborately carved nineteenth-century gravestones envelop a largely intact burial mound built two millennia before the first of those stones was set in place.

Mound Cemetery is a very nice example of what historic preservationists call "adaptive reuse." Throughout much of the Southeast and Midwest, many European settlers viewed ancient earthworks as inconveniences and impediments, destroying them in great numbers to prepare land for agriculture or development. It is very impressive and especially fortunate that in 1801 the founders of Marietta made the remarkably thoughtful and sensitive decision to continue the native precedent, treating the area around the mound as sacred ground and continuing its use as a home for the dead.

Site Type: Burial Mound

Wow Factor: *** The overall appearance of the site is very cool, with a large burial mound surrounded by nineteenth-century gravestones.

Museum: None

Ease of Road Access: ****

Ease of Hike: ****

Natural Beauty of Surroundings: *** Old cemeteries are beautiful. This one, with an ancient burial mound in the middle, is amazing to see.

Kid Friendly: * If your kids like spooky, they will enjoy walking (respectfully) through the cemetery and reading some of the epitaphs.

Food: Bring your own.

How to Get There: Mound Cemetery is located in the middle of a residential neighborhood in Marietta, Ohio. Punch Fifth and Scammel Streets, Marietta, Ohio, into your GPS, or type that into whatever mapping program you prefer for exact directions. There's no parking lot, but you should be able to find parking on local streets.

Hours of Operation: The gates to the cemetery are open during daylight hours. There are a few entrances on the streets surrounding the cemetery.

Cost: Free

Best Season to Visit: Any time

Website: www.mariettaoh.net/site_pages/government/monuments/Mounds_of_Marietta.pdf

Designation: Cemetery; National Register of Historic Places

I.1. A view of the three largest mounds at Toltec Mounds in Arkansas. (Site 3)

I.2. You can see how wonderfully well maintained the mounds at Etowah are. This photograph was taken from the top of the largest of the platform mounds there. (Site 7)

I.3. One of two shell amulets called gorgets on display. Simply gorgeous. That makes them gorgeous gorgets, which isn't easy to say. (Site 7)

I.4. Artist's conception of the urban settlement of Cahokia in Collinsville, Illinois, at its peak. (Site 9) (Cahokia Mounds State Historic Site; painting by William R. Iseminger)

I.5. Close-up view of Monks Mound at Cahokia. (Site 9)

I.6. A reconstructed dwelling house at Grand Village of the Natchez gives the visitor an intimate view of life in the village. (Site 12)

I.7. Cemetery Mound, located in Mound Cemetery. The late eighteenth- and early nineteenth-century settlers of the town of Marietta, Ohio, placed their cemetery in the shadow of an ancient Native American burial ground. (Site 16)

I.8. This copper cutout of a bird is emblematic of the remarkably beautiful art of the burial mound builders. (Site 18)

I.9. Grave Creek Mound in Moundsville, West Virginia. At a height of 69 feet, this is one of the two tallest burial mounds in North America. (Site 21)

I.10. A close shot of the main mound at Aztalan. And yes, I was there in winter. Contrary to popular belief, it doesn't snow in Wisconsin in summer . . . at least not that often. (Site 22)

I.11. Gobsmacked *is the best word to characterize my reaction when I get to this point on the trail to Montezuma Castle in central Arizona. (Site 23)*

I.12. *This pictograph dates to the early 1800s and was painted by a Navajo artist to represent the Spanish invasion of the canyon and their massacre of his people. (Site 24)*

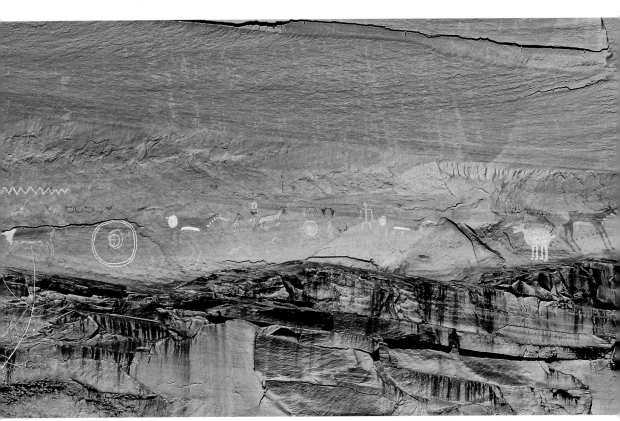

I.13. *Pronghorn antelopes, which continue to thrive in the American Southwest, were painted onto the walls of Canyon de Chelly adjacent to a structure that's appropriately named Antelope House. (Site 24)*

I.14. *Built 900 years ago, positioned like a fortress, Wukoki sits on a bedrock outcrop just a few miles from Wupatki. (Site 27)*

I.15. View from the paved trail at Navajo National Monument, looking down into the Betatakin ruin in northeastern Arizona. This is what it looks like with the naked eye. Look closely for the structures built at the base of the cave. (Site 28)

I.16. Square Tower House in Mesa Verde in southern Colorado. Take a look at that amazing structure with its four-story tower. Wow! What more needs saying? (Site 29)

Site 17 **Miamisburg Mound**

Miamisburg, Ohio

Journal Entry

April 22, 2009

The Miamisburg Mound is a monster; there's no better word for it. It is enormous, imposing, and situated in the most dramatic setting possible, atop an already high natural terrace (Figure 45). The dimensions of the conical mound itself are impressive—about 70 feet high and about 877 feet around at the base. I'll save you the math: That adds up to just a shade less than 1.5 million cubic feet of earth, moved by the basketful without any machinery or draft animals. It's much larger (eight times larger by volume) than Cemetery Mound. Impressive indeed.

What You Will See

Miamisburg Mound was built by bearers of the Adena Culture. Located in a 37-acre state park, the mound itself is the thing to see. There is no museum, and there are no additional earthworks to view.

Figure 45. The enormous Miamisburg Mound is about 70 feet high.

Figure 46. This stairway is not original to the mound, but it affords the visitor both a splendid view of the area surrounding the mound and a heart-thumping appreciation for the amount of labor invested in its construction.

Though the mounds themselves at most sites are off-limits and climbing them is frowned upon, a stone staircase has been built here to allow visitors to walk up the earthwork for a different perspective of the amount of labor that went into its construction (Figure 46). The 116-step climb is worth the work and affords an impressive view of the mound's surroundings. The mound at Miamisburg is literally an artificial mountain, and you can't help but wonder if the intention was to afford the ruler buried at its base a view of the territory he ruled in life.

Why Is Miamisburg Mound Important?

If you've ever needed to move a substantial amount of dirt with nothing more than shovels and a wheelbarrow, you will be immensely impressed by the labor invested in the construction of Miamisburg Mound. Without the use of draft animals—the native peoples of North America domesticated a number of animal species, including the dog and the turkey, but did not have horses or oxen—all that dirt had to be excavated, transported, and then piled up by hand, entirely by people-power. Imagine the effort expended in digging, moving, and then piling up nearly 1.5 million cubic feet of dirt, essentially one basketful at a time. Now consider the number of people who must have been called on to build the mound and the kind of organization and coordination of all of that labor. Think Egyptian pyramids. Think the Sphinx. Think Stonehenge. For that matter, think the Vatican or St. Patrick's Cathedral in New York City. And this is the Ohio of Native America, more than 2,000 years ago.

An archaeological investigation of the mound was conducted in 1869. That excavation revealed a burial located about 8 feet below the modern summit, a man interred in a bark tomb. A sounding down to about 36 feet located another burial vault. This 1869 dig literally just "scratched the surface" of Miamisburg's archaeological potential; no subsequent excavation has been conducted.

Based on the 1869 dig, Miamisburg mound appears to have been a living monument to the deceased rulers of this part of Ohio. The mound wasn't just a "one and done" burial chamber. Its construction was accretional, growing in stages as rulers were laid to rest, each in his or her own small wooden tomb, which was then covered with earth, raising the height of the mound and increasing its overall volume.

Located on the crest of a tall ridge that itself is about 100 feet above the surrounding territory, Miamisburg Mound must have been an impressive landmark for the Adena people of Western Ohio—both a memorial to their chiefs and a reminder and symbol to all who gazed upon it of their enormous power. The trio of Egyptian pyramids at Giza were located in such a way that they could be seen from miles away. Miamisburg Mound was like that.

Site Type: Burial Mound

Wow Factor: *** The mound is impressively large. There's a great view from the top.

Museum: None

Ease of Road Access: *****

Ease of Hike: *****

Natural Beauty of Surroundings: ***

Kid Friendly: ***** The mound is located in the middle of a park. Kids can climb to the top of the mound on the modern steps, and there's lots of open space for them to run around.

Food: Bring your own. There are picnic tables.

How to Get There: Miamisburg Mound is located, appropriately enough, on Mound Avenue in Miamisburg, Ohio. Take exit 44 off OH 725 and travel 1 mile south, or take exit 42 off I-75 and drive 3 miles west. The mound dominates the landscape; you can't miss it.

Hours of Operation: Open daily during daylight hours

Cost: Free

Best Season to Visit: Any time

Website: www.miamisburg.org/miamisburg_mound_park.htm

Designation: City park, National Register of Historic Places

Site 18 **Mound City**

Hopewell Culture National Historical Park • Chillicothe, Ohio

Journal Entry

April 21, 2009

Mound City is effectively a "necropolis"—a city of the dead. The site consists of not just one burial mound but twenty-three (there may have been more); the cluster of mounds is enclosed in a square earthen enclosure. Human remains are contained in each of the mounds. The site was used as a burial ground between 200 BC and AD 500, and interments of the most important people contained elaborate arrays of grave goods, including sheets of mica, copper sculptures, and smoking pipes made to resemble local animals. The age of the site and the nature of the artifacts found there place it firmly within the Hopewell Culture. Administered by the federal government, Mound City is one of five separate and significant mound sites that together make up Hopewell Culture National Historical Park.

Before my Spring 2009 visit, I had been to Mound City back in the early 1980s. One of the significant differences between what the site looked like in the two visits relates to one of the burial mounds. Back in the 1980s there was a trail leading into the site, up to and then *into* one of the mounds; you actually could walk into the ancient tomb. Inside, the human burial had been left intact and in place. The original log tomb had been reconstructed, so the grave itself was in an open space covered by the soil of the mound. There was a human skeleton along with grave offerings, if I recall correctly, which gave the viewer the opportunity to see the interment much as it looked when the deceased had been laid to rest likely about 2,000 years ago. I'm pretty sure there was a Plexiglas wall that prevented visitors from actually walking into the grave itself.

Certainly that was a remarkable scene, and similar open burials, consisting of human remains and accompanying artifacts that had been placed in the interment, could be found at a number of sites in the Midwest. I admit to very much appreciating at the time being able to see the intact burial, but I recognize that treating human remains as though they were little more than artifacts in a museum exhibit was troubling and more than a little inconsiderate of the feelings of the descendants of the deceased. After all, how would most Americans feel if you could walk into the Tomb of the Unknown Soldier at Arlington National Cemetery and snap selfies with the dead soldier to post to your Facebook page? Not so great, right? Taking into consideration the sensibilities of Native Americans and others, the federal government closed off the open burial at Mound City.

What You Will See

Mound City is an enormously impressive cluster of burial mounds surrounded by an earth berm about 4 feet high that encloses the approximately 13-acre necropolis (Figure 47). The entire site has been reconstructed. It was more or less decimated by construction of a military encampment during World War I, but today its overall look is very impressive and, with the aid of very precise nineteenth-century maps, an accurate representation of what the site looked like aboriginally. You certainly should take a walk around the grounds of the necropolis for a personal perspective of the incredible amount of labor that went into simply constructing the mounds themselves. Most are conical, with the largest originally being about 19 feet high and 90 feet in diameter at its base. There is one larger mound with an elongated, elliptical footprint; it contains multiple burials.

Figure 47. View of Mound City, part of the Hopewell Culture National Historical Park in Chillicothe, Ohio.

The burial practices at Mound City involved a number of steps. First, a shallow basin was dug or, in some cases, a low earth platform constructed. The body of the deceased was placed in the basin or on the platform and a log structure, essentially a charnel house, was constructed around the body. Next the building was set ablaze and the body cremated. The ashes and remaining bones were piled up and then important objects were placed around the remains—art works in clay, stone, and metal. Finally, earth was placed over the burial, often in a precise sequence of soil and pebbles, probably to ensure stability of the monument. In some cases multiple burials were placed in the same location, adding to the size of the mound. The tallest of the mounds contained the remains of ten individuals, at least three of whom appear to have been important leaders on the basis of the artifacts found alongside them.

The on-site museum is extremely well done, with lots of splendid artifacts excavated at the site on display. Of course the beauty and skill reflected in these grave goods, perhaps intended for use by the deceased in the afterlife, are impressive and reflect the importance of those buried in the mounds, perhaps their economic wealth, social status, and political power. There are a number of beautiful copper cutouts in the shape of birds (I.8). One of the burial mounds is called Mica Mound because of the beautiful cutouts made of that material in the form of headless, handless, and footless human forms; the plumed heads of birds; and human hands. One person buried in the mounds was interred with an astonishing 200 carved smoking pipes, all produced in an array of various kinds of stone. These pipes are lovely, beautiful, even whimsical works of art. Many are in the shape of animals including bobcats,

Figure 48. An example of a whimsical smoking pipe on display at the museum at Mound City.

beavers, birds (raven, falcon, owl, heron), rabbits, and frogs (Figure 48). In most cases the bowl of the pipe where the tobacco was placed is located on the animal's back. A hole was drilled from the mouthpiece to the bowl, serving to draw smoke into the lungs of the smoker. The person smoking the pipe would draw in the smoke while looking directly into the eyes of the animal represented on the pipe. Nicotine affects perception; higher nicotine content produces more of the effect. Native tobacco had a very high nicotine content, so odds are that smoking one of these effigy pipes had a mild psychotropic effect. Giving our imagination free reign, it's easy to picture the smoker making a profound connection with the spirit of the animal represented on the pipe.

Walk through either of the entrances marked by breaks in the earth wall, and imagine the burial ceremony of a local ruler some 2,000 years ago. The remains might have been brought to a wooden structure, where cremation occurred. Then, with the remains placed in a shallow pit in the floor of the structure, a substantial mound was produced by placement of thousands of basketfuls of earth in a circular footprint over the burial building, rising to a point at its apex.

Why Is Mound City Important?

Mound City reflects, perhaps better than any other site in the American Midwest, the kind of social differentiation or stratification that characterized the native cultures we today call the Adena and Hopewell. Most people in these cultures were buried in plain, unassuming graves, but some people with special status in life—likely political rulers, religious leaders like shamans or priests, and just plain rich folks—got special treatment in death. They received their own tombs and burial monuments and were interred with items that were valuable as a result of the difficulty of obtaining the raw materials as well as the length of time and amount of skill required for their production. Walk around a modern cemetery today and note the differences in the size, raw materials, and characteristics of different grave markers; it's much the same thing in the mound tombs. The memorials we construct for our deceased reflect how those people were perceived in life as well as the economic status of the loved ones who erected those memorials. The same was true for the Adena and Hopewell.

As noted earlier, "Hopewell" is the name given to a culture that developed in the Ohio Valley beginning about 200 BC. The Hopewell Culture is characterized by construction of conical burial mounds, social stratification with great chiefs or rulers whose remains were placed in the burial mounds, the creation of what appears to have been expansive ceremonial spaces enclosed by geometrically precise walls of earth, long-distance trade, and the creation of spectacular works of art from raw materials only available hundreds of miles away from the Mound City necropolis: copper and silver (Michigan), obsidian (Wyoming), mica (Kentucky), and shell and sharks' teeth from the Gulf of Mexico.

Site Type: Burial Mound, Mound Enclosure

Wow Factor: *** Though the site has largely been reconstructed, the work involved in building the original "city of the dead" is very impressive.

Museum: ***** The artifacts recovered during excavation of this and associated sites are remarkable in their beauty.

Ease of Road Access: *****

Ease of Hike: *****

Natural Beauty of Surroundings: **

Kid Friendly: **

Food: Bring your own.

How to Get There: The park is located in Chillicothe, Ohio, 2 miles north of the intersection of US 35 and OH 104. There are plenty of signs showing the way. To find Mound City using Google Earth, just punch in the following coordinates: 39 22'26.62"N 83 00'26.14"W

Hours of Operation: The visitor center is open daily 8:30 a.m. to 6 p.m. Memorial Day through Labor Day; 8:30 a.m. to 5 p.m. the rest of the year. Closed Thanksgiving, Christmas, and New Year's Day.

Cost: Free

Best Season to Visit: Any time

Website: www.nps.gov/hocu/historyculture/mound-city-group.htm

Designation: National Historical Park

Site 19 Newark Earthworks

Newark, Ohio

Journal Entry

April 24, 2009

It's almost beyond comprehension. Imagine, just for a moment, that people from another country, bearers of another culture, say the French, Chinese, or Saudis, had managed to rent out ground we Americans consider sacred; for example, the burial place of esteemed members of our society. Imagine that place was Arlington National Cemetery. Now imagine that the new lessees wanted to somehow monetize the property, to turn it into a moneymaking proposition. Suppose that the lessees thought it would be totally appropriate to alter that sacred ground where brave soldiers had been laid to rest into a new use . . . A GOLF COURSE! Maybe the top of the Tomb of the Unknown Soldier would sport a golf tee. Soldiers' graves would become hazards for golfers to work around. And the ninth hole could be set up where slain President John F. Kennedy has been laid to rest.

Figure 49. This large mound is part of the earthwork complex that today is part of a golf course. The mound sits at the far end of a circular enclosure, part of the Newark Earthworks.

Figure 50. Artist's conception of the Moundbuilders Country Club from above. The golf course came later.
(STEVEN PATRICIA)

What incredibly bad taste, you might say. But it could never happen; no one would do something so tasteless. Well, what I just described is pretty much what happened to one section of the Newark Earthworks in Ohio. You will find there an ancient sacred enclosure in which a series of mounds was incorporated into a golf course. Unreal. Well, at least the golf course is part of the Moundbuilders Country Club, so they've honored the builders with a name. Sort of.

Okay, I get it. The golf course, in a strangely ironic way, saved the sacred site. Because the country club incorporated the site into their golf course, no one could build homes or businesses there. But if it was "only" a sacred Indian site, that's probably what would have happened. People who work in historic preservation use the term "adaptive reuse" to characterize the rehabilitation and reuse of a historic structure; for example, taking an abandoned nineteenth-century factory building, refurbishing and maintaining its key historical elements, but turning the interior into a modern condominium or office complex. We have already seen how the people of nineteenth-century Marietta, Ohio, did a thoughtful job of adaptively reusing the ancient burial mound found in their community by burying their own dead in its shadow (**Site 16, Cemetery Mound**). But I just don't think "adaptive reuse" applies to using an ancient Indian sacred complex as a golf course.

What You Will See

Along with the golf tees and holes, there is a remarkable set of earthworks to see at the Moundbuilders Country Club, including a great circular enclosure of 20 acres connected through two parallel earthen walls to a much larger octagonal enclosure of about 50 acres (Figure 49). Eight platform mounds are located within the great octagon.

The area within the great circle and octagon is an active golf course and is closed to anyone who is not a member of the country club or a guest. There is, however, a public viewing platform accessible from the parking lot where you can get a decent view of the section of the enclosure where the circle and octagon are joined. Also, the country club has opened the course to non-golfers four days each year. Check with the Moundbuilders Country Club for their "golf-free" days when you can walk throughout the entire monument. Check out this beautiful painting by artist Steven Patricia for his conception of what the site looked like soon after it was constructed—and what a modern, thoughtful preservation of the place would look like today (Figure 50).

There are additional earthworks in the area. The Great Circle Earthworks—a circular space enclosed by an earthwork ring some 1,200 feet in diameter—is preserved as a park, and an adjacent visitor center contains information about the Newark Earthworks.

Why Are the Newark Earthworks Important?

Along with being a marvelous example of the geometric beauty of Hopewell mound building, the Newark Earthworks reflect the astronomical knowledge of the native peoples of the American Midwest. Standing on the large mound at the base of the circular enclosure, a viewer gazes straight up the parallel walls joining the circle to the octagon, bisecting that enclosure, and pointing to a location on the horizon measured at 51.5 degrees (to the northeast). This is the precise location where the moon rises farthest to the north in a cycle that lasts 18.6 years. No coincidence, this reflects a long series of observations by native peoples that must have taken generations.

Site Type: Mound Enclosure
Wow Factor: **** The elaborate earthworks are very impressive, but perhaps the biggest "wow" here is that anyone thought it was a good idea to incorporate a sacred site into a golf course.
Museum: *** There is a small museum near the Great Circle Earthworks, which are part of the Newark Earthworks complex.
Ease of Road Access: *****
Ease of Hike: *****
Natural Beauty of Surroundings: * I give it one star. But if you think golf courses are beautiful, you'll love this place.
Kid Friendly: *
Food: Bring your own.
How to Get There: The earthworks are located in Newark, Ohio, at N. 33rd St. and Parkview Rd., on the grounds of the Moundbuilders Country Club (125 N. 33rd St.).
Hours of Operation: The site can be viewed from the outside of the enclosure and from the viewing platform all year, during daylight hours.
Cost: Free. But duck if you hear a golfer yelling "Fore!"
Best Season to Visit: Any time, but check the schedule for golf-free days when anyone can actually explore the site rather than simply view it from afar.
Website: www.ohiohistory.org/visit/museum-and-site-locator/newark-earthworks
Designation: Private; National Historic Landmark

Site 20 Pinson Mounds State Archaeological Park

Pinson, Tennessee

Journal Entry

April 17, 2012

Pinson Mounds is an impressive ancient ceremonial center located in Madison County, Tennessee. The mounds have been preserved within a 1,200-acre state park that bears the site's name: Pinson Mounds State Archaeological Park. As I hiked the paved trail out toward Mound 28, a beautifully symmetrical truncated pyramid of earth located at the eastern side of the complex, I figured it would be a good idea to go off-trail a bit and walk around the mound. I'm glad I did. When I turned the northeast corner of the mound, I spooked a couple of beautiful white-tailed deer that bounded away from me. They weren't that happy to see me, but I was glad I got to see them.

What You Will See

Pinson Mounds was built and used as a ceremonial center for a large, dispersed population of Native Americans between 200 BC and AD 500. Depending on how you count the various earthworks, there are between fifteen and seventeen mounds at the site spread out across about 400 acres. The tallest is Saul's Mound, a platform mound with a rectangular footprint located in the Central Complex (Figure 51). Saul's Mound is about 72 feet at its highest point, making it the second-tallest existing mound in

Figure 51. The primary earthwork at Pinson Mounds in Tennessee. There is a modern wooden stairway to the top of the mound.

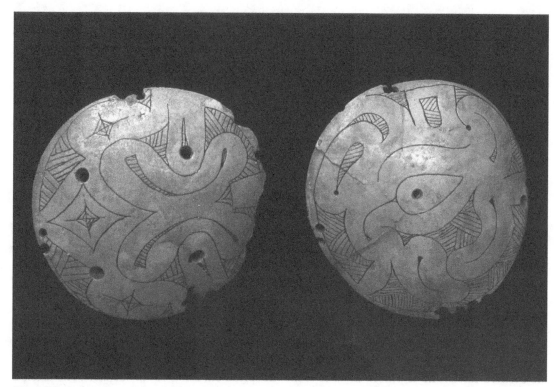

Figure 52. At first glance, I thought these incised rattles on exhibit at the Pinson Mounds museum were made on turtle shells. Oops! They're the tops of human skulls.

North America. At 100 feet, Monks Mound at **Site 9, Cahokia** is the only taller mound. Saul's Mound has a rectangular (well, rectangularish) footprint measuring 370 by 300 feet, with each corner pointing in a cardinal direction. This alignment implies that the builders positioned the mound this way intentionally, possibly to mark the summer and winter solstices, as well as the vernal and autumnal equinoxes. There is a modern set of wooden stairs you can climb to the top of Saul Mound.

The other earthworks at Pinson include several other platform mounds, including the very impressive 33-feet-high Ozier Mound in the Western Group and Mound 28 at the site's eastern margin. I guess to minimize weathering, trees have been allowed to grow freely on the mounds, which detracts a bit from their appearance. Most of the site is accessible along a narrow macadam path. Because its main trail is paved, Pinson (like **Site 3, Toltec** in Arkansas and **Site 23, Montezuma Castle** in Arizona) is at least partially wheelchair accessible. Some mounds are accessible along short dirt paths.

There also is a semicircular enclosure at the site, located in what is called the Eastern Citadel, circumscribed by a 5-foot-high embankment delineating an area of about 1,500 acres. A large platform mound is located within the enclosure.

A very nice on-site museum displays some of the artifacts found during excavation of the site, including two beautiful inscribed rattles from one of the burials (Figure 52). At first I thought they had been made from turtle shells. Turned out they were made from human skull fragments. Very cool, though a little bit creepy.

As at **Site 10, Angel Mounds** in Indiana, the museum at Pinson is built in the form of a platform mound and is actually covered with sod. From a distance it really gives the viewer the impression of an authentic mound. Oh, and the "Please Don't Climb on our Museum" sign is a cute touch.

Why Is Pinson Mounds Important?

Pinson Mounds is a terrific example of the complexity of Mississippian ceremonial centers and the amount of labor it must have taken for its construction. Archaeological excavations at the site produced little in the way of the ordinary refuse one would expect at a habitation site. Like some of the other mound builder ceremonial sites in our odyssey, Pinson was not a city or even a large village. It was a place inhabited by only a very few people, who likely were important functionaries in the religious lives of the dispersed population of farmers who viewed Pinson as a sacred place.

Site Type: Platform Mound
Wow Factor: *** Saul's Mound is impressive. The modern wooden stairway affords visitors a nice perspective of the site.
Museum: **** There are some stunning artifacts on display that were found at the site.
Ease of Road Access: *****
Ease of Hike: **** The main trail through the site is paved, making the trail very flat, easy, and even wheelchair accessible.
Natural Beauty of Surroundings: **** Beautiful wildflowers abound. When I walked around the back of one of the mounds, I encountered two deer browsing on the grass.
Kid Friendly: *** Lots of room to explore and a very nice museum should interest most kids.
Food: Bring your own.
How to Get There: Pinson Mounds is located in Pinson Mounds State Park, 460 Ozier Rd., Pinson, Tennessee. It's about 2 hours and 20 minutes southwest of Nashville, off I-40, and 1 hour 45 minutes northeast of Memphis, also via I-40.
Hours of Operation: Grounds open daily 7 a.m. to sunset. Museum open Monday through Saturday 8 a.m. to 4:30 p.m.; Sunday 1 to 5 p.m. (Check website for winter hours.)
Cost: Free
Best Season to Visit: Just about any time of year is good, but it will be hot and humid in the summer.
Website: http://tnstateparks.com/parks/about/pinson-mounds
Designation: State park; National Historic Landmark

Site 21 Grave Creek Mound Archaeological Complex

Moundsville, West Virginia

Journal Entry

April 19, 2014
Grave Creek Mound is, depending on whom you read and how you measure it, either the largest or the second-largest burial mound in North America, with **Miamisburg (Site 17)** being the other contender. Grave Creek Mound is officially measured at 69 feet high, a foot shorter than Miamisburg. However, Grave Creek Mound is 927 feet in circumference at the base, making it larger in that metric than Miamisburg by 50 feet and rendering it a little larger by volume as well. Whatever. They're both honking big and impressive burial mounds. Like Marietta's **Cemetery Mound (Site 16)**, Grave Creek Mound is located in the middle of a city. The juxtaposition of an ancient burial monument surrounded by factories, residential neighborhoods, and even an adjacent prison seems very strange, but it does reveal how conscious the early European settlers of Moundsville (yeah, they named their city after the huge mound found there) were of the meaning and spiritual importance of the mound. They could have taken the mound's soil and used it as topsoil and cleared the ground for agriculture or development, but they didn't, ultimately making it the centerpiece of a park and museum.

What You Will See

Grave Creek Mound is an impressive Adena Culture burial mound located within the confines of an old industrial city in West Virginia (I.9). You can climb to the top of the mound on a spiral of steps added to allow the archaeological tourist a better perspective of its monumental character. By the time you get to the top, you're heart will be thumping, and the view is pretty impressive. The mound contains something like 60,000 tons of dirt, symmetrically mounded to a height of 69 feet. It took a lot of work to build the mound. The very nice, eclectic Delf Norona Museum on-site includes an interesting mix of local historic material (when I visited there were mannequins wearing antique dresses), but there are also substantial exhibits about the site's archaeology. Check out the models of the mound showing the locations of burials found there during excavation.

Why Is Grave Creek Mound Important?

Along with being a significant example of an Adena burial mound, the Grave Creek Mound is ironically important for its association with an archaeological fraud. The motive was money, and the strategy exploited the desire to believe that someone other than local Indians were responsible for the mound's construction. Remember the discussion earlier in this book of the mythical race that was supposed to have been the true builders of the mounds? The Grave Creek Tablet fit into that mind-set (Figure 53). The owner of the mound actually sold what amounted to mining rights to the monument, and there was an expectation that it contained fabulous treasures like those found in Egyptian tombs. No such treasures were found, but human burials with ceramics were recovered, indicating to any rational person that the mound was an Indian tomb. During these early excavations, a small stone tablet inscribed with a mysterious script was found in the excavation. Any one of a number of self-styled experts identified the ancient language in which it was written (none agreeing on which language it was), and many proposed translations, none of which were even vaguely similar. Check them out:

Figure 53. The Grave Creek tablet was a fake, perpetrated to convince people that ancient Europeans had traveled to America and built burial mounds. This photograph is of a modern replica; the original is missing.

Translations 1857–1875

The Chief of Emigration Who Reached These Places (or This Island) Has Fixed These Statutes Forever.
   —Translated by Maurice Schwab

The Grave of One Who Was Assassinated Here. May God to Avenge Him Strike His Murderer, Cutting off the Hand to His Existence.
   —Translated by Jules Opert

I Pray (to) Christ His Most Holy Mother, Son, Holy Ghost Jesus Christ God.
   —Translated by Buckingham Smith (from a Catholic cipher)

You know something fishy is going on with an ostensibly ancient inscription when you get this rather broad array of entirely different translations. None of them are even vaguely similar. That's because the inscription is entirely fake and, let's face it, meaningless. Certainly it's an interesting thing to ponder at the site. By the way, the original tablet has gone missing. You'll see a copy in the museum along with some of the suggested translations. It's a hoot.

Site Type: Burial Mound

Wow Factor: ** The mound is impressively tall.

Museum: **** The museum is really impressive, with lots of information about local history; but the display on the Grave Creek Tablet is less skeptical than I might have hoped.

Ease of Road Access: *****

Ease of Hike: *****

Natural Beauty of Surroundings: * There is a nice view of the surrounding city from the top of the mound.

Kid Friendly: ** There are lots of fun exhibits in the museum; the little displays showing how the mound was made are interesting.

Food: Bring your own and picnic outside.

How to Get There: Grave Creek Mound is about as far west as you can get in West Virginia, 15 minutes south of Wheeling, just east of WV 2 at 801 Jefferson Ave. in downtown Moundsville. It's across the street from a historic prison, which is also open for a visit.

Hours of Operation: The museum and grounds are open Tuesday through Saturday 9 a.m. to 5 p.m. At other times you can do a simple drive by and see the mound even when the museum is closed.

Cost: Free

Best Season to Visit: It snows in West Virginia in winter. No surprise there. But just about any time of year is good when the weather is decent.

Website: www.wvculture.org/museum/GraveCreekmod.html

Designation: State park; National Historic Landmark

Site 22 **Aztalan Mounds State Park**

Aztalan, Wisconsin

Journal Entry

February 19, 2011

Aztalan is located in a state park in the town of that same name, east of the town of Lake Mills, Wisconsin. My visit was actually a little strange on a number of levels. Prior to this winter trip, all my site visits to Aztalan Mounds had been in spring or summer. It was a bit of a shock to see a mound site with a coating of snow—and being absolutely freezing while walking around. Beyond the weather, Aztalan was strange because it looked a lot like a miniature version of **Site 9, Cahokia,** replete with a primary temple mound, a plaza with that main mound at one end, and smaller platform mounds demarcating that plaza. Strange or not, it certainly impressed me that, so far from Cahokia and the core region of platform mound building societies, here was a genuine geographic outlier exhibiting the reach of their culture.

Figure 54. The main mound at Aztalan, in Wisconsin, is a miniature and distant version of Monk's Mound at Cahokia.

What You Will See

Located in a state park, the site includes an impressive multitiered primary platform mound and two smaller, though still impressively monumental, platform mounds (Figure 54, I.10). You will also be able to see a section of the palisade that has been reconstructed in its original footprint as determined through archaeological excavation. Unfortunately the site was sold for $22 in 1838 and altered significantly as farmers plowed and planted over the mounds and wagonloads of potsherds were used as roadbed fill in the surrounding region. That nonsense ended in the twentieth century, professional archaeological investigation of the site commenced, and the site was purchased by Wisconsin for a state park.

As you can see in the photos, I was there in winter and we were the only people at the site. At the time of my visit, the only information available on-site was located in a little shelter that provided some signage describing Aztalan along with a map. There is an ongoing effort to construct a permanent interpretive center at the site, and currently there is a temporary one. Also, artifacts from Aztalan can be seen at the nearby Aztalan Museum (separate fee).

In a number of specific features, Aztalan looks very much like other Mississippian mound builder ceremonial centers. In fact, some it was built self-consciously as a miniature version of Cahokia, with a primary multitiered platform mound and several other monumental earthworks, all surrounded by an extensive palisade.

Why Is Aztalan Mound Important?

Aztalan is another one of those ancient sites in the continental United States that was viewed by its early European visitors as too large, too sophisticated, and requiring too much communal labor to have been constructed by local native people who these visitors and settlers viewed as primitive. So upon first encountering this site, those Europeans named it Aztalan, which while wrongly implying a cultural and historical connection to the Aztecs (the site's name is a word in the Aztec language of Nahuatl), is actually pretty interesting. According to the Aztec's own version of their history, before settling in the basin of Mexico where the modern Mexico City is located, they came from a land to the north. The Aztecs certainly were referring to a region immediately north of that location. But Wisconsin sure is north of Mexico so, the argument went, the Aztecs didn't travel to Wisconsin to build the site; they originated in Wisconsin, built Aztalan, and then traveled south to Mexico. Not bloody likely.

One of the most important things about Aztalan is its location. The site is located far from the Mississippian mound builder heartland. Aztalan is located more than 340 miles from Cahokia and is the farthest north of the platform mound ceremonial and population centers.

Virtually every great civilization relies on trade, sometimes long-distance trade, to access raw materials not naturally available in its core area. Some archaeologists, in fact, view Aztalan as a colony of people sent from Cahokia a little before AD 1100 to facilitate their obtaining one of these materials. Located more than 340 miles from Cahokia (that's by modern highways; the ancient trip must have been far longer), Aztalan is in a region where native copper—not an ore that needs smelting but a pure variety of the metal, ready to use as is—was locally available and mined by people for thousands of years. The idea here is that in a strategy we see even in recent history, Cahokians established a colony in the region in order to more economically and reliably gain access to and exploit copper. Pretty cool.

Site Type: Platform Mound

Wow Factor: ** The primary mound is small but nicely symmetrical.

Museum: There is a temporary interpretive center at the site. The long-term plan is to build a permanent center.

Ease of Road Access: *****

Ease of Hike: *****

Natural Beauty of Surroundings: ***

Kid Friendly: ***

Food: Bring your own.

How to Get There: Aztalan Mounds is located in Aztalan State Park, 2 miles off I-94 near the town of Lake Mills, Wisconsin. It's about an hour drive from either Milwaukee or Madison. Coming from the west on I-94, reach CR B by going south on WI 89 to Lake Mills. From the east off I-94, take WI 26 south to Johnson Creek and then to CR B.

Hours of Operation: Grounds open daily 6 a.m. to 10 p.m.

Cost: You'll need a vehicle pass for the park. See website for details.

Best Season to Visit: Of course it's cold in Wisconsin in winter . . . and snowy. I visited the site in February. There was snow on the ground, and it was cold. But it wasn't bad.

Website: http://i94.biz/aztalan/aztalan.html

Designation: State park; National Historic Landmark

Cliff Dwellings, Great Houses, and Stone Towers

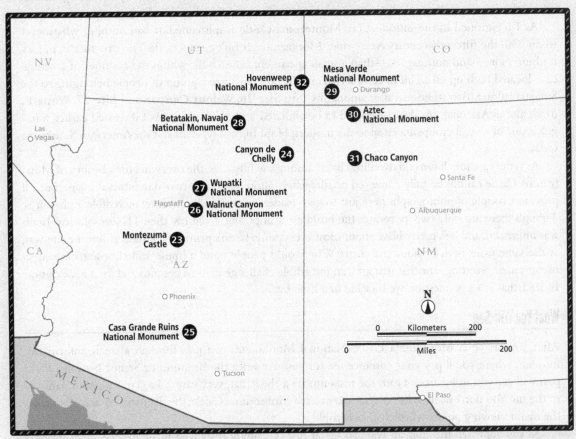

Figure 55.

(MAP BY ALENA PEARCE)

Site 23 Montezuma Castle

Camp Verde, Arizona

Journal Entry

July 30, 2009

There is a word, used almost exclusively by British speakers of English, spoken in reaction to something that is absolutely, mind-blowingly impressive—either in a good or a bad way. That word is gobsmacked. I just love how it sounds. It denotes a combination of surprise and amazement, but times 10. Every time I visit Montezuma Castle and experience the dramatic "reveal" when reaching the point along the trail where the ruin virtually explodes into view above me I am, well, gobsmacked.

As I mentioned in the introduction, Montezuma Castle is misnamed. It had nothing whatsoever to do with the fifteenth-century Aztec ruler Montezuma. It isn't even a castle. The structure is, in fact, nothing more—and nothing less—than a small apartment house built within the confines of a natural cave located high up on a cliff in central Arizona. Its builders were a group of people belonging to the Sinagua culture. Two additional sites among my fifty, **Site 26, Walnut Canyon** and **Site 27, Wupatki** (both also in Arizona), are also considered to be affiliated with that culture. As I discussed earlier, Sinagua is one of several groups ancestral to the modern Hopi Indians who inhabit the American Southwest today.

As is the case for all the cliff dwellings listed among my fifty sites, the overwhelming beauty of Montezuma Castle cannot be fully conveyed or adequately appreciated in a two-dimensional image, but I'll provide a couple of photographs here just to give readers an impression of how incredible a place it is. Though there are only twenty rooms, the building is imposing. Even my then 11-year-old son Jacob was impressed, and he's pretty blasé about most everything. Jacob's primary question about the site was, at the same time, both obvious and smart: Why would people build a house and choose to live in so inconvenient a setting, one that was such an incredible challenge to even get into and then back out of? Indeed, that is a key question we'll tackle in a little bit.

What You Will See

After you arrive at Montezuma Castle National Monument, you pass through a small, informative museum where you'll pay your entrance fee (or your America the Beautiful or Senior National Parks pass will get you in for free). From the museum it's a short, flat, very easy hike across a paved pathway to the site. You don't need to be an avid hiker to see Montezuma Castle; the flat pathway actually makes the major viewing points wheelchair-accessible.

As you approach the ruin, all you can see at first is a subtly shadowed niche located three-quarters of the way up the cliff ahead of you and to your right. You continue walking a very short distance along that path and then, bam (I-11)! You are standing directly below the structure, which appears almost to be floating above you from your vantage point on the trail (Figure 56). As I said, I'm gobsmacked every time.

The site's general appearance is quite beautiful, and its setting is extremely dramatic. I'm convinced that this was quite intentional on the part of the builders. After all, why would ancient architects be any different from modern ones? I think it's little more than temporal conceit to assume that ancient buildings were designed only with practical or utilitarian considerations in mind. Highly functional of course, Montezuma Castle also is truly beautiful in its simplicity and filled with thoughtful touches, including a front wall that is curved inward, matching the concave surface of the cliff in which it is

Figure 56. Walk on the paved trail at Montezuma Castle National Monument for the payoff: this great view of the small but beautiful cliff dwelling.

secreted. I bet the ancient builders and residents of the structure thought it looked pretty amazing too. Though there are only twenty rooms spread out across five stories—Montezuma Castle is far smaller and less grand than most of the cliff dwellings at **Site 29, Mesa Verde** (Colorado)—its construction nevertheless was an impressive and massive undertaking. Built in about AD 1100, the site was occupied for more than 300 years. It was abandoned after AD 1425, possibly as the result of a prolonged drought.

When Montezuma Castle was first opened to the public in the early twentieth century, visitors were allowed to climb up the cliff and explore the interior of the ruin. That practice ended in 1951. The building had begun to deteriorate as a result of so many people traipsing through the fragile, more than 600-year-old site, so it was closed to the public. Binoculars or a telephoto lens will come in handy for your visit. With the close-up view thus afforded, you'll be able to clearly see the building's elegant masonry as well as the exposed ends of some of the original sycamore logs used as roof and ceiling beams.

You can get up-close views of the remains of ten additional structures as you continue along on the paved trail, including Castle A, a larger but not as well-preserved building consisting of more than forty rooms located at the base of the cliff. The site, then, was not just a single impressive structure but an entire neighborhood.

If you have the time, you should definitely walk the length of the loop trail back to your car. You'll get a variety of interesting views of the "castle," have opportunities for great photos, and see a nifty little diorama in a kiosk along the way. If you have a bit more time, you can drive an additional 11 miles to a fascinating companion site, Montezuma Well. The well is a natural feature, a lake that resulted from the collapse of a cavern. Look closely and you'll see two cliff dwellings built by the Sinagua in a niche above the well (Figure 57). More than a million gallons of water flow through the well every day (so

Figure 57. A drive of about 11 additional miles brings you to Montezuma Well, a natural spring-fed body of water with cliff dwellings built into the walls.

these Sinaguans, in fact, were not "without water"), serving as an irrigation source to farmers both ancient and modern.

Though named for the dryness of their home territory, the Sinagua were farmers who relied on water to grow corn, beans, and squash as part of a broad diet that included a significant component of wild plants and animals. Rainfall in the area was undependable for agriculture, so the Sinagua developed sophisticated irrigation strategies involving small dams and lengthy channels to direct water to their planting fields from sources like the nearby Beaver Creek as well as Montezuma Well. Some of their irrigation channels continue to be used to this day.

Why Is Montezuma Castle Important?

At least one of the reasons you should see Montezuma Castle is its setting. Imagine people with no mechanical assistance or animal power building a small, elegant, five-story apartment complex in a naturally eroded alcove situated about 90 feet up a crumbly cliff. Now imagine daily life there. Tending to their agricultural fields, hunting wild game, fetching water, collecting clay for pottery making, visiting neighbors—all these daily tasks involved a nearly 90-foot climb down and then back up with the use of ladders as well as hand- and footholds carved into the rock. That brings me back to my son Jacob's question: Why would people go to all that trouble? The answer is pretty simple: The difficulties presented by Montezuma Castle's setting were more than compensated for by the advantages that setting provided. In its natural alcove, the building is shaded from the brutal Arizona summer sun. Its positioning is also important for the protection it afforded its residents; it must have been very difficult for enemies to mount a sneak attack on a building located in a niche 90 feet up a cliff. The thickness of the walls as well as the dearth of windows further rendered the structure impervious to the slings and arrows not of outrageous fortune but of nasty neighbors. Bottom line: When you're up there, you're largely safe from enemy attack.

The thick walls and very few windows were also smartly conceived to keep it cool inside during the day and warm at night. Modern architects and builders in the Southwest mimic some of those same strategies, utilizing thick exterior walls with a high thermal mass in today's energy-efficient construction practices. Finally, the building is more than high enough to avoid the surging waters of Beaver Creek when it floods. Montezuma Castle, therefore, reflects the ingenuity, capability, and adaptability of the ancient Sinagua people and for that reason alone is an important site that's worth a visit during your archaeological odyssey.

The US government has long formally recognized the site's significance. After the passage of the American Antiquities Act in 1906, President Theodore Roosevelt was given the power to officially designate places in the United States as "National Monuments." Roosevelt was a true visionary about the need to preserve for future Americans places that exemplify our nation's natural and cultural heritage, and he wasted little time in naming monuments. The first place so designated was Devil's Tower in Wyoming (that's the volcanic mountain that plays a major role in the Steven Spielberg movie *Close Encounters of the Third Kind*). El Morro in New Mexico, a striking sandstone promontory covered in historical graffiti, was number two. On December 6, 1906, Montezuma Castle was the third place to be designated by President Roosevelt as a national monument. As of this writing, there are 109 places so designated (a number that likely will continue to grow), twelve of which are included in my fifty sites.

Site Type: Cliff Dwelling

Wow Factor: ***** It's a small cliff dwelling, but the setting is gorgeous.

Museum: ***** There's a terrific National Park Service museum on-site.

Ease of Road Access: ***** It's a very short drive off the highway on a paved road; well sign-posted.

Ease of Hike: ***** The hike to Montezuma Castle is very short and paved. It is wheelchair friendly.

Natural Beauty of Surroundings: **** The surrounding Arizona desert is notable for its stark beauty. The presence of Beaver Creek, which attracted human settlement to the area in the first place, provides a nice habitat for lots of greenery.

Kid Friendly: *** There's nothing particularly geared toward little kids, but the hike is easy and short, which helps with short attention spans.

Food: Bring your own. There's no food service in the park.

How to Get There: Montezuma Castle is located just a few minutes off I-17, about a 90-minute drive north from Phoenix. Take I-17 north from Phoenix to exit 289. Drive east through two traffic circles for approximately 0.5 mile to the blinking red light. Turn left onto Montezuma Castle Road.

Hours of Operation: Open daily 8 a.m. to 5 p.m.

Cost: See website. There is no additional fee for Montezuma Well.

Best Season to Visit: Central Arizona can be brutally hot in summer, so you might want to visit in any other season. However, the hike is short, not particularly challenging, and there's is an air-conditioned museum on-site.

Website: www.nps.gov/moca/index.htm

Designation: National Monument

Site 24 **Canyon de Chelly**

Chinle, Arizona

Journal Entry

March 17, 2015

> *I grew up here, raised by my grandmother. The canyon was the center of my world. It was my school. My book. My museum. My playground. I have walked its entirety. I know every rock, the ruins, the art, the plants, and the animals who live here. Mostly, I know my people. My grandmother raised me here to be a story teller, to share the tale of our people with the Bilagáana, the White people, so our history might be understood and never forgotten.*

Our brilliant Navajo guide, Harris Hardy, told this to us as we stood in front of a beautiful and heartbreaking nineteenth-century pictograph panel depicting a group of horseback-riding Spaniards in

Figure 58. The incredible beauty of Canyon de Chelly in northeastern Arizona, a place filled with the communities of both ancient and living peoples. The Mummy Cave Ruin is pictured here.

Canyon de Chelly (pronounced de-SHAY). The painting shows a red-cloaked priest bearing an image of a cross in the midst of a contingent of men wielding rifles (I-12). Artfully rendered in pigment by the Navajo artist, these invaders, Harris told us, were depicted as celebrating their recent massacre of more than one hundred Navajo women and children who had been hiding in a rock cliff alcove now called Massacre Cave. Bullet holes still mark the margins of that cave. On the cliff above it, a Navajo woman is said to have encountered a Spanish soldier. When he assaulted her, she grabbed him and sent them both over the cliff edge to certain mutual death.

Located on the Navajo Indian Reservation in northeastern Arizona, Canyon de Chelly is a splendidly beautiful locale where history, culture, and natural beauty join to create an experience that should not be missed (Figure 58). Canyon de Chelly is not a dead place. It is not an abandoned ruin. It is a world where the past and the present coexist. Navajo families continue to work their farms that dot the base of the canyon, living alongside the remnants of the houses of the people who lived here in antiquity.

What You Will See

Canyon de Chelly offers a wealth of possibilities to the archaeological time traveler. For instance, a drive along South Rim Road affords access to a number of short trails that lead to excellent overlooks of several ancient dwellings including First and Junction Ruins, both relatively small sites ensconced in small clefts in the canyon wall (Figure 59). Another stop affords a view of White House, a larger ancient apartment house built on the floor of the canyon with a separate upstairs section ensconced in the cliff. Farther along on the south rim is the aptly named Sliding House ruin, which looks as though it's in the midst of a slide down the face of the canyon. A drive along North Rim Road provides access to views of Ledge Ruin, the large complex of rooms called Antelope House, the large cliff dwelling in Mummy Cave (also called the House Under the Rock), and the smaller ruin in Yucca Cave.

If you've made the commitment to see Canyon de Chelly, I implore you to do more. The canyon is on the Navajo reservation, and Navajo people's homes, barns, and fields are located there. The canyon is not public land, and the Navajo are not on display as museum pieces; they are people living out their lives. However, they welcome visitors who are respectful of their culture and who wish to learn more about the Navajo people and their history. To this end, the Navajo allow visitors to hike down to White House Ruin (accessible from South Rim Road) on their own. The round-trip from the trailhead takes about 2 hours—and remember that whatever slope you walk down into the canyon, you'll need to hike back up.

And there is much, much more to see and much, much more to learn in Canyon de Chelly. I highly recommend signing up for a tour (run by several local companies) led by a Navajo guide. Using a Navajo guide provides an infinitely more immersive experience, and you'll see so much more. You'll be able to experience up-close the ruins you could see only from a distance along the rim roads. Beyond this, the canyon walls are sprinkled with amazing works of rock art—like the one Harris Hardy took us to as described in the Journal Entry above. Antelope House, visible from the overlook located along North Rim Road, is called that because of a truly remarkable wall of pictographs depicting a number of realistically rendered, large-scale though not quite life-size pronghorn antelope, a species that still thrives in the American Southwest (I-13). Your Navajo guide can take you right to Antelope House, where you'll have a close encounter with the gorgeous paintings on the rock wall adjacent to the ancient structure of four pronghorns among other images of sheep, horses, and dogs. There's rock art all over the place in Canyon de Chelly, and Harris was happy to tell us the stories underlying all of them. It was amazing.

Figure 59. First Ruin (seen here) is one of several amazing cliff dwellings seeming to cling to the walls of Canyon de Chelly. These structures predate the Navajo presence in the canyon.

Why Is Canyon de Chelly Important?

Canyon de Chelly is a truly remarkable place. It's not just a single site; it's an inclusive territory with a series of interconnected villages in which Ancestral Puebloans lived between AD 200 and AD 1300. After they left, Canyon de Chelly wasn't unoccupied for long. That's when the people who call themselves the Diné—commonly referred to as the Navajo—moved in.

In Canyon de Chelly you will see a discrete territory occupied by at least two different groups of Native Americans during the course of the past 2,000 or so years. You will be able to view several cliff dwellings as well as some larger free-standing structures on the floor of the canyon. You'll also be able to see historical Navajo farmsteads characterized by their own form of architecture—the hogan. It's this continuity that renders Canyon de Chelly so important in any archaeological odyssey.

I think the great significance of Canyon de Chelly resides, in part, in the deeply intimate and personal connection between the ancient wonders you will see in Canyon de Chelly and the people who today call it home. The ancient ruins, the magical works of art, along with the fence posts, pastures, cornfields, traditional Navajo houses, recent homes and farm buildings, and especially the proud and resilient residents of the canyon, are part of a great web of life and history, a web deeply rooted in this place and one that transcends time.

Additional Note

Tours that lead into the canyon are run by private companies and fees are charged for that service. The tours aren't cheap, but they are more than worth it. We used Canyon de Chelly Tours and they were fantastic. For prices and tours visit http://canyondechellytours.com. Be sure to tip your guide. You can also hire a Navajo guide for a horseback ride into the canyon. We used Justin's Horse Rental (www.facebook.com/Justins-Horse-Rental-623254347709579/timeline/).

Site Type: Cliff Dwelling, Great House, Pictographs

Wow Factor: ***** The combination of cliff and ground pueblos and petroglyph and pictograph panels makes Canyon de Chelly a destination that no archaeological tourist should miss.

Museum: ***

Ease of Road Access: *****

Ease of Hike: **** The minor hikes from parking areas along the rim are easy. The one unguided hike you can take (to White House Ruin) is about 2.5 miles round-trip; you descend about 500 feet and need to hike back up. The hike itself should take about 90 minutes. I'd call it moderately strenuous.

Natural Beauty of Surroundings: ***** The overlook of Spider Rock alone makes this a five-star destination.

Kid Friendly: ***

Food: There's food available in the town of Chinle (pronounced CHIN-lee), which is immediately adjacent to the park.

How to Get There: Canyon de Chelly is located on the expansive Navajo Reservation. It is about 3 miles from AZ 191 in Chinle, Arizona. AZ 191 is accessible from I-40 in Arizona and NM 264 in New Mexico.

Hours of Operation: The visitor center, located at the intersection of North Rim and South Rim Roads, is open daily 8 a.m. to 5 p.m.

Cost: Free. Though administered by the National Park Service, Canyon de Chelly is on the Navajo Reservation. It is the policy of the tribe not to charge for access to the monument.

Best Season to Visit: Spring and fall

Website: www.nps.gov/cach/index.htm

Designation: National Monument; Navajo Nation

Site 25 Casa Grande Ruins National Monument

Coolidge, Arizona

Journal Entry

July 30, 2009

Frederick Law Olmsted Jr. was a hotshot landscape architect in a family of hotshot landscape archi-tects. His father, Frederick Law Olmsted, was codesigner of Central Park in New York City. So Junior certainly had the pedigree going for him and, as is clear from even a cursory perusal of his professional biography, an especial fondness for and interest in enhancing the natural beauty of our national parks. So it beggars the imagination trying to comprehend what he was thinking when he designed the mon-strosity that is the "ramada," the metal canopy that monumentally looms over the ancient ruins of the great house at Casa Grande. It sort of looks like an elevated landing pad for a helicopter. Built in 1932 at a cost of $28,000, Olmsted's roof replaced a wooden structure that was intended to preserve and protect from the elements the huge structure that served as the major habitation for most of the residents of the village. In that Olmsted certainly succeeded. But in terms of designing a roof that melted into the back-ground, that disappeared when visitors came to the site to appreciate the ancient building, well, epic fail. The raw materials of the canopy, with its iron girders and colossal metal posts, are entirely out of keeping with the organic look and feel of the great house. Beyond this, the monumentality of the roof effectively shrinks the scale of the building, making it look puny when in fact it was monumental for its time. But that's no reason not to include Casa Grande in my fifty-site odyssey. It really is an impressive site and, outside of **Site 27, Wupatki** and **Site 31, Chaco Canyon,** about the best preserved of the great houses of the Southwest.

What You Will See

Casa Grande means "great house" in Spanish, and it certainly is. Though the great house is the largest structure at the site, the village in which it was located was essentially a large compound with a num-ber of buildings, all surrounded by a village wall more than 8 feet high. Built more than 700 years ago, unlike the pueblos at **Wupatki** and **Chaco Canyon,** where stone was the primary building material, the raw material used for both the buildings and the village wall at Casa Grande was caliche, a kind of natural concrete (Figure 60). The Great House at Casa Grande is very impressive, a four-story apart-ment building. The long axis of the building is about 60 feet long, and it has been estimated that more than 6 million pounds of caliche were used in its construction—a free-standing four-story structure, the largest within a compound encompassed by a wall several feet high. Only the core of the building reaches up to four stories; a skirt of three stories surrounds the four-story core. There are several other, smaller buildings located in the compound, most to the northeast of the great house. The second-largest structure in the village is located in its southwest corner and is actually incorporated into the village wall. South and east of the great house is a large, open plaza of about 2 acres where village residents might have congregated for trade, religious rituals, and social interactions. The area outside the village walls was farmland in a dry landscape.

Casa Grande is categorized as a Hohokam community. The Hohokam were experts at dry-land farming, and archaeologists have found hundreds of miles of irrigation canals and ditches built and used by them to transport water to their fields where they grew corn, beans, and squash. Casa Grande likely

Figure 60. With the village wall in the foreground and the weirdly roofed great house in the middle, you can imagine what this thriving community was like 800 years ago. Well, if you ignore the metal roof.

housed a few hundred people at its peak in the mid–1300s and appears to have been largely abandoned by about AD 1450.

You can walk partway into the building and gaze up its four levels. Though the floors and ceilings are gone now, you can get a nice perspective of the overall appearance of the interior of the great house. As you walk around the village compound, you'll see the remains of the other, smaller structures as well as the remnants of a wall that encompassed the compound. The folks at Casa Grande were serious about security; there was no opening in the tall, enclosing wall, so access to the village must have been by ladder.

The on-site museum is absolutely terrific, and you'll see some very useful depictions by artists of what this wonderful community must have looked like at its peak.

Why Is Casa Grande Important?

Before there were national monuments, national parks, or national historical parks, in June 1892 President Benjamin Harrison designated Casa Grande as the first prehistoric and cultural preserve. In 1918 President Woodrow Wilson included the site in the listing of officially decreed national monuments.

Casa Grande has long been officially recognized for its significance. It is the largest and most impressive village site of the Hohokam people. Built in AD 1300, Casa Grande itself is a testament to the architectural and engineering skills of the Hohokam. Along with engineering the caliche into a usable building material, the people of Casa Grande brought more than 600 large wooden beams—some of these beams more than 12 feet long—into the site. The tree species that contributed these beams—cottonwood, juniper, pine, and fir—don't grow nearby but had to be obtained from the mountains, about 50 miles away, reflecting the great skill and organizational abilities of the Hohokam people.

Site Type: Great House

Wow Factor: ** The great house at Casa Grande is pretty massive. The ruin maintains enough of its integrity to convey a good idea of what the impressive walled village looked like when it was occupied more than 650 years ago.

Museum: ***

Ease of Road Access: *****

Ease of Hike: *****

Natural Beauty of Surroundings: *

Kid Friendly: **

Food: Bring your own.

How to Get There: Casa Grande is located in Coolidge, Arizona, right off I-10, midway between Phoenix and Tucson (about 1 hour from each of those cities). Take exit 211 from Tucson or exit 185 from Phoenix and then just follow the signs to the site.

Hours of Operation: Open daily 9 a.m. to 5 p.m. Closed on Thanksgiving and Christmas.

Cost: See website.

Best Season to Visit: Any time but summer

Website: www.nps.gov/cagr/index.htm

Designation: National Monument

Site 26 Walnut Canyon National Monument

Flagstaff, Arizona

Journal Entry

April 14, 2013

When I first walked down the 240 steps from the rim of Walnut Canyon to reach the trail that brings you to the cliff dwellings, my reaction was, "Are you kidding me?" First, it just seems crazy that people would go to all the trouble of constructing their houses in such a ridiculously difficult and apparently precarious setting. I mean, **Montezuma Castle (Site 23)** was challenging enough; this was crazy. Second, it is clear that the residents created an unimaginable degree of inconvenience just to accomplish the ordinary tasks in their daily routines. No one wants to concern themselves with the potential of falling to your death when you get up in the dawn hours just to exit your house to pee. It was dangerous enough for vigorous, healthy young adults. I simply can't imagine what it must have been like for the elderly, much less for parents of squirmy, adventurous, curious kids. I mean, holy crap; one false step, one wrong move, and down you go to the bottom of a step-sided, rocky canyon. Today, no zoning commission would ever sign off on this project. And forget about insurance; that's not going to happen. Nevertheless, at around AD 1100 people began to scale the walls of the canyon and then to build homes in the horizontal, narrow seams of eroded rock that characterize both walls.

The precarious nature of the location of the dwellings and the challenges and dangers presented by a life in the cliffs begs the question: Why? Why did the residents of Walnut Canyon build their houses in rock alcoves hundreds of feet above the canyon floor?

What You Will See

Walnut Canyon presents the visitor with one of the most incredible settings of any of the Southwest cliff dwellings (Figure 61). Dozens of attached dwellings sit nestled in a series of shallow linear niches

Figure 61. Long view of the cliff dwellings located in natural niches throughout Walnut Canyon.

Figure 62. The trail down into Walnut Canyon brings you right up to some of the strings of structures. You can even walk into some of them.

scattered across the strata of the steep canyon walls. Have you ever seen photographs of rock climbers who actually overnight in the middle of a climb, literally hanging from the cliff face as they sleep? Walnut Canyon is a little like that.

At its deepest, the floor of Walnut Canyon is about 350 feet below the top. The niches in which the cliff dwellings were built consist of a limestone softer than the surrounding rock. The niches were eroded as Walnut Creek cut down into its streambed.

A paved path and steps—the Island Trail—lead from the visitor center down to the level where the visitor can encounter twenty-five of the cliff dwellings. This provides an up-close and personal perspective of the structures (Figure 62). You can even enter into a few; note how much cooler it feels inside a dwelling even when it's sweltering outside. The path also provides spectacular views of the interior of the canyon; with the naked eye or, even better, a telephoto lens or binoculars, you can gaze across the canyon and peer into ancient structures on the opposite cliff face (Figure 63). The broader, naked-eye view is instructive as well, and you can see the separate levels of alcove habitations.

The cliff dwellings in Walnut Canyon were built in about AD 1100. The structures were cleverly built along two extensive, primary stratigraphic niches along the canyon's walls. The primary building materials were limestone blocks and clay, the latter used as a mortar for binding the stone blocks together. The builders took advantage of their surroundings, the niche itself providing a ready-made ceiling, floor, and rear wall. The builders had merely to construct a wall in front of the already existing

Figure 63. Imagine these structures across the canyon when they were inhabited.

natural niche to enclose their lodgings, and then build whatever interior walls they desired to create separate apartments or rooms.

The Island Trail is a 0.9-mile loop and is not especially difficult, but those with a fear of heights might not be comfortable. As is almost universally the case, the steep 185-foot rise up out of the Canyon (with its 240 steps) is the most strenuous part of the hike.

Why Is Walnut Canyon Important?

Walnut Canyon reflects the architectural genius of the Sinagua people, who we met before at **Site 23, Montezuma Castle**. Their skill is apparent in their quarrying of materials, approach to design, and construction practices. And think about it; the houses in Walnut Canyon were built between AD 1100 and about AD 1400. So the sturdy, still-standing structures nestled in the niches are at least 600 years old. That's pretty good for a people who did all their building by hand and without the aid of machinery or even draft animals. With their construction of steep trails, ropes, and ladders, they were able to attend to their needs, bring food down into their homes in the canyon alcoves, collect and bring firewood and other necessary resources down into their residences, and ultimately create a cozy home for themselves that afforded pretty spectacular views.

It really is impossible to explain why the Sinagua people went to all the trouble to build their homes in a series of narrow niches along the walls of a cliff. The people of Walnut Canyon were agricultural and farmed the mesa top. Living in the canyon's niches was certainly inconvenient, at least from a modern perspective, but it freed up land on the mesa top for agriculture and likely provided protection from marauding enemies. And it provides the archaeological tourist an incredible place to spend a few hours and contemplate a life and a world much different from our own, a world where apparently no one was afraid of heights.

Site Type: Cliff Dwelling

Wow Factor: **** The actual structural remains at Walnut Canyon aren't spectacular, but their context—inset into the cliff walls marking a steep, narrow, deep canyon—is amazing.

Museum: ***

Ease of Road Access: ****

Ease of Hike: ** The elevation is high (about 6,700 feet), the steps leading down to the canyon trails are steep, and the climb back up will get your heart thumping, especially if you're a sea-level guy like me.

Natural Beauty of Surroundings: **** The canyon is gorgeous.

Kid Friendly: *** Kids will love the hike—and being able to enter some of the structures—but hold their hands on the trail. Well, try to.

Food: Bring your own.

How to Get There: Walnut Canyon is located 7.5 miles from Flagstaff, Arizona. From Flagstaff take I-40 East. Get off at exit 240 and go south for 3 miles to the canyon.

Hours of Operation: Open daily 9 a.m. to 5 p.m. November through April; daily 8 a.m. to 5 p.m. May through October

Cost: See website.

Best Season to Visit: Because of the higher elevation and dry air, Walnut Canyon is nice in spring and summer. It's cold in winter.

Website: www.nps.gov/waca/index.htm

Designation: National Monument

Site 27 **Wupatki National Monument**

Arizona

Journal Entry

April 14, 2013
We usually think of a volcanic eruption as catastrophic and utterly destructive, killing people and laying waste to hundreds of square miles of countryside, creating an uninhabitable landscape looking more like the surface of the moon than any place on Earth. You've certainly heard of Mount Vesuvius and the tragic destruction of the elegant city of Pompeii in AD 79 by that volcano's cataclysmic eruption. Well, that was before my time, but I do remember the eruption of Mount St. Helens in Washington State on May 18, 1980. This was the most destructive eruption to occur in the United States, at least in recorded history. More than 1,000 feet of the volcano's summit was blasted off of the mountain, with much of the remnants falling to earth as ash and rock, destroying 185 miles of roadways, 15 miles of railway tracks, nearly 50 bridges, 250 houses, and killing more than 50 people. Catastrophic indeed, but as bad as it was, the destruction was short term. The area devastated by the eruption is now the scene of abundant, new growth; grasses, bushes, and trees have filled the formerly dead zone, reflecting the endless persistence of life. After its destructive force dissipates, a volcanic eruption can be a rejuvenating force, enriching soil and resulting in an explosion of plant and animal life.

Something like that happened in central Arizona in AD 1064. In that year, as determined by dendrochronology (tree-ring dating), the mountain we today call Sunset Crater erupted in a pyroclastic explosion of unimaginable proportions, killing everything in its wake. Among the things killed in the eruption were trees whose preserved trunks bear witness in their rings to the precise year the eruption occurred. Though in the short term the devastation wrought by Sunset's eruption was extreme, in the long haul the blanket of ash that enveloped the hundreds of square miles surrounding the volcano created a rich agricultural soil that attracted Native American farmers looking for arable land in the twelfth century. The large great house called Wupatki and several smaller pueblos located within a few miles of the big site reflect the movement of people back into the area to exploit the volcanically enriched soil.

What You Will See

There are two national monuments you should visit in this part of your odyssey, Sunset Crater and Wupatki, though only Wupatki is included in my list of fifty sites. At Sunset, a geological not an archaeological site, you can hike around the volcanic cone. You'll see that, more than 950 years after the eruption, plant life has yet to reestablish itself at the top of the cone and be able to extrapolate from the missing part of the peak the enormity of the material blasted into the atmosphere.

The great house called Wupatki and the surrounding fortress-like settlements of Wukoki, Lomaki, Citadel, and Nalakihu Pueblos fill out the picture of a dynamic cultural adaptation to a postapocalyptic volcanic landscape in northern Arizona nearly a thousand years ago.

The eruptions that resulted in Sunset Crater lasted on and off for close to 130 years. Even with ongoing volcanic activity, as many as 3,000 people converged on the area after AD 1130, probably because the soil had become far more conducive to agriculture as a result of the volcanic deposits. In other words, only about sixty-six years after the eruption and cataclysmic destruction, the landscape had once again become suitable for agriculture.

Figure 64. Reminiscent of ceremonial ball courts seen in Mesoamerica, Wupatki has its own version.

The landscape around Sunset Crater is alien and bizarre. The black lava flow at the base of the volcano looks as though it was deposited last week—it looks a bit like an asphalt parking lot that was roiled by a bulldozer in the past day or two—though the major eruption of the volcano took place more than nine centuries ago. By counting the rings of the preserved remains of trees growing when the volcano erupted—and killed by the lava flow—we know that the last major eruption occurred in AD 1064.

After viewing the lava fields and black-topped volcanic cone, continue on to nearby Wupatki National Monument. There you can visit the great house, a multistoried structure that served as home to more than one hundred people (see the cover of this book). We know that construction began in AD 1106 by tree-ring dating the oldest roof beam incorporated into the dwelling. At Wupatki proper you can see the remains of a ball court, a field demarcated by a short oval wall (Figure 64). The game played on courts such as this may have been borrowed from civilizations to the south, in Mesoamerica.

From Wupatki you can drive on paved roads to a number of smaller but dramatically situated pueblos, built like fortresses atop natural red-rock platforms, including Wukoki, Citadel, Lomoki, Nalakihu, and Box Canyon (Figure 65). It's definitely worth the drive; Wukoki (I.14) looks for all the world like a fort positioned to protect the primary village site of Wupatki. Most of the hikes to these smaller individual dwellings are short and easy, but the Citadel Trail does involve a steep ascent.

Why Is Wupatki Important?

At Wupatki you have the material evidence of the response of as many as 3,000 people spread out across an area of 56 square miles to a natural disaster. As noted, the eruption of the volcano that was to become Sunset Crater was, at least initially, devastating. Over the course of decades, the cinder, ash, and lava that spewed from the mountain destroyed all in its wake. But once the mountain quieted down, nature began the process of healing and human beings began the process of adapting to the new conditions,

Figure 65. Box Canyon ruins just a few miles from the great house at Wupatki.

which included a richer agricultural soil more capable of retaining moisture in the arid climate of northern Arizona. Sunset Crater National Monument provides the visitor with a snapshot in time—a volcanic eruption, dated precisely to AD 1064; the resilience of nature, even in the face of a devastating natural disaster; and a subsequent land rush by a farming people to claim the rich volcanic soil that resulted. The great house of Wupatki, as well as the myriad smaller dwellings located throughout the region, is a reflection of the resilience of human beings when faced with a natural catastrophe, and the very human ability to find opportunities in the challenges posed by nature. Sunset Crater and Wupatki National Monuments exhibit the genius of our species.

Site Type: Great House
Wow Factor: ✳✳✳✳ The overall look and feel of Wupatki along with the surrounding smaller sites is pretty awesome.
Museum: ✳✳✳✳
Ease of Road Access: ✳✳✳✳✳
Ease of Hike: ✳✳✳✳✳
Natural Beauty of Surroundings: ✳✳✳✳✳
Kid Friendly: ✳✳✳✳
Food: Bring your own.
How to Get There: From Flagstaff, take US 89 north for 12 miles and turn right at the sign for Sunset Crater Volcano-Wupatki National Monuments. The visitor center is 21 miles from this junction.
Hours of Operation: Open daily 9 a.m. to 5 p.m. Closed on Christmas.
Cost: See website. Fee covers entry to both Wupatki and Sunset Crater National Monuments.
Best Season to Visit: Spring and fall. Summer can be hot, but the hikes are short and easy, so it's doable.
Website: www.nps.gov/wupa/index.htm
Designation: National Monument

Site 28 Betatakin

Navajo National Monument • Shonto, Arizona

Journal Entry

August 15, 2015

From a distance, through a camera lens, Betatakin looks for all the world like a perfect miniature village replete with tiny trees and little replica wooden ladders. Even today, when I show my students some of my telephoto images of the site, I feel compelled to assure them that it's not a dollhouse or shadowbox. Betatakin is a spectacular, well-preserved, large-scale village dwarfed by the massively high stone alcove in which it was built, an enormously arching natural cave that formed in the sandstone cliff face millions of years before people chose it for their home. Breathtaking seems hardly a strong enough word to describe this amazing place. The Navajo National Monument is administered by the National Park Service but is located on the reservation of the Navajo Tribe. As is the generous policy of the tribe—they view the ruins as sacred—there is no charge for visiting the ancient sites located here.

What You Will See

You begin your odyssey back to the time of Betatakin at the visitor center and museum. From the center, a reasonably easy hike on the paved Sandal Trail along the canyon rim takes you in 0.62 mile to a splendid overlook of Betatakin (I.15). The photographs I've included here were all taken from that overlook with an assortment of zoom lens (Figures 66 and 67, the latter taken with a honking huge

Figure 66. Even a small telephoto lens brings Betatakin into closer view.

Figure 67. A 600mm telephoto lens or binoculars makes it seem as though you could walk into Betatakin. In this view, the village looks like a magnified image of a shadowbox or dollhouse. But it's entirely real and full-size.

600mm lens; you won't get that image with your cell phone). Once you're done at the overlook, turn around and hike back to the visitor center. Other trails, including Aspen (0.41 mile each way) and Canyon View (0.32 mile each way), provide other vantages of the canyon.

The more adventurous, and those who aren't satisfied with the distant view afforded by the Sandal Trail, can register for a guided hike that takes you down into the canyon and right to the ruins. Expect a 3- to 5-hour, 5-mile round-trip with some fairly strenuous walking—700 feet down into the canyon and then, saving the best for last, a 700-foot climb back up at the end of the tour. It's certainly worth the trip but is not recommended for people with heart, respiratory, hip, or knee problems or other health issues.

Why Is Betatakin Important?

Many of the sites included in this book are picturesque; in fact, a beautiful or awe-inspiring appearance was one of the informal criteria I used in selecting these fifty sites. But Betatakin is remarkable even within those fifty spectacular sites. Even from—maybe especially from—the overlook, the village and its setting are truly breathtaking, a spectacular achievement of architecture as art in the late thirteenth century, when the primary construction took place.

Betatakin is important as an example of how a people carved a life out of what might seem to many of us the harsh surroundings of the canyonlands of the American Southwest. The residents of Betatakin and hundreds of other, generally smaller sites were agricultural, planting corn, beans, and squash in the rich soil that bordered the stream at the base of the canyon. Their potters produced lovely ceramics, painted with a distinctive series of black-and-white geometric designs. The residents of Betatakin worshipped in their kiva, the same kind of structure used by their Hopi descendants to this day for religious ceremonies. They painted their clan symbol on the sheer cliff face about their village. And then, at around AD 1300, the residents of Betatakin left, perhaps as the result of a long-term drought that affected the region at the end of the thirteenth century. The community was occupied only briefly, perhaps no more than fifty years, but during that short period they produced a splendid place that today we can view and marvel at.

Additional Note

While you get spectacular views of the cliff dwelling from the paved canyon rim trail, during summer there are two moderately strenuous guided hikes each day down to the ruins: one at 8:15 a.m. and one at 10 a.m. During winter there's one hike each day, leaving the visitor center at 10 a.m., when weather and staffing permit. Because the tours are limited and weather can cause their cancellation, always call ahead (928-672-2700) to reserve a spot and confirm the schedule.

Site Type: Cliff Dwelling

Wow Factor: ***** The Betatakin cliff dwelling is mind-blowing. To get a deep appreciation of its beauty from the trail, you'll need binoculars; to take a great photo, you'll need a big telephoto lens. Sorry; that camera on your smartphone just won't cut it. Or you'll need to sign up for the hike down into the canyon.

Museum: ****

Ease of Road Access: *****

Ease of Hike: *** The rim trail hike to the overlook where you can get a great view of the cliff dwelling is pretty easy; it's paved, making it reasonably accessible by wheelchair.

Natural Beauty of Surroundings: **** Gorgeous views from along the rim trail

Kid Friendly: ***

Food: Bring your own.

How to Get There: Betatakin is located in the Navajo National Monument. Take US 160 to AZ 564. Plug this address into your GPS for specific directions: Navajo National Monument, Shonto, Arizona.

Hours of Operation: Open daily 8 a.m. to 6 p.m. late May through mid-September; 9 a.m. to 5 p.m. mid-September through late May

Cost: Free

Best Season to Visit: Summer is hot but dry. The hike along the rim is pretty easy, so heat shouldn't be a problem if you're in good health.

Website: www.nps.gov/nava/index.htm

Designation: National Monument

Site 29 **Mesa Verde National Park**

Cortez, Colorado

Journal Entry

August 5, 2009
Okay, this may sound weird, but I've come to think of these fifty sites kind of like children. I love each of the sites equally; each one is unique and special and worthy of our attention, study, and visitation. But I'll admit something I would never admit about my kids; ultimately, I do have a favorite. If I had to recommend just one site—just one of these amazing places—that you should visit, I'd suggest Mesa Verde. Mesa Verde simply is an enormously special place. Awesome is an insufficient word to describe it.

What You Will See

Constructed and inhabited primarily between AD 1190 and AD 1300, the Mesa Verde cliff dwellings are situated in naturally carved alcoves overlooking a deep canyon. Most cannot be visited. You can only enjoy them from a distance by stopping along roads in the park (all paved) that hug the edge of the mesa, pulling into parking areas, and looking across the canyon. Mesa Verde is one of the places in our odyssey that, in theory anyway, you can experience by "windshield survey," where you spend most of your time in the car, stopping at overlooks and exiting the car for a better view and some photographs. But please don't do just that unless you are physically incapable of hiking, because there are five major cliff structures that, with a little hiking and in some cases just a little bit of climbing on ladders, you can actually walk into.

You'll need to begin your visit with a stop at the Visitor and Research Center, where you'll pay your entrance fee. You'll also want to purchase tickets there for scheduled ranger-guided hikes to Cliff Palace, Balcony House, and Long House (more about that later). You can't visit those sites without a ticket. Once you're done at the visitor center, continue driving on Ruins Road. There are a number of overlooks along the way with beautiful views, but no ruins are visible.

When you get to the Far View area, your best bet is to continue south on Chapin Mesa, one of two locations where you'll be able to see lots of amazing cliff dwellings (the other being Wetherill Mesa). The first site you'll encounter is called Cedar Tree Tower. It's down a short side road on your left (east) and a brief hike to the masonry tower. Get back on the road south (turn left from the Cedar Tree Tower access road), and in short order you'll come to Spruce Tree House, the first and probably best preserved of the cliff dwellings. The road you're on comes to a four-way intersection. Follow the signs to the right for Spruce Tree House. Once parked you can visit the Chapin Mesa Archaeological Museum, where you'll see displays of some of the beautiful artifacts excavated in the area. Next it's an easy, short hike to the cliff dwelling. There are a bunch of switchbacks, and the hike back to the parking area is uphill just about all the way, but it's not so bad. Spruce Tree House is a large dwelling site, worth the walk (it's a self-touring site and the National Park Service doesn't restrict access). You can actually climb down into one of the roofed kivas. It's a good idea to get this up-close encounter with an easily accessible cliff dwelling first, before seeing a bunch of them from afar.

Note: As I write this in July 2016, Spruce Tree House is closed to the public for safety reasons. Hopefully it will be reopened by the time you read this book. Even if you can't walk into the very impressive cliff dwelling, you can still see it from the nearby trail. Check the Mesa Verde website for updates.

There is a 2.4-mile-long trail from the Spruce Tree House complex to Petroglyph Point, home to the densest concentration of rock art at Mesa Verde. It's not a spectacular art panel, but it's a nice, only moderately strenuous hike, so go for it if you're interested.

After you're finished here, get back in your vehicle and continue south (make a right from Spruce Tree House) onto the Mesa Top Loop, a one-way road from which you'll be able to see many of the most impressive cliff dwellings in the park. (There actually are more than 600 cliff dwellings at Mesa Verde, but you won't see more than a small fraction of them.) All the cliff dwellings visible from each turnoff are signposted with photographs or illustrations that will allow you to identify each one. In no particular order, you'll be able to see the following cliff dwellings on the side opposite your point along the loop:

1.   House of Many Windows
2.   Site 634
3.   Sunpoint Dwelling
4.   Sun Temple (a freestanding structure on the mesa top)
5.   Oak Tree House
6.   Hemenway House
7.   Sunset House
8.   Mummy House
9.   New Fire House
10. Fire Temple

Not visible from the loop road itself is one of the most elegantly beautiful of the Mesa Verde cliff dwellings: Square Tower House. After the parking area marked "Navajo Canyon View," on the right you'll see the car park and trail to Square Tower House (I.16). Do not, under any circumstances, miss the opportunity to see this. The trail to the overlook is easy and short. The last time I was there, I actually saw a couple of young teenagers on the trail (no, not my kids) thoroughly engrossed in their handheld video games. The second they got to the overlook and gazed down at Square Tower House, the gaming came to an abrupt halt and they clearly were impressed by the view. The structure got its name from a four-story tower built into the back of the alcove in which it is situated. It's breathtaking. Though ordinarily you cannot access Square Tower House, there have been a few ranger-guided hikes to it. I have never had the opportunity to hike to the site, but if you are there when one is offered, I highly recommend it. Be forewarned; I have read that the hike is somewhat strenuous.

Once you are done with your telephoto encounters with distant cliff dwellings, get ready to see a couple of them up close and personal. Hopefully you've remembered to purchase tickets for the scheduled tours of the cliff dwellings known as Cliff Palace and Balcony House.

Once you've completed the loop, the road brings you back to the main drag, this time heading north. Before you reach the turnoff for Spruce Tree House, you'll turn onto the road marked "Cliff Palace Loop" on your right.

From the overlook where your guided tour group will gather, Cliff Palace looks surreal, almost like a fairy castle (Figure 68). Across a distance of about the length of a football field, in a natural alcove at the base of the cliff, you can see the remnants of a profusion of square rooms, round kivas, and elegant towers, some round, some square. The entirety of it is just mind-blowing.

Now, I can't lie; access can be moderately challenging: You have to climb down to the bottom of the canyon, and there are ladders to deal with, height, and, in summer, heat. And of course you're going to have to climb back up. But it is an astonishing place, and everyone should get over whatever fear they might have and walk among the ruins (I.17). Trust me; it's not that scary.

Figure 68. Secreted in a cave at the base of a cliff, looking for all the world like a splendid palace, sits the dwelling called (what else?) Cliff Palace.

Once you've accomplished that trek, get back to your car and continue on the Cliff Palace Loop to your next stop: Balcony House. Make no mistake; Balcony House is a lot scarier for anyone with a fear of heights (Figure 69). If the Cliff Palace hike freaked you out, you're going to have a problem with Balcony House. Get over it, because it is amazing. I admit to having a bit of trepidation about the exposed heights my first time. I came to the 30-foot wooden ladder modeled on the actual ladders used by the ancient inhabitants and wasn't sure I could do it. The fact that a five-year-old kid comfortably climbed up right in front of me was tremendous inducement to me to gut it out. Ultimately, it really wasn't that bad.

The structure gets its name from the cedar balcony between the first and second stories of the main structure that has survived all this time. The view from the site is just splendid; and despite all the trouble it must have presented in building and merely traveling to and from wherever you had to go, I think the view made it worth the effort.

If you possibly can, plan for at least part of a second day at Mesa Verde in order to visit the second cluster of cliff dwellings. These are located on Wetherill Mesa, which is adjacent to Chapin Mesa (Figure 70). A 40-minute car ride from the Far View area along Wetherill Mesa Road, a steep and meandering mountain road, brings you to a ranger station and parking lot. You have to leave your vehicle there; you can't drive your own car. From there a tram takes you to Long House, the second-largest (to Cliff Palace)

Figure 69. You'll need to climb a ladder to get to Balcony House with a park ranger. Scary? Maybe a bit. Worth it? You bet.

Figure 70. If you have a couple of days at Mesa Verde, check out the less-crowded ruins on Wetherill Mesa. This is a photograph of the largest ruin there: Long House.

cliff dwelling at Mesa Verde. Like Cliff Palace and Balcony House, the trek to Long House is a ranger-guided tour for which you'll need to sign up and pay a nominal fee. The hike to Long House isn't too bad.

You can visit Step House on your own. There is a ranger on duty down at the dwelling, where there also is a partially reconstructed kiva. The hike down to Step House has lots of, well, steps and also switchbacks. The hike back up is a little steep, but most of the path is paved, so it's not too challenging and certainly worth the trip.

Along the tram route there are overlooks of a few very impressive cliff dwellings, including Kodak House, Long House (the one you can visit, but the overlook provides a stunning panoramic view of the site), and the Nordenskiold Ruin. The hikes to the overlooks of Kodak and Long House are very short, and the tram that takes you to the trailhead waits several minutes for pictures. You can always pick up another tram if you want to spend more time hiking and photographing. They run regularly, but you have to wait for a tram; you cannot hike on the tram road. The hike to Nordenskiold Ruin is longer but not arduous; it's a round-trip of about 1.5 miles from the Wetherill Mesa ranger station and a little bit less than that from the tram stop.

If you have only a single day at Mesa Verde, I highly recommend spending your time at Chapin Mesa visiting Cliff Palace and Spruce Tree House. I also advise you to suck it up, get past any fear you might have of heights, and visit Balcony House. You definitely should drive the Mesa Loop road and stop at EVERY overlook to see each of the very impressive ruins visible across the canyon. With a second day, don't miss Wetherill Mesa. One ranger I spoke to estimated that only about 15 percent of Mesa Verde visitors make it to Wetherill Mesa, so you don't experience the crowds you do back on Chapin, and the sites are pretty impressive here as well. There is a snack shop at the ranger station (nothing major: cold beverages, trail mix, chips, that sort of thing).

Mesa Verde is a world-class destination on our archaeological odyssey, with amazing things to do and see for everybody.

Why Is Mesa Verde Important?

In the course of writing this book, as an archaeologist I have had occasional pangs of guilt about telling you that a site is important simply because it is so cool. But I'm over it. Mesa Verde is important to see because it is an amazing thing to see; actually, it is many amazing things to see. The builders of the cliff dwellings were accomplished architects and engineers. Using the material at hand, without the advantage of mechanized help during construction, and without the power afforded by beasts of burden, they created a self-contained world in a canyon cutting through a green mesa in southern Colorado. They produced their own food and made their own tools, weapons, containers, clothing, etc. They lived there in apparent harmony for centuries. And then they left.

You simply can't come away from Mesa Verde without enormous respect for the genius of the people who planned, designed, and constructed the cliff dwellings and for the work, effort, and artistry required to complete the task. These folks were intelligent, hardworking, creative, and dedicated. It is a privilege, so many years after they left the mesa and canyon, to be able to experience the remnants of that intelligence, work, and creativity

Why did they go to the trouble? It really isn't clear. Native peoples, the ancestors of those who built the cliff dwellings, lived on top of the mesa beginning as far back as AD 600, but they didn't start living in the cliff face alcoves until nearly 600 years later. In placing their homes in those alcoves, were they attempting to simply save farmland on top of the mesa? That seems unlikely. All that trouble, in both the construction and the inconvenience posed by the location of their homes for everyday tasks—not to mention the challenges of keeping your kids from falling off the cliffs—suggests a more serious rationale. Perhaps it was for defense. After all, as we saw at **Site 23, Montezuma Castle,** secreting your house in an inaccessible cliff would seem a pretty good strategy for protecting yourself from nasty neighbors. Whatever the cause, the result is an amazing thing to see during our trek through time.

What happened at the end of the thirteenth century to cause the residents of Mesa Verde to abandon their cozy cliff homes? That's another puzzler, but it likely had something to do with a prolonged drought that befell the region between about AD 1250 and AD 1300. Tree rings show that beginning in the late thirteen century, rainfall decreased precipitously and stayed low for a very long time—a couple of dozen years, in fact. For a farming people in an already dry region, that drop in precipitation must have had a devastating effect on their subsistence base. Perhaps they held out as long as they could, leaving when the prospect of starvation became too real. Even if the drought wasn't catastrophic—and there is evidence that the people of the Four Corners region had lived through other droughts—perhaps it was the coup de grâce, the final straw, that, combined with myriad other factors, including population increase, warfare, or even the pull of a new religion from the south, convinced most people to abandon the cliffs.

Whatever the ultimate cause of their departure, oral traditions of the Hopi people who now live in the pueblos of northern New Mexico to the south of Mesa Verde tell of a historical mass movement from the north. Archaeology of northern New Mexico supports the notion that the Mesa Verdeans moved there, searching for permanent watercourses that, even during times of drought, had sufficient water to fill irrigation canals to feed their fields.

Additional Note

Beyond the entrance fee, there are additional but nominal fees for the complete Mesa Verde experience. In order to keep crowds to manageable proportions, the National Park Service controls the number of people who can visit three of the most impressive and therefore most popular cliff dwellings at any one time. They accomplish this by limiting access; you cannot visit Cliff Palace, Balcony House, or Long House by yourself. You have to sign up in advance for a ranger-guided tour. You do that in person in the park at the Mesa Verde Visitor and Ranger Station, the Morefield Ranger Station, or the Chapin Mesa Archaeological Museum. You can also purchase tour tickets outside the park at the Colorado Welcome Center in Cortez, Colorado. I'm sure the sale of tickets generates very little income for the park, but it serves the valuable purpose of controlling the crowds at these three cliff dwellings.

There also are a number of fee-based ranger-led backcountry hikes to sites not ordinarily seen by visitors. There also is an amazing twilight tour to Cliff Palace; when I took that tour, the ranger played the role of one of the Wetherill brothers, the first white people to see the cliff dwellings. He even dressed the part! For a complete listing of all these tours, check this link on the Mesa Verde website: www.nps.gov/meve/planyourvisit/tour_tickets.htm.

Finally, have a careful look at the National Park Service map of Mesa Verde for detailed directions to each of the overlooks and hikes (www.nps.gov/meve/planyourvisit/maps.htm).

Site Type: Cliff Dwelling (like, for serious!)

Wow Factor: ***** The cliff dwellings themselves along with their setting render this place a 6 on a 5-star scale of wowness.

Museum: *****

Ease of Road Access: *****

Ease of Hike: Varies. The hike down to Cliff Palace is moderate. The hike up to Balcony House is a little scary, but not too strenuous. The hike to Petroglyph Point is moderately strenuous.

Natural Beauty of Surroundings: ***** The scenery at Mesa Verde is stunning.

Kid Friendly: *****

Food: Food is available at the Metate Room at Far View Lodge (nice sit-down place) and the more casual (and less-expensive) Spruce Tree Terrace Cafe and Far View Terrace Restaurant.

How to Get There: From the west (Cortez, Colorado), head east on US 160 for 10.3 miles (15 minutes) to the well-signed Ruins Road, on your right. From the east (Durango, Colorado), head west on US 160 for 35.5 miles (46 minutes) until you reach Ruins Road, on your left. Turn onto Ruins Road and follow it uphill to the top of the mesa. You'll drive on this road to the park headquarters for about 45 minutes. The ride from Cortez to park headquarters is about 1 hour. From Durango, it's about 1.5 hours.

Hours of Operation: Mesa Verde is open daily year-round. The visitor center hours vary seasonally; check the website. The cliff dwellings are open during visitor center hours.

Cost: See website.

Best Season to Visit: Mesa Verde is fantastic virtually year-round, but it can snow here in winter. Hikes down (or up) into the cliff dwellings also vary seasonally (www.nps.gov/meve/planyourvisit/upload/interp_program_sch_2015_v8.pdf).

The on-site hotel, Fairview Lodge, is open mid-April through mid-October. You'll be able to see the cliff dwellings at other times; you just won't be able to stay at the hotel. The campground is open early May through early October.

Website: www.nps.gov/meve/index.htm

Designation: National Park; World Heritage Site

Site 30 Aztec National Monument

Aztec, New Mexico

Journal Entry

August 7, 2009

As was the case with Montezuma Castle, the name "Aztec National Monument" is a misnomer. Aztec is a terrific example of an Ancestral Puebloan great house and has nothing to do with the Aztec civilization encountered by the Spanish invaders of Mexico in the early sixteenth century. Just as was the case with Montezuma Castle, Europeans were so impressed by the architecture of the ruins that they assumed it must have been the work of the great indigenous Mexican civilization and not the work of local Indians. That assumption could not have been more wrong, but the name has stuck.

On my 2009 visit to Aztec, an Indian woman and her daughter were selling very cool pieces of art that they were making in the shade of a veranda at the site. The art was the equivalent of portable petroglyphs, incised carvings of various designs of both animal and geometric figures on pebbles.

Figure 71. View of the Great House at Aztec National Monument in northern New Mexico.

What You Will See

A very easy 700-yard trail takes you around and into the Aztec Great House (Figure 71). You'll be able to see the beautiful masonry—all accomplished without the benefit of metal tools—produced by the village's ancient inhabitants. Note the use of a darker, green-hued stone in a thick band across exterior walls. This is purely for decoration and reflects the masons' aesthetic sense by adding a contrasting color to their work. You will also be able to walk into and through parts of the structure and get a brief feel for what it must have been like to call Aztec home.

Excavated by archaeologists in the 1950s, most of the artifacts recovered at the site actually are housed at the American Museum of Natural History in New York City. Fortunately, some of the most impressive of the items recovered there are on display at the on-site visitor center and museum.

The unique feature you'll see at Aztec is the kiva (Figure 72). The presence of a kiva isn't itself unique. As indicated in the Ancient America chapter, a kiva is the equivalent of a church, a sacred building in which important ceremonies related to Ancestral Puebloan spirituality were conducted. The great house villages ordinarily have multiple kivas, likely belonging to individual extended-family residents. You'll see lots and lots of kivas during your archaeological odyssey through the American Southwest. Casa Rinconada at **Site 31, Chaco Canyon** is the largest and by most measures the most elaborate.

With the exception of the Great Kiva at Aztec, all the other kivas you'll be seeing—aside from recent, subtle efforts at stabilization—have been left as they were found when the sites in which they are located were designated as national parks, national monuments, or national historic monuments.

Figure 72. The exterior of the reconstructed great kiva—a place of worship and ceremony—at Aztec.

Figure 73. The interior of the reconstructed great kiva at Aztec.

And largely, that's a good thing. Though there are occasional murmurs about "fixing" ancient ruins (Stonehenge, for example), I think that it is usually best to leave the sites as they are. I agree with author Ray Bradbury who, when describing a fictional ancient city on Mars in his book *The Martian Chronicles*, describes it as "Perfect, faultless, in ruins, yes, but perfect nonetheless."

Okay, but in the case of the Great Kiva at Aztec, I'm going to give the park service a pass on this. Admittedly, it is a little disconcerting and out of place, a perfect masonry building in the midst of an ancient ruin. Instead of leaving it as is, they have completely reconstructed the Great Kiva, the primary house of worship of the residents of Aztec. But they've done a wonderful job. I think it's interesting and informative to be able, as an archaeological tourist, to enter this "church" and see it as the ancient residents of Aztec did in order to gain an appreciation for the spiritual life of the people who lived here nearly 900 years ago (Figure 73).

Why Is Aztec Important?

One of the largest of all the ancient pueblo structures in the Southwest, Aztec is a splendid example of an Ancestral Puebloan great house. There are close to 500 rooms here, including living and storage spaces. Parts of the pueblo were three stories high, and the exterior wall surrounding the great house was as much as 30 feet tall. Aztec was not a primitive or ad hoc project. The entire building complex appears to have been planned out by architects and designers, much in the manner of our modern construction projects. Even from a modern sensibility, Aztec appears to have been a beautiful, impressive, and monumental building.

Through the application of dendrochronology—tree-ring dating—we know that most of the structure was built during the four-year-period AD 1111 to AD 1115. The village was occupied by several hundred people for about 160 years and was abandoned by about AD 1275.

Site Type: Great House

Wow Factor: **** Aztec is a well-preserved ruin. The masonry is beautiful, you can walk through some of the structure, and the reconstructed kiva is very impressive.

Museum: ****

Ease of Road Access: *****

Ease of Hike: *****

Natural Beauty of Surroundings: **

Kid Friendly: ****

Food: Bring your own.

How to Get There: Aztec is located on Ruins Road, 14 miles east of Farmington, New Mexico. Take NM 516 east from Farmington to the city of Aztec. Turn left onto Ruins Road, which is located at the third stoplight in Aztec, before you cross the river.

Hours of Operation: Open daily, 8 a.m. to 6 p.m. Memorial Day through Labor Day; 8 a.m. to 5 p.m. Labor Day through Memorial Day

Cost: See website.

Best Season to Visit: Spring and fall, but summer and winter are okay as well.

Website: www.nps.gov/azru/index.htm

Designation: National Park

Site 31 Chaco Canyon

Chaco Culture National Historical Park • Nageezi, New Mexico

Journal Entry

March 9, 2015

There are two primary rationales for writing this book. The first is to inform you, the reader, of the amazing and spectacular archaeological legacy left behind by the first inhabitants of what was to become the United States. Fair enough. The second, rather obviously in a book that advertises itself as a "time travel guide," is to encourage you to conduct your own treks through American antiquity, to get off your collective butts and see for yourselves the still-visible shadows of that past. With that in mind, it might seem contradictory that I also sometimes feel just a trace of ambivalence about encouraging you to visit some of those places, especially those that are geographically isolated. That ambivalence is manifested in a long-standing controversy about the attendance figures at Chaco Canyon National Historical Park and whether the federal government should attempt to make access to the site easier. Chaco is an amazing place, and I truly want you to go there. But part of what makes it such a wonderfully evocative place is how alone you can feel there while encountering the past.

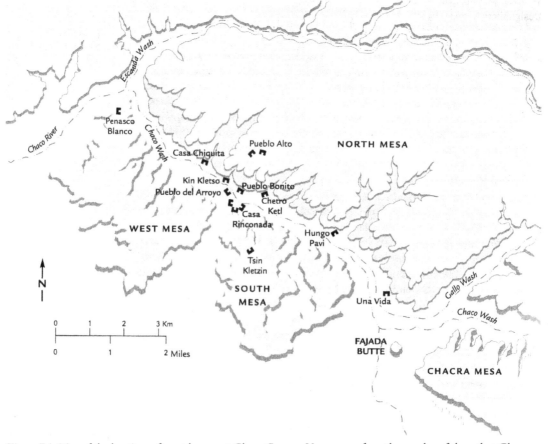

Figure 74. Map of the locations of great houses at Chaco Canyon. You can see from the number of them that Chaco was an important hub of culture in the ancient Southwest.

Chaco is remarkable. The ancient Chacoans constructed a series of more than a dozen truly monumental great houses—large, free-standing, many-roomed, multistoried structures—situating them in the unexpected, stark landscape of a desolate canyon in northwestern New Mexico (Figure 74). It's a federal facility with a wonderful on-site visitor center and a bunch of well-maintained hiking trails. However, considering how incredibly mind-blowing the archaeological remains in the canyon are, attendance figures for this site are pretty low. In 2015 there were just a shade under 39,000 visitors for the entire year. Compare that to another of my fifty sites, **Site 29, Mesa Verde National Park,** where the 2015 attendance was close to 550,000, about fourteen times the figure for Chaco.

I have been to both places multiple times; they are both amazing, but my experiences at the sites have been entirely different. When you go to **Mesa Verde,** and I strongly encourage you to do so, you likely will encounter large crowds of visitors. If every one of them bought a copy of this book, then I'm okay with the crowds. Kidding! Wherever you go, there are tons of people. My best analogy might be this: I love Walt Disney World, but my experience there is always tempered by long lines and the enormous crowds (okay, and the price of a bottle of water). Chaco is different. It has never been crowded there during any of my visits. There isn't a lot of traffic on the park road; and during hikes to and through the great houses, you might not even run into another person or family. Perhaps it sounds silly, but walking around at Chaco, it can almost feel as though you are discovering for the first time the remarkable architectural achievements of the inhabitants.

At least in part, Chaco's relatively low attendance figures result from the fact that a long stretch (about 13 miles) of the primary access road is unpaved, can be a little rough, and is impassable after it rains. Further, there are few facilities at park headquarters. There is a primitive campground, but unlike Mesa Verde, there is no motel on-site. Unless you plan on camping there, you need to plan on leaving the park the same day you arrive. That can make for a very long day indeed. The park service further recommends that you not drive a recreational vehicle on the unpaved access roads. I have this bizarre image of driving the road into Chaco and passing the rusted-out hulks of broken-down RVs with still clothed human skeletons in the drivers' seats. Gross, I know.

There has been a long-running discussion about paving the entire primary access road, which would certainly make travel to Chaco substantially less problematic. With paving, food and motel chains would be more likely to build facilities near the beginning of the access road to serve the likely surge in visitors. And therein lies my ambivalence. I certainly want to encourage you to visit Chaco. However, too much success in that will change the experience for those willing to go to the trouble to visit it as it is now. In a small way, right now you have to "earn" Chaco with a longish drive on an unpaved road. Maybe that's a good thing. But if it prevents more people from experiencing Chaco, maybe it's not.

What You Will See

Built between AD 850 and AD 1150, the great houses of Chaco are astonishing bits of architecture and art. They are massive; must have required a tremendous amount of cooperative, communal labor; and reflect a great sophistication of engineering and construction. After reaching the visitor center, paying your entrance fee, and looking at the exhibits, you can drive the 9-mile paved park road loop, which takes you to five of the primary great houses at Chaco: Una Vida (there's also a cool petroglyph panel on the cliff above the building), Hungo Pavi, Chetro Ketl, Pueblo Bonito, and Pueblo del Arroyo. A 2-mile round-trip hike from the Pueblo Arroyo parking area brings you to two more impressive structures: Kin Kletso and Casa Chiquita. The masonry incorporated into each of the great houses is quite beautiful, consisting of quarried and "dressed" stones; interestingly, each house's stonework is unique. The individual stones used in the construction of some of the houses are flat

Figure 75. Casa Rinconada, the largest kiva at Chaco Canyon. Though many of the Chacoan great houses incorporate small and medium-size kivas, Casa Rinconada is a separate, free-standing structure. It's located just a short distance from the largest of the Chacoan great houses, Pueblo Bonito.

slabs; in others the stones have been shaped into bricks; and some houses change up the individual courses or layers of stones, producing interesting linear patterns. Along with the many interconnected clusters of rectangular rooms, each great house also has several of the round ceremonial structures called kivas. These circular rooms have a bench along the base of the interior wall, niches positioned along those walls, sockets for large wooden beams or posts that held up the roof, masonry vaults, and a stone-lined hearth on the floor. Check out the reconstructed kiva at **Site 30, Aztec National Monument** for a peek at what the many Chaco Canyon kivas looked like. Case Rinconada (Figure 75), accessible along a short trail from Pueblo Bonito, is an enormous free-standing kiva with an additional cool feature—an underground passageway that leads from outside to the floor of the kiva. One can imagine priests dressed as spirit beings entering the kiva from that tunnel, as if arriving from the underworld. Amazing. Though the roofs and ceilings are gone, the walls of some of the great houses are in good condition; you can walk through them, affording an up-close and personal view of the living spaces of the Chacoans. It's all very, very cool.

Though you can conduct essentially a car tour of five of the major buildings, parking and taking very short hikes up to them, I also highly recommend getting out of your car and doing a little more

Figure 76. The Chacoan great house called Kin Kletso, viewed from the trail to the top of the mesa on your way to the Pueblo Bonito overlook.

serious hiking. My favorite trail, and the one I most highly recommend, takes you to the top of the mesa and the Pueblo Bonito overlook (Figure 76). Pueblo Bonito alone is worth the price of admission to Chaco; the largest of the great houses, it contains more than 800 rooms in a single, three-story structure (I.18). You can walk through the building following the park service trail, but the best way to see Pueblo Bonito is from above (I.19). The mesa trail lets you see it that way. I admit that it is a bit strenuous, but not overly so—the elevation difference from the bottom of the trail to the top is only about 240 feet. Making your way to the top is a tiny bit scary, but only briefly at the beginning. As you hike up the trail, in a very short distance from the trailhead you will reach a rock crack through which you will walk to the top. It's not so narrow that you'll be afflicted by claustrophobia; and if you have a fear of heights, you'll feel much safer as soon as you reach the crack. You do have to scramble over some boulders along the way, and there is some minor hand-over-hand climbing involved. Once you reach the mesa top, you'll pass out of the crack and then walk a bit to the overlook. The mesa is wide; if you are afraid of heights, just don't walk close to the edge and you should be fine. In 0.7 mile the trail splits; the trail to the left brings you to a mesa top great house, the Pueblo Alto Complex. If you hike up to Pueblo Alto, the trail loops around back; in 2.5 miles you'll be at the other end of

Figure 77. The Supernova Pictograph at Chaco. The moon was in its crescent phase when the star exploded (perhaps depicted here as a star-shaped pictograph) in the night sky over Chaco in AD 1054.

the trail you began on. If instead of taking the trail to the left you continue straight along the rim of the mesa, you'll arrive shortly at the Pueblo Bonito overlook. The view is awesome and provides a particularly useful perspective of the 800-room dwelling. The only word I can use to adequately describe the view: Wow.

Petroglyph Trail is a very short and easy hike (0.3 mile one-way) along the cliff face behind and between two of the great houses, Chetro Ketl and Pueblo Bonito. There's a parking lot about midway between these two great houses from which you can access both structures and check out the Petroglyph Trail as you walk between them. There are some cool petroglyphs there; my favorite is the image of a mountain lion.

Another area with even more interesting rock art can be found farther to the northwest on a hike past the great house Casa Chiquita. The entry to that trail (signed "Petroglyph Trail" though it's not the Petroglyph Trail mentioned above between Chetro Ketl and Pueblo Bonito) is about 1.25 mile from the Pueblo del Arroyo parking lot. The rock art is spread out across a distance of about 0.3 mile. That petroglyph trail brings you back to the main trail you were on originally (the Peñasco Blanco Trail). From there you can turn left and hike back to the Pueblo del Arroyo parking lot (a bit more than 1.5 miles, making that entire trek a 3-mile hike). If you continue past the end of this petroglyph trail and turn right, in about 1.5 miles you'll come to a side trail to the left that brings you to another mesa-top great house, Peñasco Blanco, and another trail to the right that brings you to the very impressive supernova pictograph. From the Pueblo del Arroyo parking lot, past Casa Chiquita, through the petroglyph side trail, to the supernova pictograph, and then back to the parking lot is about 6.5 miles. It's long but flat, and well worth it. (Check out the map on the Chaco Canyon National Park Service website for more information about these and other trails at the site: www.nps.gov/chcu/planyourvisit/upload/CHCU_park2006%20UPDATE.pdf.)

Why Is Chaco Canyon Important?

Chaco is unique. Nowhere else did the native peoples of the American Southwest build such a dense concentration of large structures, and we're not sure why they did so. You'd think, *Okay, it's something like a part of a modern city where there's a dense concentration of apartment houses,* but that explanation doesn't hold up. Interestingly, there's not an abundance of household debris in the canyon. The archaeological evidence, or lack of it, actually seems to indicate that the population of the canyon was substantially lower than might be expected based on the number of apartments available in the dozen or so great houses located there. So what was the function of those great houses, if not for habitation? It may be that all the labor that went into constructing all those rooms in all those great houses was intended for ceremonial reasons. The building themselves are aligned to points on the horizon of astronomical significance, important points marking the rising and setting of the sun and the moon during the year. It's almost as though the Chaco great houses are part of a giant celestial calendar. Other evidence related to a calendar is located midway up Fajada Butte, southeast of the biggest concentration of structures. There the inhabitants etched a spiral petroglyph onto the rock face right behind a crack in a rock. The sun streams through that crack, forming what researchers have called a "sun dagger" that crosses directly through the spiral on the day of the summer solstice.

The great houses are an example of "public architecture" and may have been intended to mark the canyon as the spiritual and economic center of the Chacoan cultural universe, a place of pilgrimage where residents, not of Chaco but of more than a hundred inhabited great houses located many miles away from the canyon, came together to spend some time, trade, have festivals, and worship. Chaco does seem to have been the center of that universe for a period of time. Analysis of aerial photographs of the region reveals the presence of an elaborate and sophisticated system of roads leading to and from Chaco.

One more thing. If you take the trail from Pueblo del Arroyo past Kin Kletso and then past Casa Chiquita, out beyond the Petroglyph Trail you'll see an interesting pictograph panel with what appears to be a crescent moon and a starlike object nearby. Based on the appearance of the pictograph and the timing of the construction of the Chaco great houses, it has been suggested that the pictograph is a representation of something the people at Chaco actually saw in the sky: a supernova that resulted from the explosion of a star in what we call the Taurus constellation (Figure 77). Today called the Crab Nebula, the star exploded in an unimaginable paroxysm in AD 1054. We know exactly when it exploded because Chinese astronomers also saw it and recorded it in their journals. It was, they said, bright enough to be seen in the daytime sky and as bright as a quarter-moon at night. The location of the star pictograph at Chaco, juxtaposed with the image of a crescent moon, matches what we know about the phase of the moon when the star exploded. It cannot be proven definitively that the pictograph you'll see at Chaco is a painting of this celestial event, but it certainly is a fascinating possibility.

Site Type: Great House, Petroglyphs, Pictographs

Wow Factor: ***** The great houses at Chaco should not be missed. Pueblo Bonito is one of the most impressive buildings produced by Native Americans.

Museum: *****

Ease of Road Access: *** Part of the road is unpaved. It's not terrible and you won't need four-wheel drive, but it can be bumpy.

Ease of Hike: There are lots of hikes in Chaco, from very short walks from turnouts and parking lots to ruins of great houses to much longer and far more strenuous hikes with lots of elevation changes. Check the website for details.

Natural Beauty of Surroundings: ***** Starkly beautiful. By the way, Chaco has been designated a "dark sky region." It's a great place to see the stars at night with very little light pollution.

Kid Friendly: **** Energetic kids will love Chaco. There are lots of places to expend energy, as well as lots of lizards and little furry critters.

Food: Bring your own.

How to Get There: The best way to access Chaco is from the north from US 550, which you can pick up in Bloomfield, from the north, or Cuba, from the southeast (that's Cuba the town, not the island nation). From mile marker 112.5 on US 550, head south on CR 7900/7950. Take a right onto CR 7950 when it peels off CR 7900, which continues straight (to another site, Pueblo Pintado). CR 7950 will take you to the visitor center. Altogether, once you turn onto CR 7900/7950, it's about 21 miles to the visitor center, 13 of which are on a dirt road whose maintenance is a bit, um, casual.

You can also access Chaco from the south. From NM 9, go north on NM 57. This route is rougher, on 20 miles of not-so-well-maintained dirt road.

Hours of Operation: Open daily 7 a.m. to sunset. The visitor center is open 8 a.m. to 5 p.m. Chaco is closed on Thanksgiving, Christmas, and New Year's Day.

Cost: See website.

Best Season to Visit: Summer is hot, but you never know. I've been to Chaco in August and the temperature didn't get above the high 80s. Spring or fall might be better.

Website: www.nps.gov/chcu/index.htm

Designation: National Historical Park; World Heritage Site

Site 32 **Hovenweep National Monument**

Utah

Journal Entry

August 4, 2009

Even in a region where superlatives deservedly apply to so many of the archaeological remains listed in this guide, Hovenweep stands out as a unique—and uniquely marvelous—reflection of the architecture of the native peoples of the American Southwest. Not cliff dwellings or great houses, beginning a bit after AD 1200, the builders of Hovenweep constructed a series of seven major masonry towers along the north and south rims of a small canyon in eastern Utah. They also built two towers within the canyon itself.

About a 1.5-mile hike starts at the visitor center and takes you down into the canyon and then up again to the other side. From there you travel around the rim and get a close view of almost all the ruins, including Hovenweep Castle (large and impressive) and Twin Towers. It's a very, very cool place. The hike brings you back to the visitor center. Hovenweep is one of the most interesting of the Ancestral Puebloan ruins.

What You Will See

At Hovenweep you're going to see some very impressive examples of the architectural skill of the native peoples of the American Southwest. From the very informative visitor center, it's a short 300-yard stroll to the beginning of the Rim Trail that circles Little Ruin Canyon (Figure 78). For most of its 1.5-mile loop, the trail affords a flat and easy, unpaved hiking surface that follows the rim of the canyon (I.20).

Figure 78. A broad view of some of the towers at Hovenweep National Monument. The names of the structures don't really float above them.

Figure 79. Looking up as you walk along the trail across the bottom of the canyon, you can see a number of the towers and other structures that seem to cling to the edge of the cliff.

However, across a short stretch it is a little steeper, descending into the canyon and then climbing back out (Figure 79). There's also a short (0.5-mile) loop off the main trail to Tower Point. If you take the main trail as well as the Tower Point Loop, it's about a 90-minute hike. With stopping for photos, figure it can take as little as a couple of hours, though you might want to spend more time there.

The Rim Trail takes you right up to the seven towers that dot the canyon's rim. On the north side you'll see in sequence as you hike to the west: (1) Stronghold House, (2) Unit Type House, (3) Tower Point (you'll see this tower only if you take the Tower Loop Trail), and (4) Hovenweep Castle. After passing south around the western end of the canyon, you'll turn back east and see (5) Hovenweep House, (6) Rim Rock House, and (7) Twin Towers (my favorite; Figure 80). You can also take the hike in the other direction, starting with Stronghold House and, instead of walking west along the rim, taking the trail down into the canyon and then up onto the south rim. Either way, along the trail you'll also get great panoramic views of each of the seven rim towers from the opposite side of the canyon as well as Round Tower and the very well-preserved multistory Square Tower, located within the canyon itself. It's all quite beautiful and unique in its concentration of towers. Incredible; that's the best way to describe it.

Figure 80. This photograph of one of the iconic structures at Hovenweep, the Twin Towers, as seen from across the canyon. A short hike from the trailhead down into the canyon, and then back up the other side, brings the visitor right up to the Twin Towers.

Why Is Hovenweep Important?

Hovenweep is unique. You won't see this remarkable concentration of towers anywhere else in North America. It's not entirely clear why, between about AD 1230 and AD 1275, the ancient inhabitants constructed so many towers and fortresslike structures. All of them are "intervisible," meaning you can see each structure from each other one along the rim of this canyon. Some of the towers (for example, Hovenweep Castle and Unit Type House) were inhabited and have windows whose positions appear to have been designed to align with the rising of the sun at the solstices and equinoxes. Tall towers would have provided a clear view of sunrise, so that might explain the architectural form. A calendar based on the sun that told farmers when to begin preparing the fields, when to plant, and when to harvest would have been a valuable tool for those living in an agriculturally challenging region like the Southwest.

Perhaps the towers were built as lookouts, defensive structures that provided residents a broad view of the surrounding territory and ample notice of the appearance of potentially dangerous strangers. Towers might also have functioned as communication beacons, with a warning flame set at their apexes when danger approached. We can continue to speculate, but for our purposes it's enough to know that Hovenweep is an amazing place.

Site Type: Stone Tower

Wow Factor: **** The Hovenweep towers are very impressive.

Museum: ***

Ease of Road Access: *** There are some unpaved roads along the way, but they are well maintained. You won't need a four-wheel-drive vehicle or one with particularly high ground clearance.

Ease of Hike: *** You'll hike down into the canyon and back up to do the entire trail. It's a very nice and pretty easy hike.

Natural Beauty of Surroundings: ****

Kid Friendly: ****

Food: Bring your own.

How to Get There: Hovenweep is located in southeastern Utah, hard fast against the border with Colorado. From US 191 in Utah, take UT 262 east. Where UT 262 cuts south (to the right), continue straight instead. Pass the Hatch Trading Post and take the road to the right, following the signs to Hovenweep.

From the Colorado side, from US 491 take the road labeled either CC or BB to CR 10. Take CR 10 west and follow the signs to the visitor center.

Hours of Operation: Open daily 8 a.m. to 6 p.m. April through September; 8 a.m. to 5 p.m. October through March

Cost: See website.

Best Season to Visit: Any time is good, but it can be pretty hot in summer.

Website: www.nps.gov/hove/index.htm

Designation: National Monument

Rock Art

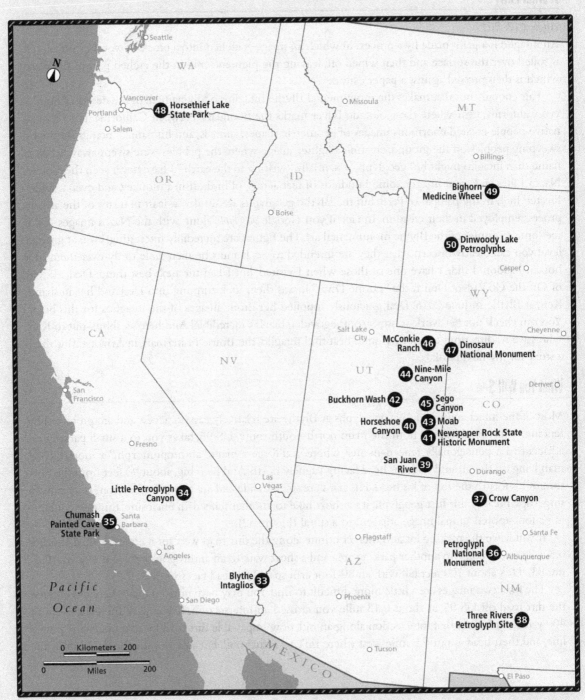

Figure 81.

Site 33 Blythe Intaglios

Blythe, California

Journal Entry

August 12, 2011

An intaglio is a print made by a process in which an image is etched into a block of wood or metal. Ink is rolled over the surface and then wiped off, leaving the pigment only in the etched part of the plate, which is then pressed against a paper canvas.

Fair enough, but that makes the monumental Blythe Intaglios oddly named. In the desert of Southern California, near where the Colorado River marks the boundary between California and Arizona, native people created enormous images of geometric shapes, animals, and humanlike beings simply by sweeping pebbles off the ground, creating a lighter image where the pebbles were swept away. A better name than intaglio might be "geoglyph," essentially, "writing in the earth." I have never seen the famous Nazca Lines and giant images, some hundreds of feet across, of birds, fish, a monkey, and even a spider located high in the pampas of Peru, but the Blythe geoglyphs are similar, at least in terms of the artistic process employed in their creation. In fact, if you Google *geoglyph*, along with the Nazca images you'll see some examples of the Blythe monumental art. The figures are incredibly interesting; even at ground level you can clearly discern what they are intended to be. It must be incredible to fly over them in a hot-air balloon. I didn't have one of those when I visited, but I had the next best thing: Desi Ekstein of On the Go Video! Desi is the "Drone Diva." It was sheer luck running into Desi and her husband, Ken, at Blythe in June 2016. Desi graciously supplied her drone images of the intaglios for this book. You can check out her work at http://onthegovideo.biz. It's incredible! And here's a shout-out to Ken, who gave us directions to another quite beautiful intaglio, the Bouse Fisherman, in Arizona. But that's a story for my next book.

What You Will See

Most of the intact and impressive geoglyphs at Blythe are relatively easy to access and are protected by fencing. A dirt road leading from the main north–south route, US 95, takes you to a small parking lot adjacent to a pentagonally fenced-in area where you'll see a giant "anthropomorph," a monumental man lying on the ground with his head facing vaguely north. And he *is* big, about 90 feet from the bottom of his feet to the top of his head. His arms are spread wide and are about 70 feet from fingertips to fingertips. Nearby this first geoglyph, it's a short hike to another fenced-in enclosure, this one containing a four-footed animal image adjacent to a spiral (Figure 82).

If you leave the parking lot and then continue along the dirt road west for a little less than another 0.5 mile, you'll come to another parking area and a short walk to an anthropomorph to the north (Figure 83). He's about 100 feet tall with an 80-foot arm span. His head faces southwest.

The final two images are a little more difficult to find. You may have noticed that when you entered the dirt road off US 95, at about 0.13 mile you crossed an intersection. If you park there, walk about 400 yards south from that intersection along an old, now impassable dirt road located under the power line, and then head about 0.5 mile west (there isn't an actual trail, but just aim for the flat bluff in the

Figure 82. Intaglios of a four-legged animal and a geometric figure at Blythe, California. The animal is about 40 feet across. (COURTESY OF DESI EKSTEIN, ON THE GO VIDEO!)

distance), you'll find the largest of the anthropomorphs. He's a whopping 170 feet tall and nearly 150 feet across his outspread arms (Figure 84). He's a true giant. Nearby there's another four-footed animal (you can see it at the top of the photograph). Both of these images are also enclosed by fences. (Punch in 33°47'42.37"N 114°32'11.85"W in Google Earth for the precise location of these two intaglios.) Do not, under any circumstances, climb over the fences or in any way disturb any of the images. Please. You can still see tire tracks where, before the fences were erected, some idiot thought it might be fun to go four-wheeling over a sacred site.

These geoglyphs are truly gigantic and impressive. Now consider this: The Blythe Intaglios were unknown to anyone but local Indians until 1932, when a pilot overflew them. I can't imagine his reaction and that of the people he told about the amazing things he had seen from the air above the desert north of Blythe.

Figure 83. A monumentally scaled spirit being at Blythe. The anthropomorph is about 100 feet tall. (COURTESY OF DESI EKSTEIN, ON THE GO VIDEO!)

Figure 84. Two of the Blythe Intaglios. The anthropomorph is more than 170 feet tall, with an arm span of more than 147 feet. (COURTESY OF DESI EKSTEIN, ON THE GO VIDEO!)

Why Are the Blythe Intaglios Important?

I've mentioned this in our discussion of **Serpent Mound** and **Rock Eagle Effigy Mound.** All over the world, not just in North America, people have produced images on the ground, whether through piling stones, sweeping away stones, mounding up soil, cutting into chalk, or even through the architectural footprint of a building. The Blythe Intaglios are an example of this form of art. Medieval churches, effigy mounds, and geoglyphs appear to reflect the belief of people in various places and times—that the gods live on high and it is the job of human beings to produce beautiful works of worship that can be seen in their entirely only by those spirit beings.

It would be a cliché to simply say the images in the Blythe Intaglios are mysterious. They're not all that mysterious to the local Mohave Indians, whose ancestors produced them beginning perhaps 1,000 years ago. They tell us that the four-footed animals are representations of *Hatakulya*, a mountain lion who is one of the beings who helped the creator god produce the universe. The humanlike images are of *Mastamho*, supreme creator of the Earth.

Site Type: Geoglyph

Wow Factor: **** I rate the Blythe Intaglios at four stars. If you can see them from above, from a hot-air balloon or a small, low-flying plane, they deserve five stars.

Museum: None

Ease of Road Access: ****

Ease of Hike: ***** The well-maintained access road to the geoglyphs brings you very close to four of them. A short hike (0.5 mile one-way) across relatively flat ground gets you to two more figures.

Natural Beauty of Surroundings: **** The area is a semidesert, beautiful in its starkness.

Kid Friendly: ***

Food: Bring your own.

How to Get There: The geoglyphs are located about 17 miles north of I-10 (the interstate that runs from Los Angeles to Phoenix). Travel north from I-10 in Blythe on US 95. After Cottontail Road (on the right) and before you reach South Riverview Road (also on the right), the dirt road (on the left) leads directly to the three most accessible of the intaglios. The road is well marked with stone pillars and a large sign reading, obviously, "Blythe Intaglios."

Hours of Operation: The Blythe Intaglios are located on Bureau of Land Management property and are accessible daily, year-round.

Cost: Free

Best Season to Visit: It's hot in summer (like the surface of the sun hot), but the hikes are short, so just about any time of year is good.

Website: www.blm.gov/az/st/en/prog/cultural/intaglios.html

Designation: BLM property

Site 34 Little Petroglyph Canyon

Coso, California

Journal Entry

August 13, 2011

We've seen far too many examples of vandalism in our fifty-site odyssey, ranging from kids defacing ancient sites by tagging them with their initials or signatures, yahoos who damage art by shooting it, and the extreme example of an inexplicable attempt to erase an ancient art panel in its entirety (Courthouse Wash in Moab). So I was very pleasantly surprised that among the literally thousands of petroglyphs I was privileged to see during my guided hike through Little Petroglyph Canyon with archaeologist Mike Baskerville, with one noticeable exception I'll discuss later, I saw virtually no graffiti. When I commented on this gratifying and unexpected turn of events, Mike simply laughed and reminded me that Little Petroglyph Canyon (also called Renegade Canyon) is located in the Naval Air Weapons Station (NAWS), a 1-million-acre military base in Southern California. "If anybody sneaks onto the base to do anything they shouldn't, we shoot them first and ask questions later." Point well taken.

The one bit of graffiti I did see was, I hate to admit, actually pretty interesting. In the late 1940s and early 1950s, some scientists working for the Atomic Energy Commission were stationed at NAWS. Apparently, during their time on the base, one or more of those scientists hiked out to see the rock art during their off-hours and decided to make an addition of their own. They shouldn't have done it of course, but at least they didn't incise their work over any older art. They found a blank bit of stone and, well, expressed themselves. Their "art" can still be seen, and it was more than just a little funny in its anachronism: $E = MC^2$ (Figure 85). If Giorgio Tsoukalos, the weird-haired bullshit artist of *Ancient Aliens* fame, were to find out about this, he might explain it as a message from extraterrestrial visitors. Please don't tell him.

Figure 85. The only graffiti I saw in Little Petroglyph Canyon. It was left by physicists stationed at the Naval Air Weapons Station in the 1940s, not ancient aliens.

What You Will See

Located in the Coso region of Southern California, about 3 hours east of Los Angeles, Little Petroglyph Canyon (Little Pet) almost certainly has the greatest number of individual rock art images among the sites in our fifty-site odyssey. I've seen estimates in the neighborhood of 20,000 images. And Little Pet is only one of four canyons on the 36,000-acre preserve on the base with a large concentration of ancient rock art. It's estimated that there are at least 100,000 individual petroglyphs and as many as 1 million spread out across the four canyons. That's not a typo. In any event, the Coso region has the densest concentration of ancient art just about anywhere in the United States, quite possibly the world. In your hike through Little Petroglyph Canyon, you'll see ancient art on basically every available rock surface, and there are a lot of those, for about 1.5 miles. The oldest art in the canyon may be as much as 10,000 years old. Some of the re-patination of the incised lines in the art—where the process that results in the veneer on the surfaces of the basalt has begun to cover the art—suggests that the art began in earnest by about 6,000 years ago.

There's an astonishing array of images etched into the volcanic rock that brackets the trail through the canyon (I.21)—basalt, like the raw material used by the artists at **Site 36, Petroglyph National Monument** and **Site 38, Three Rivers,** both in New Mexico. I will not provide a blow-by-blow description of all the art we saw; that would take an entire book or, actually, a series of books. Briefly, here's a non-exhaustive listing of the categories of art we saw:

1. Lots of bighorn sheep shown from the side (Figure 86)
2. Lots of bighorn sheep shown from the front, with their horns looking like the wings of a bird flying toward you
3. Some snake images
4. A possible turtle
5. Lots and lots of atlatls, a tool used to increase the distance and accuracy of a spear, characterized by large, circular weights and hooks
6. Plenty of geometric shapes
7. Images of what appear to be rugs with complex designs; lots with tassels on their bottoms
8. Simple stick figure people, some aiming bows and arrows at sheep
9. Simple stick figure people, some pointing what appear to be swords at sheep
10. My favorite images at Little Pet are the many, detailed, absolutely trippy anthropomorphs (Figures 87, 88). None of them look like the Fremont images we've seen in Utah; they don't have the triangular bodies with broad shoulders and narrow waists of the Fremont style. The bodies of the Coso anthropomorphs tend to be rectangular, with the long axis vertical; richly detailed designs are etched into their bodies, and their heads bear all kinds of interesting headdresses. These images are called patterned body anthropomorphs (PBAs), and they are astonishing.

Figure 86. Bighorn sheep, a dog, a medicine bag, and a bowling ball with too many finger holes adorn this rock face in Little Petroglyph Canyon in Southern California. Okay, it's not really a bowling ball.

Figure 87. The spirit beings of Little Petroglyph Canyon are unique, different from everything else seen on our fifty-site odyssey.

Trust me; I've only scratched the surface here. You absolutely have to see this amazing place for yourself. You'll be blown away by the beauty and quantity of the ancient art.

Why Is Little Petroglyph Canyon Important?

I think it's fair to respond to the question "Why is Little Petroglyph Canyon important?" or, more broadly, "Why is the rock art located in the greater Coso region important?" with, "You might as well ask why the Metropolitan Museum of Art in New York City is important, or the Louvre in Paris, or the Hermitage in St. Petersburg." These places, all of them, are repositories of physical manifestations of the great creativity and imagination that characterize the human mind. More than simply art galleries, though they are impressive and, indeed, important as such, these places also are windows into the human soul, however you want to define what that is. As humans, in all times and all places, we observe the world around us, process what we have observed, and then we question it. We attempt to understand the reality around us, to give meaning to our world and our place within it. As humans we insist there is more to it than simply we are born, we live, and then we die and disappear. We feel we are deeper than this, that we are part of something awesome and eternal. We think, we dream, and we imagine. Part of what makes us human is the impulse to make those thoughts, dreams, and imaginings concrete, to paint them on canvases, sculpt them in clay, record them on paper, and, as seen so often in our fifty-site odyssey, to scratch, etch, peck, or paint them onto soaring stone cliff walls. Go to Little Petroglyph Canyon to see a vast

Figure 88. More amazing art in Little Pet.

and thrilling plethora of the thoughts, dreams, and imaginings of the ancient peoples of California. You won't regret it.

Additional Note

Here's the deal with Little Petroglyph Canyon: You can't go there on your own. Remember; it's on a military base, with all kinds of secret military stuff going on. However, you can see the rock art because the military graciously has arranged with a local museum to allow tightly controlled, limited-access tours to Little Pet. Since 1966 the Maturango Museum in nearby Ridgecrest, California, has led tours for small groups of visitors. You need to sign up for a tour through the museum. They don't take reservations over the phone. Download the tour application form (www.maturango.org/Resources/petrodates.pdf), fill it out, and either e-mail (matmus9@maturango.org) or fax it to the Petroglyph Tour Coordinator at (760) 375-0479. The wonderful folks at the museum will contact you and provide you with all the details of your tour. Expect to arrive at the museum early in the morning; tours generally leave the museum at 6:30 a.m. (the museum's address is 100 E. Las Flores Ave., Ridgecrest, California). Your group will need to carpool to the canyon trailhead. From the museum it's a 5-mile drive north to the entrance of the base and then another 40-mile drive to the trailhead into Little Petroglyph Canyon.

Little Petroglyph Canyon has the highest entry fee of any of the sites in this book—by far. It's steep, but it covers the expense of having a number of certified tour guides along with you. There's a discount if you're a member of the museum. It is an absolute necessity to sign up for one of the organized tours well in advance of your planned trip. The tours fill up quickly and long before their scheduled dates. Because of the paperwork required by the US Navy, the museum cannot accommodate walk-ins. Each visitor 18 years of age and older must fill out a five-page (!) form (http://maturango.org/Resources/petrobaseaccess.pdf), which gets submitted to the base for approval. Further, you must be an American citizen to go on a tour of Little Pet; anyone on the tour 16 years and older must show a valid ID indicating that he or she is an American citizen. Kids must be 10 years old or older to go on a tour—no little ones and no pets. Additional information about the tours can be found at www.maturango.org/Resources/Petroglyph%20tour%20information.pdf.

Yeah, I know. There are a lot of rules and paperwork; it may seem a bit overwhelming at first. If you have any questions, call the Petroglyph Tour Coordinator at (760) 375-6900, Wednesday through Friday 10 a.m. to 1 p.m. and 2 to 4 p.m., or e-mail matmus9@maturango.org.

Trust me, the art is truly amazing and more than worth the hassle.

Site Type: Petroglyphs

Wow Factor: ***** Mind-blowing number of beautiful and amazing works of ancient art.

Museum: None on-site; affiliated with Maturango Museum

Ease of Road Access: *****

Ease of Hike: ** The hike has some interesting spots where you'll need to scramble a little over rocks. But it's not that bad.

Natural Beauty of Surroundings: ****

Kid Friendly: The guided tours do not accept anyone under the age of 16.

Food: Bring your own.

How to Get There: As noted above, the answer to "How to Get There" is: "You don't." You will be brought there by your guides from the Maturango Museum.

Hours of Operation: Accessible only by guided tour. To check tour schedule and availability, visit the museum website at http://maturango.org/petroglyph-tours/.

Cost: See website.

Best Season to Visit: Determined by the US Navy and the Maturango Museum. Check their website for the latest schedule.

Website: http://maturango.org/petroglyph-tours/

Designation: US naval air base

Site 35 **Chumash Painted Cave State Historic Park**

Santa Barbara, California

Journal Entry

August 15, 2011

When you hear or read the phrase "painted cave," it usually signifies the art placed on the walls of the large and deep solution caverns of Europe in the cultural period called the Upper Paleolithic, which developed during the late Ice Age. Place names like Lascaux, Altamira, and Chauvet evoke memories of the multitude of PowerPoint slides many students endure in the first few classes of Art History 101. Dating back as much as 35,000 years ago, this iconic art—among the first representational and naturalistic depictions produced by ancient human beings—is exemplified by depictions of animals including horse and woolly mammoth, cave bear and lion, elk and woolly rhinoceros.

So when you hear or read the phrase "painted caves," you likely do not think of ancient art painted on a shallow cave high in the hills overlooking Santa Barbara, California. Yet there Chumash Painted Cave sits, high above the Southern California coast. The images are beautiful and absolutely worth a visit (Figure 89).

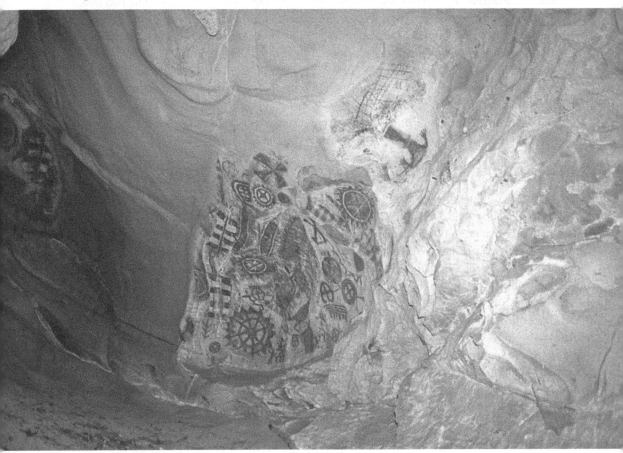

Figure 89. It's only a single pictograph panel, but the painting visible in Chumash Painted Cave in the hills overlooking Santa Barbara, California, was well worth a visit.

What You Will See

The site itself is well signed. Once you arrive, attempt to wedge your vehicle into the tiny pullout on the left that can accommodate about two cars. Two subcompact cars. The cave is located up a short, steep hill on the left side of the road. The cave is protected by a heavy iron gate blocking the entrance, placed there in response to the damage wrought by graffiti-writing vandals over the years. There are two, small circular gaps in the gate to accommodate cameras. That works pretty well for positioning your camera or cell phone. A problem posed especially for photographers, however, is the lack of light in the cave. There is no artificial lighting, and because of the surrounding topography and thick canopy of trees, the sun doesn't exactly illuminate the place. But once your eyes become adjusted to the low light level, you'll be able to see just how fascinatingly beautiful the art is (I.22). If you want to get some decent pictures, bring a tripod or at least be ready to steady your camera sufficiently for a longish exposure.

The art at Chumash Painted Cave is not nearly as old as that adorning the Upper Paleolithic cave walls of Europe; it's only several hundred years old and was produced by the local Chumash Indian tribe. The overarching theme of the Chumash Painted Cave art doesn't look like anything we've seen earlier in this book. The primary, repeating theme of the art in Chumash Painted Cave is the circle; there are several, and most are elaborately ornamented. Painted in very bright and fresh tones of red, white, and black, some of the circular images are spoked and some have a series of pointed tips along their circumferences. One stands out in its simplicity—a circle, filled in entirely in black (though some recent idiot scratched a name onto it). You'll also see a series of pretty trippy geometric shapes. The two images that evoke some comparisons to the Barrier Canyon art are floating anthropomorphs, predictably without arms or legs. These guys are boldly striped in black and white paint and likely are spirit beings of some sort. The reds in the paint pigment were produced by grounding chunks of the mineral hematite (an iron oxide). The whites are from gypsum. Black was produced from ground-up charcoal and the mineral manganese oxide. The binder, the liquid used to keep all the ground-up pigment together, consisted of animal fat, plant material, even water.

The cave is small and there's not a ton of art, but it remains the best example of extant Chumash art open to the public. If you're in Southern California, you shouldn't miss it.

Why Is Chumash Painted Cave Important?

It's always a crapshoot when those of us who are not members of the culture that produced ancient art attempt to explain it and address questions of its importance and meaning. In this case, the art is certainly important and significant because it is beautiful and exemplifies the commonality of the human threads of imagination and creativity. But what was the art's importance to the Chumash artists who painted the cave wall? What message were they leaving behind? What is the meaning of the art? It is incredibly difficult to answer these questions.

However, based on the traditions of the Chumash as recorded by Europeans who settled in Southern California and interacted with them beginning in the seventeenth century, it is clear that they were interested in the sky and incorporated astronomical observations into their traditions and beliefs. This has led to the suggestion that the circular images painted in this cave and in other places in Southern California are intended to be depictions of the sun. In this interpretation, the spikes emanating from most of the circles' circumferences are solar rays, perhaps as envisioned by a shaman during a trance. Maybe. If this is the case, then what is the meaning of the black, featureless circle in the middle of the art panel?

Analysis of a small sample of the black paint in that circle indicated it probably was painted in the late 1600s. That's very interesting. Astronomers tell us that on November 24, 1677, a total eclipse of the sun would have been visible in Southern California. To a people who were clearly interested in the skies above them, a total eclipse would have been a momentous experience, one that could be expected to be passed down in oral history and, perhaps, memorialized in a painting. It's impossible to test this hypothesis definitively, but it is an interesting speculation. Eclipse or not, the art is fascinating, and that's enough to make it important.

Site Type: Pictographs

Wow Factor: *** The cave is small and gated, but the painted images are very cool.

Museum: None

Ease of Road Access: ***** The 2-mile drive on Painted Cave Road is uphill with lots of switchbacks, fabulous views, and scary turns along a very, very narrow road. Driving a big RV? Forget about it. The cave area is well signed, with only a very few pull-offs for a handful of cars to park.

Ease of Hike: *****

Natural Beauty of Surroundings: **

Kid Friendly: **

Food: Bring your own.

How to Get There: Traveling either north or south on the Pacific Coast Highway (CA 1/US 101), take the State Street exit to CA 154 (north). After about 6 miles, turn right onto Painted Cave Road.

Hours of Operation: Open year-round, 24/7

Cost: Free

Best Season to Visit: Any time

Website: www.parks.ca.gov/?page_id=602

Designation: State historic park

Site 36 Petroglyph National Monument

Albuquerque, New Mexico

Journal Entry

July 18, 2014

Living in the East, I am used to large cities being surrounded by extensive suburbs which are, in turn, surrounded by even more distant exurbs filled with workers with soul-crushing rush-hour commutes to the big city.

Albuquerque, New Mexico (Weird Al fans: The towels are oh so fluffy, but the air does not smell like warm root beer), isn't like that. There is a downtown and a ring of residential neighborhoods surrounding that downtown. But rather than slowly petering out at its margins, the city—bam—just abruptly ends at a boundary marked by a starkly beautiful, otherworldly volcanic landscape. It is an urban geography wholly unfamiliar to an Easterner.

Searching for the trailhead to one of the petroglyph concentrations at Petroglyph National Monument, I drove through a neighborhood of densely packed middle-class homes, thinking I had gone wrong somewhere. My GPS told me I was about to enter a national monument, but I was still in a city. The road ended in a cul-de-sac and a small parking lot. Once I left my car, with the neighborhood behind me, I abruptly left all signs of civilization behind and entered an entirely different place—and an entirely different time—a place and time where remarkable artists depicted their world, both physical and spiritual, in thousands of finely carved incisions into rock. I had fallen off a metaphorical cliff, leaving behind Albuquerque and the modern world and entering Petroglyph National Monument. You should too.

What You Will See

The primary reason for Petroglyph National Monument's existence is the rock art. It is a very well-developed and user-friendly place. There's art that can be seen by virtually anyone, regardless of your physical stamina; there are short hikes and long hikes, steep hikes and flat ones. Take your pick, or do them all.

Obviously enough, the art you'll see at Petroglyph National Monument consists of petroglyphs (duh). All the art has been incised, carved, or pecked into the basalt boulders that dominate the landscape. The interior of the basalt is a light brown or tan, but erosion casts a dark shadow or patina over exposed surfaces. Using those rock surfaces as their canvas, ancient artists scratched through that thin dark patina, exposing the lighter toned rock interior and in this way created images of animals, people, spirit beings, and geometric shapes. It is estimated that the petroglyphs range from about 700 to 400 years of age.

The park has a small visitor center with a shop, but the center is not adjacent to any of the trails where you will see petroglyphs. Still, it's a good idea to stop there for a bit of orientation. The ranger there will provide you with a map and some useful advice about accessing the trails.

There are essentially three primary areas for petroglyph viewing.

Boca Negra Canyon

This is the most developed part of the park, and there are three very easy trails. The *Mesa Point Trail* leads from the parking lot up to about 115 feet elevation; you'll see petroglyph images on the loose boulders and bedrock outcrops all along the well-maintained trail. There are wood and/or rope barriers and even some paved concrete steps. The Mesa Point Trail takes only about 30 minutes. The *Macaw Trail* is very short (it takes barely 5 minutes) and shows a few petroglyphs including the quite beautiful, eponymous Macaw petroglyph (Figure 90). *Cliff Base Trail* is also pretty short, taking only about 15 or 20 minutes, and there are some beautiful images, including an amazing human face mask at the end of the trail. These trails are easy, but none are paved so none are wheelchair accessible. But even kids and people unaccustomed to hiking should have an easy time of it. (Take your time on the Mesa Point Trail; it is uphill, and the elevation of Albuquerque is about 5,000 feet.)

Piedras Marcadas

The parking lot for this trail is tucked into the corner of a residential and commercial zone in Albuquerque. The trail is only about 1 mile long, maybe a little more (each way), but it is in sand and can be a bit tiring. The trail follows along the base of an escarpment of basalt boulders, and there are hundreds upon hundreds of very cool images scattered across the boulder slope. There are plenty of anthropomorphs, lots of images of animals, a lot of birds, and humanlike faces and masks (Figure 91).

Figure 90. Petroglyph National Monument is located in Albuquerque, New Mexico. Here you can see the macaw petroglyph. Macaws are tropical, and the bird's presence in this ancient art indicates contact with people to the south.

Figure 91. There are lots of faces and masks etched into the basalt boulders that characterize Petroglyph National Monument. Here's a very interesting one wrapped around an edge of a boulder.

You can see lots of images from the trail, but it's a special treat if you enjoy scrambling up and down the scree slope. Some very short side trails take you up to where you can get a close-up view of the art. Certainly binoculars and a telephoto lens will come in handy here, but you should try to hike up into the boulders for a closer look. None of the hiking is very high or scary, but it gets extremely hot in a hurry in New Mexico in summer and there's very little shade. Actually, there's no shade, not even a little. Bring lots of water. And slather on the sunscreen. In my opinion, the petroglyphs visible along the Piedras Marcadas Trail are among the best you'll see at Petroglyph National Monument. The monument's website says you'll see about 300 petroglyphs. That must be off by a factor of 10. I don't pretend to have counted them, but I'm pretty sure there's a lot more than that. One of my favorites on this trail is a series of human handprints (Figure 92). Very cool.

Rinconada Canyon

I had been on the Rinconada Canyon Trail years ago, but during my 2014 visit, the trail was closed for maintenance. Apparently the trail had been washed out by a fierce storm in the area a couple of years before. Fortunately the Rinconada Canyon Trail has reopened as of October 2014. I can't say much about this trail other than it has lots of petroglyphs. So many petroglyphs.

Figure 92. That's my hand juxtaposed with handprint petroglyphs at Petroglyph National Monument. (And no, I'm not touching the art, I'm hovering over it. Please, never touch the art.)

Why Is Petroglyph National Monument Important?

The art at Petroglyph National Monument is impressive, and there's a lot of it. Although we might not understand the precise meaning of the rock art images, we can at least recognize the great creativity and imagination expressed in those images. Art, whatever its specific meaning or significance to those who produce it, conveys the humanity of the artist, and that makes all, maybe especially ancient art, important. The people who once lived here didn't tell the stories of their people and culture in words; they accomplished that in their art. Visit Petroglyph National Monument and read the stories bequeathed to us by those ancient artists.

Additional Note

Directions to the visitor center are provided below. To get to the trailheads:

   Boca Negra Canyon Trails. From the visitor center, make a left and head north on Unser Boulevard. Pass Montaño Road on the right. Take your next right onto Artisco Drive NW. That will take you in short order to the parking lot for Boca Negra Canyon. There's a nominal fee to park here.

   Rinconada Canyon Trail. From the visitor center, make a right and head south on Unser Boulevard. In about 1.25 miles you'll come to the road to the parking lot for the trailhead on the right (west), opposite St. Joseph Avenue on the left.

   Piedras Marcadas Canyon Trail. From Unser Boulevard, turn onto Montaño Road (you passed that on the way to Boca Negra Canyon). Turn left onto Riverview Trail, which becomes Golf Course Road. After a bit you'll pass a major intersection with Paseo Del Norte Boulevard NE. Continue on Golf Course Road for a little more than 0.5 mile and then make a left onto Jill Patricia Street NW. In

I.17. *Cliff Palace at sunset. (Site 29)*

I.18. *The spectacular remains of Pueblo Bonito in Chaco Canyon. (Site 31)*

I.19. You'll need to hike the trail up to the top of the mesa to get this view of the largest great house in the South-west: Pueblo Bonito. The name means "beautiful house," and it is that. (Site 31)

I.20. Here you can see some of the Hovenweep towers hugging the cliff's edge as well as the freestanding square tower sitting at the bottom of the canyon. (Site 32)

I.21. *A typical scree of basalt boulders covered with ancient rock art in Little Petroglyph Canyon. (Site 34)*

I.22. *Chumash Painted Cave in all its colorful glory. (Site 35)*

I.23. The best-known petroglyph panel along the main trail at Crow Canyon. The Navajo spirit being and corn plant, both on the left, are especially beautiful. (Site 37)

I.24. Etched into one of the thousands of volcanic boulders at Three Rivers, this image bears a resemblance to Tlaloc, an ancient Mexican rain god. (Site 38)

I.25. This photograph may be the most beautiful one in the book: a petroglyph of a bighorn sheep, pierced by three arrows, forever frozen on a volcanic boulder and set against an amazingly blue sky. (Site 38)

I.26. Words fail me. The best I can muster for these more than 6-foot-tall spirit beings at Horseshoe Canyon is OMG. (Site 40)

I.27. More of the more than two dozen anthropomorphs in the Great Gallery of Horseshoe Canyon. Look at the one on the left with two critters painted onto his chest. (Site 40)

I.28. When you drive through Nine Mile Canyon, don't you dare blink or you'll miss some of the art. Thousands of individual images festoon the north wall of the canyon. The figure on the left of the panel is often called the Juggler. On the right are a couple of bighorn sheep, one of which is being aimed at by a bow and arrow–wielding hunter. (Site 44)

I.29. Just past the Fremont panel in Sego Canyon is this crazy-beautiful Barrier Canyon pictograph panel. (Site 45)

I.30. The so-called Three Kings panel at McConkie Ranch (yeah, I see more than three figures as well) is located on a dizzyingly high and inaccessible rock face. You'll need a telephoto lens or binoculars to get a good view of it. Your cell phone camera will be useless. (Site 46)

I.31. Rock art just doesn't get any better than this amazing panel at McKee Springs showing a shield-wielding Fremont anthropomorph. (Site 47)

about 300 feet you'll see a driveway on the right. There are no signs, and it may seem as though you're going into the parking lot of a business, but don't sweat it. If you followed these directions correctly, you are there. Take a right into that driveway and then an immediate left into a small parking lot for the trail.

Site Type: Petroglyphs

Wow Factor: **** The concentration of rock art along the several trails located in Petroglyph National Monument is incredible. The art is virtually everywhere you look.

Museum: ** It's really more of a visitor center than a museum.

Ease of Road Access: *****

Ease of Hike: *** The trails vary in difficulty.

Natural Beauty of Surroundings: ****

Kid Friendly: ****

Food: You're essentially in downtown Albuquerque; there are lots of choices for eating out.

How to Get There: The visitor center is located west of downtown Albuquerque. Take I-40 to Unser Boulevard, exit 154, and drive north 3 miles to Western Trail. Turn left onto Western Trail and continue to the visitor center. Alternatively, take I-25 to the Paseo del Norte, exit 232, and head west to Coors Road. Go south on Coors Road to Western Trail; turn right onto Western Trail to the visitor center.

Hours of Operation: The visitor center is open daily 8 a.m. to 5 p.m. Closed on Thanksgiving, Christmas, and New Year's Day; also closed during severe weather. The trails are open on the same schedule.

Cost: Free except for a nominal parking fee at Boca Negra Canyon.

Best Season to Visit: Summer is ridiculously hot in Albuquerque, but it is dry. Like inside an oven. If you need it cooler, spring and fall are better choices.

Website: www.nps.gov/petr/index.htm

Designation: National Monument

Site 37 Crow Canyon

Blanco, New Mexico

Journal Entry

March 8, 2015

In a broad sense, a Navajo visiting the region they call Dinétah in northwestern New Mexico is analogous to a Jew, Christian, or Muslim going to Eden. The Navajo believe that Dinétah, particularly the canyons south and east of the modern-day town of Farmington, is the place where the world and the Navajo people were created.

The Navajo call themselves Diné; the word simply means "people." *Dinétah* means "among the people." Archaeology shows that the ancestors of the modern Navajo people originated in the north and migrated into the Four Corners region of the American Southwest relatively recently, perhaps only 600 or 700 years ago, bringing with them a culture and language very different from the local, indigenous residents, who today are represented by the Hopi and Zuni tribes. The Navajo, however, disagree, tracing their creation to Dinétah.

Hiking the trails in Crow Canyon, walking through the thick sand of the deeply incised dry washes, glimpsing the small stone structures called *pueblitos*, and gazing at the incredibly rich rock art, it certainly can seem as though you are walking back to the beginning of time.

What You Will See

A visit to Crow Canyon is all about the rock art. It's beautiful and unique, and much of it is crisply carved into deeply red and brown surfaces, revealing the lighter rock beneath. A major reason the art looks so fresh is that it was fairly recently carved, dating from the 1500s to the mid-1700s. The rock art is easily reached and occurs in three significant clusters.

Main Panel

This area is usually called the "Main Panel," but it's actually made up of several panels along the rock face, extending for about 0.75 mile. When driving to the art along the access road, you'll come to a fork about 1 mile after crossing Largo Wash (see directions below). When you reach the fork, head as straight as you can, saving the route off to the east (right) for later. In about 0.25 mile from the fork, the road curves to the right (east), passes

Figure 93. The depiction of a corn plant in the main petroglyph panel at Crow Canyon.

Figure 94. The depiction of an important Navajo deity with the horns of a bighorn sheep in the main petroglyph panel at Crow Canyon.

a gas well pad, and ends in a cul-de-sac and parking area. The trailhead to the first cluster of rock art is located just to the east of the parking area. It's a very short walk along the trail to the beginning of the art along the south-facing cliff. As you walk east along that cliff, you'll encounter groupings of astonishing images of geometric images, animals, birds, animal and human footprints, bows, arrows, and depictions of various and recognizable Navajo deities. My absolute favorite panel (I.23) includes what is very clearly the depiction of a corn plant (Figure 93) adjacent to a recognizable Navajo deity: He resembles a horned man wearing what appears to be a rounded hump with a series of feathers emanating from it (Figure 94). It's very cool. The round-trip hike is an easy slog of about 1.5 miles.

The Warrior

After hiking along the ridge and returning to your car, drive back to the fork in the road. Bear left (east) and follow that road for a little less than 1 mile, where you'll come to a little pullout on the right. Park your vehicle; look off to the north and you'll soon see a gorgeous panel called "the Warrior" (Figure

Figure 95. This large warrior image at Crow Canyon, complete with a circular shield, bow, and arrow, likely predates Navajo occupation of the Southwest.

95). He has horns or is wearing a horned headdress and is holding a large, circular shield. There are a couple of spears next to him that appear to have feathers attached to their bases, and if you look closely, he also is holding a bow (perhaps it is strapped to his back). Cross over the road and walk up to the art for a closer view. This art likely was not produced by Navajo artists; it is more likely the work of ancestors of the modern Hopi.

44 Panel

Back in your car, continue along that road until you reach another cul-de-sac (it's about 0.8 mile from the Warrior panel; in other words, about 1.3 miles from the fork in the road) and a trailhead to another series of images. The trailhead is signed "44 Panel," a reference to one of the petroglyphs that looks like an upside down 44 directly above a right-side-up 44. This hike is a little more of a trudge, not because of its length (it's only about 0.8 mile each way) but because much of it is through soft sand. The best analogy I can give you is walking on a beach. Tiring. Follow the arrows interspersed along the trail. Most of the art you'll see along the way on your left isn't particularly impressive, but the hike is more than worth it. You will be rewarded when the trail brings you closer to the cliff,

Figure 96. At the end of the 44 Panel Trail at Crow Canyon is this wonderful petroglyph panel depicting a hunter with a bow whose giant arrow has pierced the body of an antlered animal, likely an elk.

and at its end there are some amazing petroglyph panels. One clearly shows a tableaux of a hunter with a bow facing down an antlered critter, probably an elk, he appears to have just shot; there's a proportionally gigantic arrow piercing the animal's body (Figure 96). Two bison appear in the same panel. The hike back is through the same sandy wash.

Why Is Crow Canyon Important?

Continuity. Among the most important elements underlying the importance of Crow Canyon is cultural and historical continuity. The art at Crow Canyon reflects the traditional beliefs of a living people, the Navajo, who view Crow Canyon as the center of Dinétah, the place where their world began. Modern Navajo recognize the imagery at Crow Canyon. They recognize the image of Monster Slayer, holding his bow in one hand, a rattle in the other, and wearing his feathered headdress. They also recognize the symbol of Monster Slayer's twin, Child-of-the-Water; together they are the Hero Twins of Navajo belief. Modern Navajo also recognize the symbolism of corn plants rooted in stylized depictions of rain clouds. They also recognize the male god with a feathered hump on his back.

The imagery at Crow Canyon is not obscure or occult or shrouded by time. It represents a fairly recent point along a continuum of religious expression and belief, reflecting a connection between a modern people and their own past. When you visit Crow Canyon and gaze at the art etched into its rock walls, you are not looking at the indecipherable imagery of an extinct people. You are viewing the expression of belief by a living, vibrant people. You are looking at . . . continuity.

Additional Note

From US 64 in Blanco, New Mexico, turn south onto CR 4450 and set your trip odometer to 0. Drive south for about 3.6 miles from that intersection. Here CR 4450 curves to the right (west) onto a single-lane bridge over Largo Wash and then curves back around to the left (south), becoming CR 4990. Continue on CR 4990 for about 14 miles after crossing the Largo Wash bridge. It's a gravel road but very well maintained; there are bouncy sections and you'll kick up a lot of dust, but it's no challenge to drive it. At about 14 miles from the bridge you'll see a sign for Crow Canyon on your left. Here's where it can get dicey. You turn left at the sign and cross (east) back over Largo Wash. Most sources recommend a high-clearance four-wheel-drive vehicle to safely cross the wash. I drove over it in a high-clearance two-wheel-drive vehicle and it was fine, but you'll need to be very careful. The wash itself is narrow at the crossing, only about 200 feet across, but after a rain it becomes a soupy gumbo that you won't be able to make across without getting seriously stuck. You're in the middle of nowhere, and it's going to be absurdly expensive to get a tow truck there to get you out. You're just going to need to use your common sense when you get to this part of the drive.

Once you successfully cross the wash, you'll turn left (heading back to the north) onto a bumpy but passable dirt road. It's about 1 mile on that road (following the east margin of the wash) until you reach the fork in the road mentioned earlier. My suggestion is to follow the north (left) fork to the natural gas well pad and cul-de-sac and the parking area to the right for the Main Panel. After you've hiked that trail, return to your car and head back to the road fork. Turn left (east) and follow that dirt road to the Warrior panel and then to the trailhead to the cul-de-sac and trail to the 44 panel. The biggest issue, again, is to be very careful crossing Largo Wash. Rain and a wet wash are going to ruin your day.

Site Type: Petroglyphs

Wow Factor: **** Some of the art is incredibly impressive.

Museum: None

Ease of Road Access: ** Actually, road access is *** when dry and zero stars when wet. After a recent rain, the access road across the wash is impassable.

Ease of Hike: **** The main concentration of art panels is accessible by a very easy and relatively short hike. The hike to the 44 panel is a tiring slog through sand.

Natural Beauty of Surroundings: ****

Kid Friendly: *** Lots of room to run around, and the area is littered with cow poop. Your kids will probably think that's hilarious.

Food: Bring your own.

How to Get There: The site is accessible from US 64 in Blanco, New Mexico. For detailed directions from Blanco, see the "Additional Note" above.

Hours of Operation: There are no specific hours for Crow Canyon, but use common sense and go there during daylight hours. Arrive after sunrise; leave before sunset.

Cost: Free

Best Season to Visit: Any time, as long as it isn't raining and hasn't rained recently.

Website: https://farmingtonnm.org/listings/dinetah-rock-art-pueblitos/

Designation: Bureau of Land Management property

Site 38 Three Rivers Petroglyph Site

Tularosa, New Mexico

Journal Entry

June 19, 2014

When I began my archaeological odyssey in 2008, Three Rivers Petroglyph Site wasn't on my radar. I had never even heard of it. Years before I had visited **Petroglyph National Monument** near Albuquerque and had been pretty impressed by the extensive and beautiful rock art there. No surprise; it was, after all, a designated national monument, one of only 109 in the United States, and one of the only such sites awarded that status as a result of its ancient rock art. I returned to Petroglyph National Monument in June 2014 to conduct a more intensive site visit expressly for this book. Then I drove south to see a few more sites for this and another project. After a careful perusal of Google Earth, and in a last-minute decision, I decided to make a brief stop at another rock art location, Three Rivers Petroglyph Site. I didn't expect much. It's not in a national park, it's not listed as a national monument, nor is it listed as a national historical park. There's no museum or gift shop. It's just some Bureau of Land Management (BLM) property with a trail through it. I figured, hey, what the heck. It's not too much out of my way; it is open to the public. I might as well give it a quick look, check it off my bucket list, maybe include it here as an "honorable mention."

Ha! Three Rivers Petroglyph Site is mind-blowing, presenting about the densest concentration of astonishingly cool rock art I have seen during my journey through time. Three Rivers was so amazing that after a side trip to Carlsbad Caverns and Roswell (that's another book!), I stopped again on my way back to Albuquerque to look at more of the art. And then I returned in spring 2015. And I want to go back again. I'm obsessed.

What You Will See

The Three Rivers site, like Petroglyph National Monument, presents a ton of rock art etched into the surfaces of large volcanic boulders. The BLM surveyed the art at Three Rivers and counted more than 21,000 separate and distinct images in the rocks. A very easy trail—a not-very-steep hike up to the volcanic ridge where most of the art is located—takes you into the midst of literally thousands of examples of rock art in the most intimate setting imaginable. The art isn't up on a cliff or locked away behind a fence. It's right there, directly in front of you, mostly at eye level or below. Some of it is amazingly fresh looking as a result of the density and durability of the volcanic basalt into which it has been etched, scratched, or pecked. There are myriad geometric designs, including circles and squares with intricate internal designs and plenty of sets

Figure 97. The art seen at the Three Rivers Petroglyph Site in southern New Mexico is mind-boggling. Some of the animal depictions are realistic. Others are totally trippy, including this combination of a bird and a cloud terrace.

of parallel zigzag lines. And there are animals, so many animals: bighorn sheep, lots of different kinds of birds, insects, snakes, lizards, fish, rabbits, an aardvark, and a coyote (Figure 97). Some of the animal images are surreal. Check out Figure 98. I have no idea what the animal on the lower left is supposed to be. The same is true for the critter in the center of the boulder in Figure 99. There also are handprints and footprints etched into the rock surface. And there are people, or at least images that look like people or humanlike spirit beings. Some are portraits of people. Some are in profile. Some are full-bodied people. A couple of the humanlike images bear a strong resemblance to the Mesoamerican rain god, Tlaloc (I.24). The southern New Mexico location of Three Rivers isn't that far from the Mexican border, so it's not surprising that religious ideas and gods may have migrated north of that modern, arbitrary border.

Some of the humanlike images are anatomically explicit males; and sorry guys, they have penises at least as long as their legs. Yikes! My favorite image is iconic of the site—a beautifully rendered bighorn sheep pierced by three arrows still attached to their shafts (I.25). Like many of the animal depictions at Three Rivers, the artist depicted this wounded bighorn with an intricately carved geometric design in its body.

The style of the art is identified as belonging to the Mogollon people, one of the groups who can today be traced to the modern Hopi Indians of the region. Rock art is notoriously difficult to date,

Figure 98. Whatever the identity of the animal depicted on the lower left, it is not of this world.

Figure 99. The people who produced the images at Three Rivers were amazing artists. Here is one of thousands of images of animals, both real and imaginary, that grace the boulders located at the site.

and archaeologists usually rely on dated habitation sites near the rock art, especially if we find art of a style similar to the petroglyphs on pottery or in the form of figurines found near datable charcoal (like the Pilling Figurines I discussed earlier). On this basis, the rock art at Three Rivers has been dated to a 500-year period between AD 900 and AD 1400.

The main trail follows the top of the volcanic ridge, but you'll want to take lots of the short side trails among the boulders to see as much of the art as you can. The main trail takes you to an arched, covered shelter with benches located only about 0.5 mile from the parking lot; you'll appreciate that shelter in the heat. If you stop here and turn back to the parking lot, you will have seen a lot of the art, but not all of it. The trail continues beyond the shelter, and some of the coolest art is farther along on the trail. It's up to you, but I highly recommend continuing on and seeing as much of the art as you can.

The main trail follows the basalt ridge. But for the whole experience, you also need to walk the base of the east margin of the ridge. There's lots more art there. Figure 1 is a photograph of a petroglyph located at the base of the ridge.

Because of the context of the art, Three Rivers is an especially great place to bring kids, even pre-teens. The art is just so accessible on so many levels; much of it is at eye level or below, even for a kid. It's all over the place, secreted behind boulders, hidden around corners, and tucked away in niches; it's actually easier for a kid to reach some of the art than for an adult. Finding cool art panels and pointing them out to their parents can be a fun activity. Be aware that the igneous rock that characterize the ridge is hard and can have sharp-edged corners, so scampering around between boulders affords the potential for cuts and scrapes. With some care taken, kids can have a blast; but always remind them, no matter how cool the art looks, no touching!

Why Is Three Rivers Important?

Certainly there are lots of formal, technical reasons Three Rivers is an important site. But for me, all those reasons are embedded in the same explanation: It's all about the art. In all honesty, that reason alone is reason enough to visit this site.

Archaeologists want to be able to explain the past, to understand the cultures and even the minds of past peoples. It's in our job description; it's in our DNA. The art produced by ancient people screams out for interpretation, for explanation. Were ancient people merely documenting what they saw during their lives? Was it hunting magic, an attempt to ensure success in the hunt by capturing the spirit of the animals on a two-dimensional canvas of stone? Was it a form of worship, a way of honoring the spirits represented in the art? Were the images painted on or etched into rock surfaces all over the world in antiquity representations of hallucinations experienced by the artists as the result of ingesting psychotropic substances or just due to fasting or intentional sleep deprivation? Did they interpret what we call hallucinations as a window into another world or another reality? It is difficult to say with any certainty. Accepting that uncertainty, however, in no way detracts from how incredibly cool the art is.

I'm perfectly okay with viewing the art at Three Rivers as a result of simply the very human need to produce it. No matter what the other specific cultural reasons may be for what the artists at Three Rivers produced—and whether we will ever be able to figure those reasons out—I'm guessing that artists stepping back to view their work thought to themselves, Damn! That's good! And it's damn good that today, centuries later, we can hear the echoes of that self-review reverberating among the volcanic boulders that were the canvases of those prolific artists.

Additional Note

Let's face it; Three Rivers Petroglyph Site is in the middle of nowhere. I suppose that's one reason it's not Three Rivers Petroglyph National Monument, with a museum, gift shop, slick four-color brochure, and terrific website. No matter. It is more than worth the 3-hour trip from Albuquerque.

Site Type: Petroglyphs

Wow Factor: ***** *Amazing* is the only appropriate word for the rock art located at Three Rivers. You'll be blown away by its beauty.

Museum: None, but there is a small building where the site managers often are available for guidance.

Ease of Road Access: ****

Ease of Hike: ***

Natural Beauty of Surroundings: **** The site is located in the midst of a stark, volcanic landscape.

Kid Friendly: *****

Food: Bring your own.

How to Get There: From the north, take US 54 south from Carrizozo, New Mexico, to CR B30, which will be on your left in about 26 miles. From the other direction, drive north on US 54 from Tularosa, New Mexico, for a bit more than 17 miles. CR B30 is located on the right. A sign at the intersection of US 54 and CR B30 directs you toward the site, and there's a little store on the north side of the intersection. Once you turn east onto CR B30, you'll cross railroad tracks and it's a 5-mile drive on a paved road to the parking lot, on your left.

Hours of Operation: Open 8 a.m. to 7 p.m. April to October; 8 a.m. to 5 p.m. October to April

Cost: See website.

Best Season to Visit: It's crazy hot in southern New Mexico in summer (but it's a dry heat—like that makes it easier to take when it's 115°F). There's zero shade for most of the trail.

Website: www.blm.gov/nm/st/en/prog/recreation/las_cruces/three_rivers.html

Designation: Bureau of Land Management property

Site 39 San Juan River

Bluff, Utah

Journal Entry

August 13, 2015

From the perspective of a New Englander, steeped in our regional pride of being one of the earliest parts of the country settled by Europeans (well, English-speaking Europeans), the road sign that welcomes visitors to the town of Bluff, Utah, conveys a humbling message. In my home base in Connecticut, towns like Windsor (1633) or Farmington (1640) proudly trumpet the age of their founding. But seriously, we've got nothing on the town of Bluff. The sign says it all: "Bluff, Utah, Est. 650 AD." The town sign is a clever reminder that Europeans were not the first people in America and that some communities—Acoma Pueblo and Taos Pueblo, both in New Mexico, are other examples—have been continuously occupied since long before the migration of Europeans to the New World. When colonists settled in Saint Augustine or Jamestown or the Pilgrims arrived in Plimoth, Bluff was already an established community. Had its residents been aware of the arrival of those European settlers, they might have thought, *Well, there goes the neighborhood*. Evidence of the great time depth of Bluff's native occupation abounds in the hills and deeply incised washes around the town. You can experience much of it in your travel through time.

What You Will See

There are a number of spectacular sites in and around the town of Bluff, including a couple of impressive cliff dwellings and some truly spectacular rock art. Easiest to access is the large petroglyph panel located in Sand Island Park. There's a campground, a boat launch, and a short dirt-road drive to view the rock art. You'll see lots of images of bighorn sheep, people riding horses, and some very interesting anthropomorphs wearing elaborate headgear.

Next, but a bit more challenging, you can visit the rock art panel called "the Wolfman." Located outside of town, it is accessible from a well-maintained dirt road (no four-wheel drive is necessary) and a relatively short hike along a cairn-marked trail on an exposure of bedrock. The first short leg of the trail brings you to the lip of Butler Wash—a narrow, steep-walled valley with running water only seasonally and often only after a severe storm. A short hike along the bedrock brings you to an overlook where you can see a lovely little cliff dwelling on the other side of the wash. The walls of the wash are steep, but don't worry; you're not going down into it. Just take a couple of photos of the cliff dwelling from your vantage point on the rim of the wash; a telephoto lens and binoculars will be helpful.

Once you've viewed the cliff dwelling, walk north (to your left) to encounter the real highlight of your visit. Follow the cairns along the western margin of the wash. Trust me; the trail is only a little scary as it takes you gently, and not deeply, into the wash. There's a little bit of rock scrambling and squeezing through a couple of rocks, but nothing too severe; and for most of the hike, you're not very close to the edge of the wash. Up ahead, on a flat, dark panel of rock on your left, you'll see some truly beautiful rock art, very well preserved except for the bullet holes (idiots!). The best view is available by following a trail to a bit below the art, but you also can walk right up to it. The "Wolfman" who lends his name to the panel is pretty cool—he looks half-human, half-predator, standing upright on human feet but possessing hands with long, sharp outstretched claws, seemingly posed to attack. The other art placed in two separate panels along the cliff wall is even more impressive, with a person wearing a headdress or a feather (Figure 100) and beautifully rendered geometric shapes, one that looks for all the

Figure 100. Though this is not the Wolfman image, this beautiful art is immediately adjacent to him in Bluff, Utah.

world like a cut-open cantaloupe. Astonishing stuff—and the entire round-trip hike will take you only a little more than an hour.

Bluff also offers an immersive full-day experience along the San Juan River. Wild Rivers Expeditions is located in Bluff, and one of the trips they offer (some lasting days) is a one-day, 26-mile float from Bluff to Mexican Hat, Utah. The vast majority of the trip, taken in large inflatable rafts, is on flat water, but I should warn the squeamish among you that there are two sets of rapids. They are very brief, but the second (called 8-Foot Rapids, not because it's only 8 feet long but because of the height of the splash) got us soaking wet. But the trip is by far the easiest way to see amazing rock art—the Upper and, especially, Lower Butler Wash panels (Figure 101)—and an isolated cliff dwelling called River Ruin. The rock art is located close to the confluence of Butler Wash and the San Juan River. (The Wolfman panel is located upstream from that location.) The entire experience was great fun. The day trip includes a guided trip down the river, a number of stops and hikes, lunch, and a drive back to your car from Mexican Hat. Our guide, Greg Lameman, a young Navajo man, was extremely knowledgeable. Once he learned of our interest in seeing rock art and wild bighorn sheep, he went out of his way to accommodate us. It was a spectacular experience and I highly recommend it.

The office for Wild Rivers Expeditions is located on the south side of US 191, near the eastern edge of Bluff. They will drive you Sand Island County Park, where you'll go into the water. For more information on trips and costs, visit www.riversandruins.com.

Figure 101. The Lower Butler Wash panel of anthropomorphs wearing remarkable headdresses.

Why Is Bluff Important?

I have included Bluff, Utah, in my list of fifty sites because in a relatively small area there's just so much to see. Sure, the art, especially the Lower Butler Wash panel, is extremely impressive. But what may have been the coolest element of our stop in Bluff was our sighting of wild bighorn sheep. Among all the ancient art I've seen in my fifty-site odyssey, without a doubt the most common animal depicted by the ancient artists has been the bighorn sheep. The bighorns are impressive animals. An adult male can weigh in at 300 pounds; his horns alone can weigh as much as 30 pounds! For the first time in our odyssey, we actually saw one of them in the wild at Bluff. There's an active population of them in the hills above the San Juan River, and while there are no guarantees, it's a good bet you'll see them in your float downstream. After seeing them in the wild, it's no wonder why they were a major source of artistic inspiration for the native peoples of the Southwest.

One more thing: Just as bighorn sheep inspired lots of rock art, so did the trickster flute player Kokopelli. Though he has developed a cutesy image and you can buy lots of tacky trinkets with his depiction, Kokopelli actually was sort of a rascal. He would arrive in communities, lull everyone to sleep with his flute playing, and then have sex with the unconscious women. Think about that the next time you see a multicolored Kokopelli sticker on someone's windshield! I have seen lots of ancient Kokopelli rock art images but saw a unique version in Bluff. The anonymous artist, displaying a wonderful and whimsical sense of humor, created not just another humanlike Kokopelli but an upright, flute-playing sheep! I guess you could call him a "sheep-kopelli." You can see him in the large petroglyph panel located at Sand Island Park in Bluff (Figure 102). He's not to be missed.

Additional Note

The entrance to the Sand Island Campground is located in Bluff on the south side of US 191, a couple of miles past the center of town and before US 191 makes a sharp left turn to the south. There's a sign. Make that left into the Sand Island Campground. Before you get to the pay area and campground, there's a sign leading you to the right to the petroglyphs. To get to the Wolfman panel after you've seen the Sand Island petroglyphs, take a left back onto US 191 (west). In a little bit, US 191 makes a right-angle swing to the south (left). Instead, stay straight onto UT 163. Very shortly after that intersection of US 191 and UT 163, you'll see a road on the left that leads to the local airport. Directly across from the airport road, there's a dirt road on the right. Take that right-hand turn onto Lower Butler Wash Road. The road is unpaved but well maintained; you won't need a four-wheel-drive vehicle. There's a bit of a fork in .09 mile; curve a little to the left here. In another 0.26 mile, take the fork to the right. In 0.64 mile you'll come to a fence and a cattleguard (almost exactly a mile from where you

Figure 102. What could be cuter? Here is a bighorn sheep, standing up on his hind legs, playing the flute. He's a sheep-kopelli.

tuned off of UT 163 onto Lower Butler Wash Road). Just before the cattleguard turn left; it's a very short drive to a parking lot. From that lot you'll see three Mylar posts marking the trailhead. The trail follows the bedrock, and cairns mark the best route. Follow them to the edge of the wash in front of you and check out the cliff dwelling on the other side of the wash before turning left along the near edge of the wash to the Wolfman panel. It's a short hike.

Site Type: Petroglyphs

Wow Factor: ✴✴✴✴ The rock art you'll see in Bluff is amazing.

Museum: None

Ease of Road Access: ✴✴✴✴✴

Ease of Hike: ✴✴✴ Varies. Sand Island is easy; the Wolfman panel is moderately strenuous.

Natural Beauty of Surroundings: ✴✴✴✴✴

Kid Friendly: ✴✴✴

Food: Bring your own or eat out. I especially like the Twin Rocks Café; great food.

How to Get There: All of the rock art sites mentioned in this entry are accessible from Bluff, Utah. Bluff is located in southeastern Utah, about 120 miles south of Moab on US 191.

Hours of Operation: The Sand Island rock art is accessible during daylight hours. There are no set hours for your visit to the Wolfman panel. Obviously, daytime is best.

Check the Wild Rivers Expeditions website for their schedule. Their day trips along the San Juan start bright and early, running from 8 a.m., and should get you back to Bluff and your vehicle by 5 p.m. It's a good idea to stay the night before in Bluff.

Cost: A visit to the Sand Island petroglyphs is free. Camping there will cost you a nominal amount. A hike to the Wolfman petroglyph panel is free. If you have a high-clearance, four-wheel-drive vehicle, it is possible to get trail access to the Butler Wash rock art panels, but I highly recommend the day trip offered by Wild River Expeditions.

Best Season to Visit: It's hot in summer. No kidding.

Website: http://anasazihikes.com/Sand_Island.php; https://utahscanyoncountry.wordpress.com/2011/06/29/wolfman-petroglyph-panel-butler-wash/

Designation: Bureau of Land Management property

Site 40 **Horseshoe Canyon**

Canyonlands National Park • Utah

Journal Entry

March 22, 2014

Have you ever had the following experience? You are walking somewhere with your family, a group of friends, or perhaps a larger group of people. The folks you are with are loud and boisterous, chatting, arguing, joking, laughing, and clearly having a terrific collective time during their walk.

And then it all changes. Without any formal command it gets eerily quiet, as though you all simultaneously recognize that you are in the presence of something sacred and deserving of respectful and reverential silence. By that I do not mean that the place or thing necessarily has any specific or explicit religious meaning. Sure, it might be the arching dome of the interior of a basilica, but it also might be a stunning geological vista, a splendid and achingly beautiful sculpture, or a magnificent explosion of sunset colors. Or it may occur in the presence of a truly remarkable, exotic, alien, and mysterious work of ancient art in which we recognize the great skill of the artist, to be sure, but also the ambiguity embedded in our reaction to a creation in which we simultaneously recognize both the alien sensibilities of the artist and the essential humanity we share with him or her. And so we hush, speak only in furtive whispers, making our personal connection with the divine. This is precisely what I experienced when I encountered the phantasmagoric images secreted in an otherworldly canyon in south-central Utah.

The Great Gallery in Horseshoe Canyon isn't easy to get to; nor do I think should it be. It seems entirely appropriate to need to work some to reach it—it's about an hour's drive down a well-maintained but in some places bumpy dirt road and then a 3.5-mile trudge down and into a canyon and across its sandy bottom to reach the site—and the same hike back out and up. It's kind of a bear. Your heart will thump, especially as you climb back out when you are already exhausted from your trip down and in. But it's worth every step. The Great Gallery is the most splendid example of ancient art I encountered during my fifty-site odyssey. If your biggest bout of exercise for the day consists of getting out of the Barcalounger during a beer commercial to get some pork rinds and a Mountain Dew—and if you're truly exhausted after that Olympian feat—then maybe the hike to the Great Gallery isn't for you. But for everyone else in reasonable health, this is a place you should not miss.

What You Will See

Remember my favorite Britishism, "gobsmacked"? That term applies here in spades. You will actually see what amounts to four separate, major art galleries along the hike. These have been thoughtfully spaced out by the artists, so you'll not go too long during your journey without cool stuff to look at and ponder, beyond of course the splendid natural scenery.

1. After you reach the bottom of the canyon (there's about an 800-foot elevation drop and, unfortunately, an 800-foot climb back out at the end of your visit), you'll turn to the right (south) and after a while spot a beautiful series of red pictographs high on sheer cliff on your left (the east side of the canyon). This is High Gallery; the images are quite beautiful and well preserved, consisting of more than twenty elongated humanlike beings, perhaps spirits, most of them without arms. A telephoto lens and binoculars are a necessity, as you can't get terribly close to the images.

Figure 103. A part of the Great Gallery in Utah's Horseshoe Canyon. Though the hike to the Great Gallery is difficult, and the hike back out even more so, it was worth every step.

2. Continuing a relatively short distance, the trail crosses a stream to the west side of the canyon and you come to the second set of artworks, the Horseshoe Gallery. The gallery is in two segments, one each on either side of a large rockfall. The larger panel, on the left side of the pile of rocks, consists of beautiful images of humanlike beings, some strange unidentifiable creatures, and a couple of four-footed animals with upright, curled over tails. They look like and probably are dogs. Some of the images are a deep brick red; others are a very light red, almost pink. On the other side of the rockfall is a neat little hunting scene of a person aiming a bow and arrow at two antlered animals, likely deer or elk, and a horned critter, almost certainly a bison.

3. Keep walking south and in a bit you'll see what looks like a shallow cave, also on the west side of the canyon. This is the Alcove Gallery. This set of art is interesting but has suffered from natural weathering and vandalism (morons!). You'll still be able to see a bunch of cool images, including some more elongated beings, some of whom are sporting horns. It's not out of your way and worth a short visit.

4. Keep walking, because the artists of Horseshoe Canyon have saved the best for last. At the end of the trail you'll reach the Great Gallery. It is absolutely stunning. Hidden away in a broad overhang, beginning about 15 feet above the floor of the canyon—immediately above a stratigraphic bench on which the artists must have stood, perhaps using ladders to extend their reach—is a series of

images that will blow you away (Figure 103). Across a swath of rock wall more than 100 feet across, the ancient painters produced beautiful and positively spooky images of more than thirty larger-than-life-size humanlike spirits. All of them possess eerily elongated, armless and legless bodies, and each is otherwise unique in its appearance. One has big, googly eyes (I.26). Another has a couple of animals painted on its chest and tiny humans on its stomach (I.27). There are deep brick-red spirits, a pale white being, and images with lines and dots of black and white. There also are tiny white sheep and a few small dogs. They're all marvelous. On the day of my visit, there was a single park ranger and small handful of visitors. All of us spoke in whispers.

Why Is Horseshoe Canyon Important?

You might as well ask why the Vatican is important. Or the Dome of the Rock. Or Temple Mount. Horseshoe Canyon is important to us today for the simple reason that it was important to the fabulously talented Native American artists who produced these works as a way of showing their reverence for the divine beings who inhabited their spirit world. The artwork reflects the artistic genius of those who produced it and, almost certainly, the interior world of the ancient residents of southern Utah.

The art in Horseshoe Canyon represents the epitome of what has been labeled the Barrier Canyon style of painting that characterizes a number of sites in Utah dating to between 1,000 and 2,000 years ago. **Site 45, Sego Canyon** offers another beautiful example—smaller and certainly easier to get to—of the Barrier Canyon style. The recent dating of the site places the art during a time of great cultural change in the region, when the fundamental underpinnings of the food base were shifting from hunting and gathering wild plants and animals—note all those bighorn sheep in the Great Gallery panel—to an agriculturally based economy. It is possible that with that kind of shift and upheaval as the old ways fell to new practices and maybe new beliefs, the art of Horseshoe Canyon was intended as a form of worship to the spirits whose power was called upon to help in this momentous change in society.

It's an interesting hypothesis of course. But in the end, the most important aspect of the Horseshoe Canyon art may be that today bearers of a modern culture unimaginably different from that practiced by the ancient artists can nevertheless be moved to silence in the presence of the depictions of the spirit beings who inhabited their imagination.

Additional Note

A unit of Canyonlands National Park, Horseshoe Canyon is geographically separate. It lies to the west of the main part of Canyonlands (www.nps.gov/cany/index.htm) on a dirt road. It's generally well maintained, but expect bumps and ruts and occasional sand. A high-clearance vehicle is preferred, but the day we drove there, just about any vehicle with more clearance than a mini-car would have made the trip just fine. Take this dirt road from its intersection with UT 24 for 24.3 miles. There will be lots of side roads and turnoffs along the way. Ignore them and just follow the main dirt road. At 24.3 miles from UT 24 you'll come to an intersection on the right leading to the Hans Flat Ranger Station; there's an information kiosk at the intersection. Stay to the left (don't turn to the ranger station) and continue driving for 5.1 more miles, where you'll see a sign on the right to the Horseshoe Canyon Trailhead. Turn right and in 1.7 miles you'll reach the parking lot for the trailhead. There's a pit toilet, and you can camp right there if you like. At the end of the lot there's a sign directing you down into the canyon. From there you'll be stepping back into an amazing world of ancient art and worship.

Site Type: Pictographs

Wow Factor: ***** I'd give this place 6 stars for its "wow factor" if I could. It's simply that amazing.

Museum: None

Ease of Road Access: *** The dirt road isn't terrible, but you're better off with a high-clearance vehicle. I'm not confident a Prius or Mini Cooper would make it.

Ease of Hike: * I am tempted to lie and say the hike is fine, maybe 3 stars of easiness, just to induce you to give it a try. But you'd hate me. This hike is strenuous. It's through sand, which is exhausting, and the hike back up the 800-foot or so elevation drop is brutal. I am sorry to have to admit it, but this hike isn't for everyone.

Natural Beauty of Surroundings: ***** Arching cliffs of multicolored rock. It's gorgeous.

Kid Friendly: ****

Food: Bring your own.

How to Get There: From I-70, take exit 149 to UT 24 south. Follow UT 24 south for 25 miles to mile marker 135.5. On the left (east) side you'll see a sign for Horseshoe Canyon (32 miles). Take that left turn onto a dirt road and follow the detailed directions provided in "Additional Note."

Hours of Operation: Open year-round, 24/7

Cost: Free

Best Season to Visit: Not summer

Website: www.nps.gov/cany/planyourvisit/horseshoecanyon.htm

Designation: National Park

Site 41   Newspaper Rock State Historic Monument

Canyonlands National Park • Needles District, Utah

Journal Entry

August 12, 2015

Canyonlands is an expansive and truly beautiful national park. The opportunities for hiking are boundless, whether you are a weekend walker or a dedicated backwoodsman or woman. The eerily beautiful and evocative paintings of **Horseshoe Canyon (Site 40)** are located in a geographically separate unit of the park. As challenging (but worth the challenge) as those pictographs are to access, the large boulder called **Newspaper Rock,** with its wide array of pecked and incised petroglyphs, is easy. You drive on a paved road, you park, you walk a few feet, and the rock art is right there.

I know of at least one other ancient petroglyph panel in the United States called Newspaper Rock. That one is located in Petrified Forest National Park in Arizona. The name implies that the rocks on which the art was placed served in effect as newspapers where the makers recorded in their art important information for the viewer, information related to significant events in the history of their people. In truth, we don't know that either of those Newspaper Rocks served precisely that purpose; though in a sense, all art records information. After all, the name given the rock by the current tribe that inhabits the region, the Navajo, is *Tse' Hone*, "rock that tells a story." Whatever the precise intent of the artists, the good news rests in the fact that the practice of placing the art clustered together in a single place, on one rock face, certainly renders our visit, observation, and contemplation of the art that much more convenient. Art densely covers Newspaper Rock in Canyonlands, and it is amazing.

What You Will See

You will see an extraordinary number of incised, etched, and pecked images at Newspaper Rock (Figure 104). Across the approximately 200 square feet of the flat sandstone rock face, you will be able to see an estimated 650 distinct rock art images; that's an average of more than three images for every square foot of rock surface.

I won't give you an entire catalogue of the images, but a brief and non-exhaustive list includes:

- Human beings standing
- Human beings riding horses (one of whom has just fired an arrow at an elk)
- Bighorn sheep
- Bison
- Deer or elk
- Pronghorn antelope
- Lizards (maybe)
- Snakes
- Flying squirrels (maybe)
- Spirals
- Concentric circles
- Wheels (one of which looks a lot like a wagon wheel)
- Footprints (some look human, others like those of a bear)

Figure 104. Newspaper Rock, in the Needles District of Canyonlands National Park in Utah. Look at the bottom to see the superimposition of more-recent, fresher looking art on top of older petroglyphs.

- Apparently mythical beasts who have horns and walk on two feet
- Other geometric shapes, including dots and squiggles

As I mentioned previously, it can be very difficult to date petroglyphs. You can't apply carbon dating directly. Based on the style of the art as well as the weathering of the images themselves, it is estimated that the rock was used as an art canvass beginning a little more than 2,000 years ago and continuing until about 450 years ago (ignoring the modern graffiti). Part of the panel is a sort of palimpsest; more recent art was superimposed over older images.

Want to see some more art that few people ever visit? Drive past Newspaper Rock about 1.9 miles farther on UT 211, and park at a little pullout on the left. Below the parking pullout, there's a trail into Shay Canyon (you have to cross a small stream, but no big deal). The trail is clearly marked at first, taking you through a dry wash. Just a little past the stream, you'll be able to see art high up on the cliff face in front of you and a little to the right. One panel on a particularly dark rock is obvious once you know what you're looking for. Binoculars or a telephoto lens helps a lot. Though it looks pretty high up, the trail leading to the art panels isn't terribly difficult or scary. It's well worth the climb; there is art all along at the same level, including lots of cool images of bighorn sheep, geometrical patterns, and a bunch of Kokopellis.

Why Is Newspaper Rock Important?

The art found on Newspaper Rock, like all art of all times and places, provides a glimpse into the minds of the people who created it. Newspaper Rock is like a series of snapshots of the historical and spiritual lives of the ancient people of southern Utah. There are horseback-riding hunters. There are other animals that we know, based on the archaeological record, were hunted by the inhabitants of the region. Maybe these images were intended as sympathetic magic: By ritually "capturing" these animals in two dimensions on a rock surface, you can ensure your success in capturing the actual animals during a hunt. Beyond this, it's difficult to tell. Are the mythical creatures depicted on the rock gods or spirits? Maybe. Do the human footprints lead to a spirit world? Perhaps. Like much of the other art sites included in my fifty-site odyssey, whatever the intended meaning we can at least appreciate the art created there for its intrinsic beauty.

Site Type: Petroglyphs

Wow Factor: ★★★★ Newspaper Rock is a very dense concentration of interesting art produced over a great span of time. It's very impressive.

Museum: None

Ease of Road Access: ★★★★★

Ease of Hike: ★★★★★ The rock art is immediately adjacent to a parking lot. You can't get easier than that.

Natural Beauty of Surroundings: ★★★★★

Kid Friendly: ★★★★

Food: Bring your own.

How to Get There: Find your way to UT 211 from US 191. The closest town is Monticello, Utah. From Monticello, head north on US 191 for 14.4 miles. Turn left (west) onto UT 211 (also called the Indian Creek Scenic Byway), the main road leading to the Needles District of Canyonlands National Park. In 12.3 miles you will arrive at the parking lot for Newspaper Rock, on the right.

Hours of Operation: Open year-round, 24/7

Cost: Free

Best Season to Visit: Any time

Website: www.blm.gov/ut/st/en/prog/more/cultural/archaeology/places_to_visit/Newspaper_Rock.html

Designation: National Park

Site 42 **Buckhorn Wash**

Emery County, Utah

Journal Entry

March 21, 2014

I get it. Planet Earth has an enormous human population. The current estimate is that there are almost 7.5 billion of us needing food, water, and the other resources necessary for our survival. Let's not even get into that segment of the world's population (we know who we are!) that demands far more than subsistence—things like cars, laptops, tablets, and cell phones.

I thought about that at Buckhorn Wash when I walked the trail along the towering rock face onto which ancient Native Americans painted images of snakes, elongated spirits, and winged beings. Considering the great and growing human population, it is especially amazing to encounter rock art at places like Buckhorn Wash where you can feel utterly alone, completely isolated from the rest of the people living on the blue marble called Earth. Traffic jams, the lines at Walt Disney World, supermarket checkouts before a big storm, or the mall parking lot the week before Christmas reflect the reality of a far different time and a far different place than the beautiful and stark world of an isolated rock art site. It's exceptionally nice, I think, that places like Buckhorn Wash continue to exist on our crowded and busy planet.

What You Will See

The Buckhorn Wash art panel extends about 160 feet across the imposing, arching expanse of a flat rock face located on property administered by the Bureau of Land Management. The pictographs are about

Figure 105. Buckhorn Wash in Utah has some extraordinarily hallucinatory pictographs, including this one that includes a series of snakes, bizarrely elongated people or spirit beings, some animals that might be dogs, and a person or spirit being with wings.

Figure 106. Two of the individuals in this pictograph have wings—sprouting from their shoulders. I suppose we can't fault the name commonly applied to this panel: the Angels.

2,000 years old and reflect the Barrier Canyon art style, similar to those seen in **Site 40, Horseshoe Canyon** and **Site 45, Sego Canyon.**

The individual pictographs range in size from just a few inches high to 5 or 6 feet tall. All of the figures, like those in Sego Canyon, are shades of red. (The Horseshoe Canyon figures are primarily red, but the artists there also used black and white in their palette.)

On the far right side of the Buckhorn Wash panel, you'll see a handful of petroglyphs, a pretty cool bighorn sheep, and what looks like a man riding on the back of deer or elk. Check those out for sure, but the real draw here is the paintings.

The panel is covered with otherworldly images of elongated anthropomorphs. Unlike most of the Horseshoe Canyon and Sego Canyon figures, many of the Butler Wash beings have arms and legs. Some appear to be holding snakes or encountering or standing next to snakes. In one panel there are six extremely elongated beings with no arms, very short legs, and little feet (Figure 105). There also are a handful of sheep painted on the rock wall and another four-footed critter, a small mammal of some sort, but it's standing up on its back legs. In one section of the panel, the ancient artists painted images of two humanlike beings that have what appear to be wings growing out of their shoulders. In another panel, a smaller two-legged figure also has wings; his are unfurled (Figure 106).

Are the winged figures actually spirit beings who are an amalgam of human and bird? Are the images depicting people wearing capes intended to look like the wings of a bird? For those of you reading this and thinking, *Wow, that sounds like angels in medieval art*, well, only sort of. The wings don't originate from the backs of these beings but the tips of their shoulders. And the winged figures at Buckhorn Wash don't have arms.

Why Is Buckhorn Wash Important?

The Buckhorn Wash panel is a very nice example of Barrier Canyon pictographic art. It's well pre-served, with only a little bit of vandalism apparent. It is difficult to figure out the precise intent of the artists. Are the images intended to be spirit beings? Were the images supposed to represent visions expe-rienced by the artist during a fast or after ingesting a hallucinogenic substance? No one actually knows for sure. I will tell you one thing: If anywhere in the artists' purpose they wished to impress the hell out of people years after they painted them, mission accomplished.

Additional Note

The site is accessible from Buckhorn Draw Road, a well-maintained dirt road; but if it recently rained a lot, all bets are off. Once you get onto Buckhorn Draw Road from I-70, you'll travel in an easterly direction for a bit; but soon, in about 3 miles, the road will curve to the north. Follow the main road, Buckhorn Draw (on some maps the name changes to Cottonwood Road), for 15 or 16 miles until you reach a campground and a large bridge over the San Rafael River. Cross the bridge and follow the road for about 4 more miles until you reach the Buckhorn Wash rock art site. It will be on your right; there's a parking lot, a pit toilet, and ample signage. As long as you stay on the main road after leaving the interstate, you should be able to find the site.

You can find your way back to I-70 by retracing your steps south, or you can continue north (and then west) on Buckhorn Wash Road until you reach a T intersection with Green River Cutoff Road (UT 401). Turn left there to get to the town of Castledale. It's a long haul, but the road is fairly well maintained, and as long as you continue on the main road you'll get to Castledale. As with many of these out-of-the-way places, your GPS should work fine, but you likely won't be able to use whatever mapping app you use on your cell phone or tablet.

Site Type: Pictographs, petroglyphs
Wow Factor: ****
Museum: None
Ease of Road Access: **
Ease of Hike: ***** The parking lot is adjacent to the rock art.
Natural Beauty of Surroundings: ****
Kid Friendly: ***
Food: Bring your own.
How to Get There: Begin in Green River, Utah, and drive west on I-70 for about 29 miles. Take exit 131 onto Buckhorn Draw Road. For detailed directions, see the "Additional Note" for this site entry.
Hours of Operation: Open year-round, 24/7
Cost: Free
Best Season to Visit: Any time. As long as it hasn't rained recently and isn't raining, the roads will be fine. There's no hiking to do, so heat shouldn't be a problem.
Website: www.blm.gov/ut/st/en/prog/more/cultural/archaeology/places_to_visit/Buckhorn_Wash.html
Designation: Bureau of Land Management property; National Register of Historic Places

Site 43 Moab, Utah

Journal Entry

March 20, 2014

Arches National Park in Moab, Utah, is a gorgeous place with an amazing concentration of ethereally beautiful natural stone arches. If you've never seen Delicate Arch, arguably the most remarkable geological feature in the park, you can find its iconic image on Utah's license plates. And I definitely remember one of the *Star Wars* movies having Delicate Arch as a feature on another planet, I think one with two moons visible in the sky above the arch. Having seen Delicate Arch in person, I remember reacting to that scene in the movie: "Well, that makes sense." The landscape at Arches definitely looks as though it's on a planet other than Earth. Tatooine seems a perfectly reasonable place to find Delicate Arch.

Along with the remarkable beauty of the arches, the area has some quite impressive rock art. So this "site" in my fifty-site odyssey isn't a single location. The art is scattered in a number of places around Moab, the town in which Arches National Monument is located.

What You Will See

Wolfe Ranch

There actually is a very cool petroglyph panel inside the park. Adjacent to the parking lot for the trail to Delicate Arch is historic Wolfe Ranch. The old ranch house is still standing, and a very short trail to the north brings you to a deep brown vertical sandstone slab with a series of petroglyphs. The art depicts four men on horseback, which places the artwork sometime after AD 1540, when the Spanish invaders introduced the horse to the American Southwest. The men on horses appear to be hunting at least six bighorn sheep. The panel also shows a few more animals that look like dogs being used in the hunt.

Courthouse Wash

Outside the park is a very impressive Barrier Canyon–style pictograph, estimated to be at least 2,000 years old. The images include a bunch of anthropomorphs rendered in shades of red and white with elongated bodies—some with arms, some without; some with legs, some without. The art is spread out across an expanse of rock about 50 feet in length and 20 feet high. Most of the humanlike beings have elaborate headdresses, and there are a couple of what appear to be large white shields floating near those figures. It's a little bit of a climb up to the panel, but well worth it. There's a parking lot located about 0.5 mile from the west end of the bridge over the Colorado River on US 191. From the parking lot, take the paved Moab Canyon Pathway back toward the Colorado River. After passing over Courthouse Wash, you should be able to see the art if you look a bit to the left (northeast), up toward the top of the cliff. As a result of vandalism, the colors of the pictograph are somewhat muted, but if you basically walk upslope following the rock cairns you'll reach a location where you can take pretty decent photographs of the art. The hike from the parking lot is about 0.5 mile. If you want, with a combination of hiking and a little bit of rock scrambling—nothing terribly radical or scary—you can make your way right up to the art.

Potash Road (UT 279)

Continuing north and west on US 191, turn left (south) onto UT 279/Potash Rd. In about 5 miles you'll come to the first of three car pullouts to the left (east) side of the road, with a large number of petroglyphs on the right (west) side of the road (on the dark cliff face). The area is signed "Indian

Figure 107. The area around Moab, Utah, has an abundance of fantastic rock art. I simply love this wonderful 4-foot-long bear petroglyph. Those two proportionally tiny hunters with miniature bows and arrows don't appear to stand a chance.

Writing." Look about 20 to 30 feet up the cliff across a distance of about 100 feet north and south. You'll see lots of anthropomorphs, sheep, a bunch of people holding hands, and what appear to be tally marks. Though the rock varnish isn't particularly dark and, as a result, the images don't pop, they are pretty impressive. Next, continue up about a couple hundred feet to my favorite of the petroglyphs on Potash Road. Pull over into a cutout on the left and look upslope across the road to the west to view an impressive and rare bear petroglyph (Figure 107). It's about 4 feet long from snout to butt, and it's really quite lovely. The panel also shows a couple of bow hunters, tiny in comparison to the bear, shooting at him, and also three bighorn sheep. Drive about 0.75 mile beyond the bear and you'll reach a parking lot, this one on the right, at the entrance to the Poison Spider Trail (that name might not inspire your desire to walk there). From the north end of the lot you can see a petroglyph panel located upslope about 50 feet and to the northwest of the car park. There are lots of critters in the panel, as well as what look like conjoined "paper doll" figures. You're not done. Now drive another 7.5 miles farther down Potash Road, where you'll find a parking lot on the right for the Jug Handle Arch. If you stop right at the entrance of the lot—before you can even see the arch that, indeed, looks like a jug handle—and gaze about a third of the way up the slope, you'll see a nice little panel of art. Binoculars and a telephoto lens are a must here.

Moon Flower Canyon/Kane Creek Boulevard

From the middle of Moab on US 191, turn onto Kane Creek Boulevard. In about 3 miles you'll begin to see rock art—nothing spectacular, but it's fun trying to find it all. You'll see more on the left in another 1.2 miles. In another 1.7 miles, part of it on a dirt road, you'll see the coolest images on a separate boulder located below road level on the right. It's an image called the "Birthing Scene," and it sure does look like a woman giving birth (Figure 108). Well, giving birth to a watermelon.

Moab Man

If you're in Moab, you don't want to miss Moab Man. He's the town icon and really quite a handsome little guy (Figure 109). Just a short drive from the center of Moab, he, or maybe he's a she, is wearing dangling earrings and an antler headdress. Oh, and he appears to be waving. He looks like a nice guy. From US 191, the main drag in Moab, turn onto Spanish Trail Road. In a bit you'll come to a little rotary. At the rotary, stay on Spanish Trail Road, which ends shortly as it curves around to the right onto Westwater Drive about 1 mile from where you turned off US 191. Follow Westwater. You will be in a residential neighborhood, but you're in the right place. Drive 0.5 mile farther until you see the dark sandstone block with Moab Man and a bunch of other art in front of you. There's a small parking area in front of the rock. Take a look at the dog glyph. It looks as though he's gleefully hopping. He reminds me of Odie, the dog in the *Garfield* comic strip and cartoons.

Why Is the Moab Area Rock Art Important?

We've already encountered instances of vandalism in our fifty-site odyssey. Usually this occurs in the form of modern graffiti, where some idiots decided it would be fun to add their own "art" to the ancient examples. It's awful, to be sure, but this level of disrespect for history and culture pales in comparison to what happened to the Courthouse Wash pictographs. When you see them today, you will encounter a pale reflection of what they looked like even just a little more than thirty-five years ago. The art was severely damaged by a hideously savage attack by vandals in 1980. This was not an instance where modern thugs merely wrote over the ancient art. These dirtbags essentially attempted to erase the panel using a wire brush and an abrasive substance. I cannot imagine what inspired this level of disrespect. What could possibly engender that level of hatred? How did any human being decide that it was acceptable to plan and carry out an attack on art? What happened at Courthouse Wash is the equivalent of someone today entering

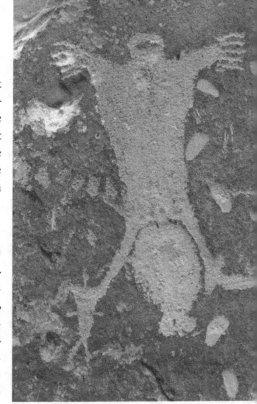

Figure 108. This one is called the Birthing Panel. You're on your own explaining what the image depicts to your kids.

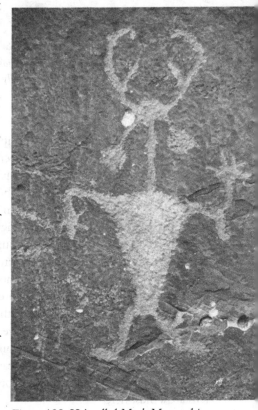

Figure 109. He's called Moab Man and is sort of the mascot for the town of Moab.

a cathedral, synagogue, or mosque and attacking a painting, sculpture, or stained-glass window to make, what? A political statement? It is incomprehensible.

Once the damage was discovered, the National Park Service did what they could to refurbish and stabilize the art. It does look better now than it did immediately after the assault, but the colors are muted. Ultimately, the vandals lost. The art still exists, and I encourage you to take the time to visit it in its current glory and think about the malicious capabilities of our species, but only briefly. Spend most of your time at Courthouse Wash contemplating the sublime nature of the art.

Site Type: Petroglyphs, pictographs

Wow Factor: **** There's a broad array of art in the locations mentioned above.

Museum: None

Ease of Road Access: *** Access to some of the art is via dirt road.

Ease of Hike: ****

Natural Beauty of Surroundings: *****

Kid Friendly: ***

Food: There are lots of food choices in Moab, from fancy dining to fast food—even Chinese food priced by the scoop. Seriously.

How to Get There: Moab is your base of operations for trips to the rock art locations mentioned above. To get to Moab from I-70, head south on US 191. From Flagstaff, Arizona, head north on US 89 to US 160. Continue east on US 160 until you hit US 191; follow US 191 north toward Moab. Follow the directions provided in the descriptions of each art location above.

Hours of Operation: The Moab-area rock art is essentially open year-round, 24/7. Of course it is best to see the art in daylight.

Cost: Mostly free. The Wolfe Ranch petroglyphs are located in Arches National Park, so you'll need to pay the park entry fee to access them (see www.nps.gov/arch/index.htm).

Best Season to Visit: It's Utah; summers are hot. Moab is extremely crowded in summer; if you don't like crowds, summer might not be your best choice.

Website: www.discovermoab.com/rockart.htm

Designation: National Park; Bureau of Land Management property

Site 44   Nine Mile Canyon

Price, Utah

Journal Entry

August 12, 2015

There's a melancholy that accompanies a trip through Nine Mile Canyon, a constant reminder of the ephemeral character of our lives. Along the road you'll see a number of abandoned, decaying farmsteads of the Mormon settlers who created their own hardscrabble world there in the late nineteenth and early twentieth centuries. That nearly self-contained world is utterly gone now. The homes where people lived and loved, nurtured children, celebrated holidays and victories, and grieved losses are now hollow shells, ironically beautiful ruins in a constant process of decay and descent into oblivion. Underlying that layer of a lost world rests another, more ancient world whose people have left phantoms of their existence in the form of stone granaries, foundations, and, most significantly, in the brilliant art left behind on the walls of the canyon that demarcated the boundaries of their homeland. Today we can peer back at that lost world, as the Bible phrases it, "through a glass, darkly," by visiting and engaging with that art. Nine Mile Canyon affords the visitor a journey through time, a journey that is well worth taking.

What You Will See

I have found a number of sources that cite 10,000 as the number of individual artistic depictions in Nine Mile Canyon; I won't argue with that (I.28). There are certainly thousands upon thousands of

Figure 110. Appropriately called "the longest art gallery in the world," Nine Mile Canyon in Utah boasts an incredible portfolio of fantastic art. This is the well-known Sand Hill Crane panel. The two cranes facing one another are at the top of the panel.

petroglyphs and a lesser number of pictographs scattered across the 40 miles of the main (Nine Mile) and side canyons, including Cottonwood, Daddy, Dry and Gate Canyons (Figure 110).

I suppose you could appreciate at least some of the art in a drive-by "windshield survey." You know what I mean: Stay in your car, driving slowly while you scan the cliff wall that demarcates the north side of the canyon. But where's the fun in that? I will list the primary places where you should pull over, get out of your car, and walk to a better vantage point for observation and photography, but this is only a very brief and not exhaustive list. The most fun is driving through the canyon with your kids and having them find the art so you can pull over for a better look.

A cardinal rule for enjoying Nine Mile is predicated on your acceptance of the fact that, as is the case at **Site 38, Three Rivers,** you are not going to see every piece of art. There's just too much of it, some of it is hidden away on isolated rock faces, and much of it is located high on the cliff. Binoculars and a telephoto lens will make your encounter with the art at Nine Mile far more satisfying. But don't be obsessive about it. Anything you miss will only inspire a subsequent visit. At least that's what I tell myself about the Owl panel I was unable to find somewhere up Dry Canyon. Damn!

Your best bet is to enter the canyon from Price, Utah. Turn onto Soldier Creek Road (there's a travel stop right there; fill your tank and get snacks and lots of water). Soldier Creek Road becomes Nine Mile Canyon Road. Once you turn onto Soldier Creek Road, zero your odometer and drive about 23.3 miles to an abandoned historic house on the left (north) side of the road. Now, on to the art (all mileage is approximate; if you just continue searching the north side of the canyon, you'll see tons of art):

1. **26.6 miles.** Encounter the first petroglyph panel. There's a little bit of a pull-off, and the art is marked by a wooden fence (on the left).

2. **31.2 miles.** There's another significant cluster of art on the left side.

3. **33.8 miles.** At a dirt road to the right, signed "Harmon Canyon," you'll see petroglyphs all over the rock face on the left.

4. **35.3 miles.** Lots more rock art on the left; look for a big snake image. Very cool.

Figure 111. A pictograph of an elk thoughtlessly vandalized by the former landowner.

5. **38.5 miles.** The road on the left goes through Gate Canyon. Keep straight on Nine Mile Canyon Road.

6. **38.8 miles.** Just past the cattleguard, look up on the left to see, you guessed it, more rock art.

7. **44.0 miles.** On the left is Rasmussen Cave. Definitely pull over and hike to the cave, where you'll see a bunch of very cool pictographs—a nice break from the thousands of petroglyphs you've been seeing! Here you will also see a reflection of the sheer stupidity and mendacity our species is capable of: a magnificent pictograph effectively destroyed by the previous property owner (Figure 111).

8. **45.1 miles.** Bear right at the fork onto Cottonwood Canyon Road. After the turn, pull over and look in front of you and to your left, where you'll see an imposing rock outcrop. Looking up to about three-quarters of the way to the top, you'll be able to see a small, dark, flat rectangle of rock. Get out your binoculars or telephoto lens and have a look. It's a little bit of a challenge, but you'll find it. It's no wonder people have called this the Santa Claus panel. And check out his reindeer (Figure 112).

9. Continue down the paved road in Cottonwood Canyon; very shortly you'll see a sign on the right for the Big Bison panel. Leave your vehicle here and follow the trail on the left side of the road for an encounter with a large bison petroglyph and then, a little farther on the trail (to the left and past a barbed wire fence), what appears to be a pregnant bison; you can see the image of a baby inside the mother.

Figure 112. You would not be the first person to see Santa and his reindeer in this art, located ridiculously high on a cliff in Nine Mile Canyon. I get dizzy just thinking about its location and the dangerous position the artist had to take in order to produce this piece of art.

10. Return to your car and drive a little farther to a parking lot on the right side. The very short trail that begins here is well signed, bringing you to a large, astonishing petroglyph panel with more than thirty bighorn sheep; some are babies, and each sheep is connected by an etched line to the sheep in front of it (Figure 113). The art is called the Great Hunt panel for a reason: There are images of four hunters, each one aiming a bow and arrow at the sheep. There's also a large horned anthropomorph and some other images I can't explain, including one that looks like a dome-topped barbecue grill and another that looks like a gas pump. If you see nothing else during your sojourn to Nine Mile (technically, Cottonwood) Canyon, see the Great Hunt panel.

11. Turn back to the intersection of Cottonwood Canyon and Nine Mile Canyon Roads. Zero out your odometer and make a right turn. Drive 2.4 miles to some more petroglyphs on your left.

12. Turn around at this point and head back the way you came on Nine Mile Canyon Road. When you reach the road to Daddy Canyon (there's a corral located there), stop and look up at the cliff on the north side. You'll see more, what else, petroglyphs.

13. Turn around and drive back out of the canyon, leaving it where you entered, near Price, Utah. Keep your eyes open for more art, now on your right. I can virtually guarantee you'll see petroglyphs you missed coming in from the other direction.

Nine Mile Canyon is an amazing place, and you'll see far more than I could possibly summarize here. Mind-blowing!

Figure 113. The Great Hunt panel at Nine Mile Canyon (it's actually a short drive down Cottonwood Canyon from Nine Mile) is one of the most famous—and most amazing—petroglyph panels in the world. It appears to tell the story of a hunt of bighorn sheep by four hunters wielding bows and arrows.

Why Is Nine Mile Canyon Important?

Nine Mile is an amazing place. Most of the art style reflects the Fremont Culture we've encountered previously and dates to about 1,000 years ago. There are lots of bighorn sheep and humanlike images with broad shoulders and narrow waists. The 40-mile stretch of canyon with its naturally stained and varnished surfaces provided a perfect canvas for ancient artists, and they came back again and again to leave their creative and imaginative images on the walls that marked the boundaries of the canyon.

Nine Mile Canyon is also important for the other evidence of use left behind by the artists. There are the ruins of at least one village in the canyon; you can see them up on the ridge at the intersection of Cottonwood Canyon and Nine Mile Canyon Roads. In a number of places you can also see ancient granaries, where the creators of the art stored their corn.

Additional Note

Once you turn onto Soldier Pass Road in Price, Utah, it becomes Nine Mile Canyon Road and will take you directly into Nine Mile Canyon. Keep on that road at all intersections or forks. After you turn onto Soldier Pass Road in Price, in about 21.6 miles you'll drive over a little bridge over Minnie Maude Creek. At 23.3 miles you'll see an abandoned homestead. Nine Mile Ranch is at 24 miles. At 26.6 miles you'll come to the first set of petroglyphs listed above. From there, follow the directions already provided for your tour of this amazing place.

Site Type: Petroglyphs, pictographs

Wow Factor: ***** In terms of both the quality and quantity of the art, Nine Mile Canyon is 5 stars from start to finish.

Museum: None

Ease of Road Access: *****

Ease of Hike: ***** Most of the art is viewable from the road; you won't have to do much hiking. A lot of the art is on private land, and you can't walk up to it.

Natural Beauty of Surroundings: *****

Kid Friendly: *** Your kids will be stuck in the car for much of the experience.

Food: Bring your own.

How to Get There: From US 6/191 (East Main Street) in Price, Utah, turn onto Soldier Pass Road (N2200E). From the west, make a left; from the east, make a sharp right. There's a gas station at the intersection. Zero your odometer in order to follow the specific directions provided above.

Hours of Operation: Open year-round, 24/7

Cost: Free

Best Season to Visit: It snows here in winter; it's hot in summer. What else is new?

Website: http://climb-utah.com/Misc/ninemile.htm

Designation: Private land; Bureau of Land Management property

Site 45 Sego Canyon

Thompson Springs, Utah

Journal Entry

March 23, 2014

Thompson Springs, Utah, is the town that time—and the railroad—forgot. In fact, the trains ceased stopping there in 1996. In the 2010 federal census, the town's population was listed as 39, and I'm guessing even that was an exaggeration. When I passed through Thompson Springs in 2014, it appeared that most of even those 39 had bailed on the place. The place today looks like a ghost town, or at least well on its way to becoming one. Coincidentally, north of Thompson Springs there is a real ghost town, an abandoned coal mining community in Sego Canyon where you can see an old cemetery, the remnants of mining shacks, the standing walls of a few abandoned buildings, and some very cool bits of an elevated wooden trestle for transporting the mined coal. Driving north on a well-maintained dirt road, just about 3.5 miles from the husk of Thompson Springs and before the ghost town, which is itself definitely worth checking out, you will encounter a fascinating trifecta of rock art panels. They are not to be missed.

What You Will See

Paiute Pictographs

You'll be able to see the rock art from the road (on both sides) as soon as you reach the parking area on the left (there's a pit toilet there too). When you pull into the parking lot, you will be facing west (looking perpendicular to the road you took to the site). Right in front of you is the first art panel, consisting of a series of beautiful pictographs on a light tan rock surface. Painted in flourishes of brick red and white, there are depictions of a couple of bison, a bighorn sheep, a couple of humanlike images, two of what appear to be impressive circular shields (one of which looks like a Lifesaver and is very beautiful) and, significantly, three images of men riding horses. As noted previously, there were no horses in North America before the Spanish arrived in the sixteenth century. There were horses in North America prehistorically, but they became extinct about 10,000 years ago. America's first settlers didn't ride horses; they ate them. Some of the Spanish horses escaped their encampments and became feral. Indians, having seen the Spanish ride horses to great effect, captured some from the growing herds of escaped animals and developed their own brand of equestrianism. So this depiction of men on horses postdates the arrival of Europeans in the region. The Paiute tribe inhabited the region around Thompson Springs historically, and they are credited with this art panel; it is figured that all the art of this panel dates to after AD 1300.

Fremont Petroglyphs

Still in the parking lot, turn 90 degrees to the right and face north. Directly in front and above you, you'll see a broad, vertical, quite dark rock surface covered with at least six anthropomorphs in the typical Fremont style (Figure 114). Two of them are exceptionally well preserved and beautiful: broad-shouldered, narrow waisted, without arms or legs, and wearing neck ornaments. Both of them are wearing headdresses with what appears to be feathers sticking up from the middle. There also are a few

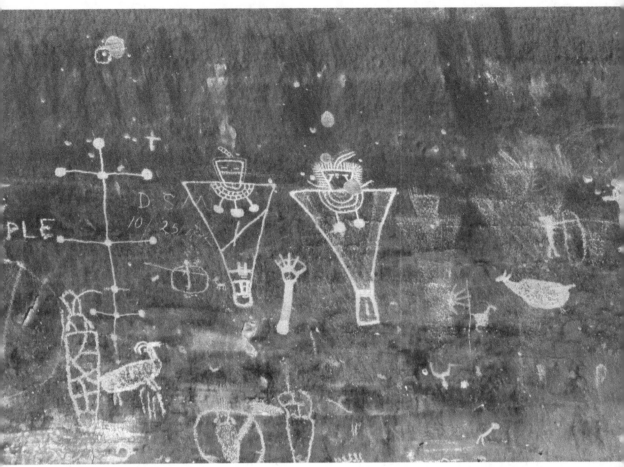

Figure 114. Sego Canyon in Utah presents the visitor with three incredible, spatially separate art panels. Here Fremont-style anthropomorphs adorn a rock wall.

bighorn sheep, one of which is being shot by a bow-wielding hunter; a broad-tailed critter that might be a beaver; a disembodied arm and hand; and some geometric patterns etched into the dark-surfaced rock face. It's altogether a very sweet Fremont art panel.

Barrier Canyon Pictographs

Walk past the Fremont art, walk to the right of that panel and turn left, and you'll encounter the coolest art in Sego Canyon: absolutely stunning Barrier Canyon pictographs of elongated, armless and legless anthropomorphs sporting horns and possessing large, circular, and hollow eye sockets (I.29). I admit it; they look very spooky and alien, not in a silly extraterrestrial sense, but in a spiritual, otherworldly way. There are more than twenty of them, all casting their eerie gaze down on their visitors. Very, very beautiful. *Phantasmagoric* is the best word to describe them. Now turn around and face east, across the dirt road. There you'll see another set of Barrier Canyon pictographs, including larger-than-life-size humanlike images. You can walk over and see them up close unless, as we experienced briefly, real cowboys are herding cattle into the pen that abuts the rock art.

Before my odyssey, I had never heard of the Sego Canyon art. I encountered it entirely fortuitously, essentially on a last-minute whim. I was in the area, traveling west on the interstate, realized the art was just a few minutes away, and gave it a shot. I am very glad I did.

Why Is Sego Canyon Important?

One of the things I found most compelling about Sego Canyon, beyond the sheer beauty of the artwork, especially the Barrier Canyon pictographs, was the fact that three temporally and culturally distinct groups of people elected to situate their art in essentially the same location. I also found it extremely telling how each group—beginning with the folks who produced the Barrier Canyon pictographs, next the creators of the Fremont petroglyphs, and then the Paiute painters—elected to honor and respect the artwork of those who preceded them, leaving the older images untouched and intact. There is no Fremont graffiti on the Barrier Canyon art and no Paiute graffiti overlaying or on the same panels with either the Fremont or Barrier Canyon art. That fact really struck me when I compared that respect to the supreme lack of respect and thought exhibited by more recent, Euro-American settlers of the area. There is English writing all over the Paiute art, Fremont petroglyphs, and Barrier Canyon art across the road, where it can readily be reached by vandals. Some people call these markings "gringo glyphs," and their existence flat out sucks. Thankfully the idiots who marked up the art weren't ambitious and didn't climb too high up the rock wall. At least the really impressive Barrier Canyon work shows less graffiti, and I didn't notice any high up among the most remarkable images.

Modern people can be thoughtless (shame on you, George Whipple; even in 1887 you should have known better). And, no surprise, they also can be pretty silly. On a recent trip to New Mexico, just for giggles we visited Roswell and stopped at the International UFO Museum and Research Center. When we arrived, the folks at the museum were concerned about a tour bus that was late arriving. When I suggested that, just maybe, they had been abducted by aliens, the woman at the ticket counter responded, without any recognition that I was joking: "No, no. They probably just got stuck in traffic." Sure. That's what they want you to believe.

Anyway, in one of the museum's displays there is a series of photographs of rock art. And wouldn't you know it? There in the middle of the display are ancient images from the Southwest that, it is suggested, just may be representations by local people of extraterrestrial visitors to Earth in antiquity! And yup; of the ten photos or prints presented in support of this hypothesis, three are of the Barrier Canyon pictographs in Sego Canyon. If that hypothesis is upheld, and the art accurately depicts them, the extraterrestrials apparently have no arms—or legs. Please! Let's accord ancient artists the simply courtesy we give their modern cohorts: Credit them for their artistry, creativity, and imagination. The Sego Canyon art provides testimony to the exhilaratingly diverse character of the human imagination. Space aliens need not apply.

Additional Note

If you continue past the art on the same road, now dirt, for about 0.5 mile, there's a fork in the road. Bear right at the fork and you'll immediately see a small cemetery to the right. That's the Sego Canyon Cemetery. Follow that road and you'll soon come to a large stone ruin. You're now in the ghost town. Continue on that road to the remnants of shacks, sheds, and pieces of the coal cart trestle. It's worth a look.

Site Type: Pictographs, petroglyphs
Wow Factor: **** All the art is impressive, but the Barrier Canyon–style pictographs are gorgeous and otherworldly.
Museum: None
Ease of Road Access: *****
Ease of Hike: *****
Natural Beauty of Surroundings: ****
Kid Friendly: ***** Kids will likely think the art is cool, but if you continue on the road to the ghost town, they'll love it.
Food: Bring your own.
How to Get There: Heading east or west on I-70, take exit 187 to UT 94 north (which becomes BLM 159 and then Sego Canyon Road) through Thompson Springs. You'll soon see a sign that says "Indian Writing" and in about 3 miles see a parking lot on the left.
Hours of Operation: Open year-round, 24/7. The Bureau of Land Management administers the property; there is no gate to enter the site.
Cost: Free
Best Season to Visit: Any time. There is no hiking involved, so even the summer heat shouldn't stress you too much.
Website: www.blm.gov/ut/st/en/prog/more/cultural/archaeology/places_to_visit/sego_canyon.html
Designation: Bureau of Land Management property

Site 46 McConkie Ranch

Vernal, Utah

Journal Entry

March 2014

The first thing I saw while driving through a light flurry of snow on the road into the McConkie Ranch property on a cool March morning wasn't anything archaeological. Nope, the first things I encountered were two beautiful mule deer, one an adult buck with a large antler rack and the other a young female. Spooked by the noise of my car, the two deer ran parallel to the road, came to a fence, and then both sailed over in an incredibly graceful, synchronized leap. They seemed to defy gravity, almost floating in slow motion as they arched over the fence. Very cool. It was a very sweet welcome to a truly remarkable rock art site.

What You Will See

I can't guarantee that you will see wildlife during your visit, but you will certainly see a ton of impressive rock art during your hikes at McConkie Ranch, at least one of which may be a depiction of a deer, or maybe an elk. Most of what you will see are beautiful, some even spectacular, examples of Fremont Culture petroglyphs, including lots of humanlike images with the standard wide shoulders and narrow waists (Figure 115). Some of these anthropomorphs are sporting headdresses with what appear to be antlers; others exhibit a variety of other decorations. There also are a bunch of fascinating and rare examples of Fremont-style petroglyph/pictograph combinations. In these cases, the artists pecked or carved images onto the flat expanse of the sandstone cliff face and then painted red and white pigmented flourishes onto those images. For example, at McConkie you'll see what looks like a bull's-eye scratched into the cliff, replete with an arrow striking into it at nearly dead center, with a painted red ring around the circumference. In a few other instances, the artists produced petroglyphs of humanlike beings wearing painted hats or carrying painted tools or weapons of some kind.

There are two primary trails at McConkie. The Main Trail is accessible from the parking lot and is less than 1 mile round-trip. It trends uphill toward the base of the cliff and curves to the left. There is quite a lot of impressive art located along the cliff. It starts slow and sort of mundane, but it gets extremely impressive as you hike along the trail. The highlight of the McConkie art is the anthropomorphic beings that adorn the walls. At the end of the trail, turn around and head back to the parking lot. From there you should head to the Three Kings Trail. Walk out of the lot and go left, at first following McConkie Road. It's a little weird because this takes you to a stile over a fence. Climb over and follow the vague trail through a field. A couple of times along the way, I really wondered if I was going right, but there are no side trails to sidetrack you. Just keep walking the track on which you started. Eventually a sign will direct you to turn left, back toward the cliff, to an abundance of exceptionally cool rock art with lots of clusters of anthropomorphs, saving the best for the end. At trail's end (it's marked) look up and in front of you. It's a little hard to see at first glance, but high up on the cliff there's an absolutely spectacular combined petroglyph/pictograph panel. It's gorgeous. The panel is called the Three Kings, though I count six humanlike figures (I.30). The largest is in the center, and he does appear to be wearing a crown. He is surrounded by spirals and is holding a large shield in his right hand. The art is big and far away; you'll want binoculars and a telephoto lens

Figure 115. Example of infrequently seen painted petroglyphs. There are several of them at the McKonkie Ranch rock art site.

for the best view and decent photographs. I can't imagine an artist getting that high on the cliff to produce the art. But there it is.

Why Is McConkie Ranch Important?

Nearly all the sites I visited during my odyssey have been preserved and are open to the public as a result of action taken by the federal or assorted state governments. In most cases the land on which the mound, cliff dwelling, great house, rock art, or monument is located has been set aside as part of a national park, national forest, national monument, national historical monument, Bureau of Land Management property, or state park. As such, these places are legally protected against development, alteration, and vandalism. In some cases, the sites are highlighted with signage, and there may even be an on-site museum.

McConkie Ranch is not in this category. The beautiful, impressive, significant, and enormous quantity of rock art on the McConkie Ranch has been preserved—and is open for public appreciation—not as the result of government action or funding. McConkie Ranch is a privately owned, working ranch. Generations of the ranch's owners, however, have been well aware of the beauty and significance of the ancient rock art on their property and have made it a point to protect and preserve that historical legacy. Further, they have opened up their ranch for the public appreciation of that art. There is a parking lot and two well-marked and maintained primary trails, all to make it easy for visitors to encounter the rock art left on the steep sandstone walls of the canyon. That's incredibly generous of the folks who own the property, whose livelihood is wholly unrelated to the rock art. They ask only that visitors stay on the trails and respect the art; don't add anything to the existing art and don't touch it. There is a special place in heaven for folks with such a deep appreciation for the spectacular artistic legacy of the ancient inhabitants of what became McConkie Ranch. Kudos to them.

So sure, McConkie Ranch is important because the art is beautiful and impressive. And sure McConkie Ranch is important because you'll see some rare examples of art that combines elements of both petroglyphs and pictographs. But an equally important aspect of McConkie Ranch is the fact that it exemplifies how one family can make a difference in the preservation and protection of our nation's historic legacy.

Site Type: Petroglyphs, pictographs

Wow Factor: **** Much of the art is fantastic.

Museum: None

Ease of Road Access: *****

Ease of Hike: ****

Natural Beauty of Surroundings: ****

Kid Friendly: ****

Food: There's a little shed by the parking lot where you can buy drinks and snacks.

How to Get There: From the center of Vernal, Utah, head west on UT 121, also known as W 500 N to the town of Maeser. Turn right (north) onto the road posted as N 3500 W. After turning, in a little more than 6 miles you'll reach the intersection with McConkie Road, on the right. There is a sign for "Indian Petroglyphs." Turn right here and in about 0.5 mile you'll reach the parking lot, on the left.

Hours of Operation: Open every day, dawn to dusk

Cost: The owners ask for a small donation. It's fantastic that they open their property to hikers and maintain the trails. Please leave them a few bucks.

Best Season to Visit: I went in March; it was snowing. Summer will be hot, but not always unbearable. Fall and spring are good choices.

Website: www.utahoutdooractivities.com/dryfork.html

Designation: Private property

Site 47 Dinosaur National Monument

Vernal, Utah

Journal Entry

March 19, 2014

Alright, I admit it; I was a weird little kid. While all my friends aspired to enter the usual professions that fascinate little kids—baseball player, firefighter, doctor, rock singer, accountant (okay, maybe not accountant)—I wanted none of that. As a kid I had a clear notion of what I wanted to be when I grew up, and it wasn't one of the jobs I listed above. And it wasn't archaeology, yet. No siree; I wanted to grow up to be a dinosaur. Not just any dinosaur, mind you. I wanted to be the apex predator, Tyrannosaurus rex. I wanted to be the eater, not the eaten. Attaining a certain level of maturity when I turned 6, the awful truth was revealed to me that even in America, where a little kid could aspire to be anything he or she dreamed of, a kid still could not grow up to become another species, and an extinct one at that.

Once I recovered from the trauma of that revelation, I discovered that although I couldn't grow up to be a dinosaur, at least I could become the kind of scientist who studies dinosaurs. I thought that was a pretty good fallback position, and from that moment I decided I would become a paleontologist. I became the dinosaur kid, devouring every book I could about dinosaurs, convincing my mother that it would further my education if she would buy me lots of plastic dinosaur figures, models of dinosaur skeletons, and the rest of the dino bric-a-brac available to a dino-nerd back in the mid-1950s. My fascination with dinosaurs never abated, but eventually my focus shifted to human antiquity. And the rest is, as they say, history. Well, technically, prehistory.

So it should be pretty obvious why I wanted to go to Dinosaur National Monument, a federal property that straddles the border of Utah and Colorado. What might not be obvious is why I'm including Dinosaur in my book about fifty archaeological sites. After all, the dinosaurs became extinct 65 million years ago, and the oldest settlement of North America dates to no earlier than 30,000 years ago, maybe even not much more than 15,000 years ago.

Well, it turns out that, as the result of little more than fortuitous happenstance, Dinosaur National Monument contains some of the most remarkable, beautiful, and well-preserved rock art I have ever seen. Some of it really is "can't miss"–quality art and relatively easy to access. Well-maintained dirt roads take you to short, fairly easy hiking trails to the best of the art sites; a very pleasant 2-mile hike gets you to another one.

What You Will See

You can enter the national monument from the town of Jensen in eastern Utah. The entrance road brings you to the Quarry Visitor Center. Here you can do dinosaur-related stuff and be taken to the Quarry Exhibit Hall, where you'll be able to check out a bunch of fossil dinosaur bones left in place by paleontologists. Continuing east on Cub Creek Road provides easy access to three rock art sites, signposted and located adjacent to the road.

Cub Creek Art Panels

1. Only about 0.5 mile from the visitor center, on Cub Creek Road (part of the Tilted Rocks Scenic Drive) there's a little bit of a pullout on the right where you'll see a shallow cave on the north side of the road called the Swelter Shelter. Go on a hot day in August and you'll know why it's

Figure 116. You can see the depictions of four lizards pecked into the rock face here at Cub Creek in Dinosaur National Monument, located in the far eastern border of Utah.

called that. There are some reasonably cool petroglyphs and pictographs there, but we're just getting started.

2. About 9 miles from the visitor center along Cub Creek Road, things get really good. There are two separate clusters of art (listed as viewpoints #13 and #14 on the scenic drive map and signed as such). Site #13 has lots of interesting petroglyphs, including some cool anthropomorphs who appear to be wearing large, breastplate-like necklaces. There also are some images of bighorn sheep and interesting geometric designs.

3. Continue driving to site #14. Pull off on the right where you see the sign, cross the road, and head uphill along a short trail. The trail brings you to some tall, flat rock surfaces that have what I believe to be the largest concentration of lizard petroglyphs in the United States (Figure 116). They are spectacular. See if you can find the one way off to the left and so high on the cliff that it's hard to figure how the artist put him or herself in position to create it. As you walk along the trail hugging the cliff, you'll see several small lizard images and one amazingly fresh, supersize lizard glyph that is more than 3 feet long. There are also the remnants of an image of the spirit being Kokopelli, the humpbacked flute player whose image has become iconic of the American Southwest.

Figure 117. Jenn Davis peruses the McKee Springs rock art in Dinosaur National Monument.

McKee Springs

The art at McKee Springs is not only my favorite at Dinosaur, the images there are some of the best I saw during my fifty-site odyssey (Figure 117). They are gorgeous. Naturally, they're a bit more difficult to get to. You actually have to leave the park as though you were headed back to Jensen. Travel south on UT 149 for about a mile past the visitor center and then make a right on the road toward Vernal. In 5 miles you'll see a road on your right. Take that right turn and drive 4 miles. At that point you'll see another road on the right. This is Island Park Road. Turn right and drive a little more than 11 miles on a usually passable dirt road (don't drive this road if it has rained recently). The bulk of the McKee Springs art is located on the left side of the road, but there is a very nice petroglyph panel located up the hill on the right side just before you come to the pullout across from the main art. The art at McKee Springs consists of lots of extraordinary anthropomorphs (I.31). Some of them are near life-size in the sense that the humanlike beings are about the size of a real human being. Some are wearing earrings; some are wearing necklaces. Several of them are holding what appear to be shields. One couple is holding hands. There are horned beings and upright creatures with antlers. There are bighorn sheep. And concentric circles. And spirals. It's absolutely beautiful artwork. I realize it's a long drive on a dirt road, but trust me on this one; you don't want to miss this bunch of art. Here it comes: I'm gobsmacked (I do like that word) when I see this stuff.

Deluge Shelter

Further from the visitor center, the Deluge Shelter is located near the Jones Hole Fish Hatchery, accessible from Jones Hole Road, north of the national monument.

Park at the fish hatchery and take the trail south toward the Green River. It is a very nice hike through some lovely geology, and the artwork is well signed. There are some very cool pictographs, including images of anthropomorphs, a dog, a bighorn sheep with incredible horns, and some geometric images. The art is very interesting, but you need to be pretty dedicated to drive the 44 miles from the visitor center to see it.

See the Cub Creek art; it's so close to the visitor center. See McKee Springs; it's more of a haul, but it's mind-blowing and worth the trip. Deluge Shelter is worth seeing, but it's not indispensable.

Why Is Dinosaur National Monument Important?

Fremont art is characterized by an abundance of anthropomorphs with broad shoulders and very narrow waists. Once you've seen Fremont anthropomorphs, you'll recognize them whenever you see them. The Fremont anthropomorphs sometimes wear headdresses and sometimes wear jewelry. Legs tend to be narrow and short. The art at Dinosaur is beautiful and very well preserved. You need to see it!

Site Type: Petroglyphs, pictographs

Wow Factor: ***** Dinosaur National Monument has some of the most amazing rock art I have ever seen. Don't miss it, especially the art at McKee Springs.

Museum: ***** It's all about the dinosaurs, and it's fantastic, including real fossil bones in a real bedrock exposure.

Ease of Road Access: *** The roads leading to the rock art are open depending on the weather. Be careful with dirt roads when it rains; Island Park Road leading to the McKee Springs rock art becomes impassible after it rains. It snows a bunch seasonally, and the roads close in the winter; always check ahead.

Ease of Hike: **** There are a number of relatively easy, short hikes for close-up access to the rock art.

Natural Beauty of Surroundings: *****

Kid Friendly: ***** Dinosaurs. What more do I need to say?

Food: Bring your own.

How to Get There: Take US 40 east out of Vernal, a bustling town in eastern Utah. In 13 miles you'll reach Jensen. Turn left (north) in Jensen onto UT 149, which will take you directly to the visitor center in about 7 miles.

Hours of Operation: Check the Dinosaur National Monument web page for a detailed schedule of visitor center hours and the ranger-led tours of the Quarry Exhibit Hall.

Cost: See website.

Best Season to Visit: Any time is good, so long as it's not snowing or raining and hasn't in a while.

Website: www.nps.gov/dino/historyculture/viewing-petroglyphs-and-pictographs.htm

Designation: National Monument

Site 48 Horsethief Lake State Park

Dallesport, Washington

Journal Entry

August 18, 2012

> *Roll on, Columbia roll on,*
> *Roll on, Columbia roll on.*
> *Your power is turning our darkness to dawn,*
> *Roll on, Columbia roll on.*

Iconic folksinger Woody Guthrie wrote "Roll On Columbia, Roll On" in 1941 as an anthem extolling the public work projects funded by the federal government to create jobs while at the same time harnessing the hydroelectric potential of the Columbia River marking the border between Oregon and Washington State. The eleven dams that resulted sparked an economic revival in the American Northwest by providing the infrastructure for irrigating agricultural fields and providing the energy that kindled an explosion of industrial development. Those dams also forever changed the river valley—affecting animal life, impacting stream drainage patterns, and inundating archaeological sites.

You may have heard of the Aswan Dam project in Egypt. For many of the same reasons our government funded the Columbia River project, between 1960 and 1970 the Egyptian government built a great hydroelectric facility that involved constructing a dam across the Nile. By impounding the river and creating an enormous lake, the project threatened an iconic monument built by the Egyptian Pharaoh Ramses II beginning in 1264 BC at the place called Abu Simbel. Modern Egyptians are understandably proud of their heritage and well aware of the importance of archaeotourism (an underpinning theme of this book) to their economy. An enormous salvage project was launched to save the Great Temple at Abu Simbel with its four colossal statues, each more than 60 feet high and weighing hundreds of tons.

Something similar, though on an admittedly smaller scale, occurred along the Columbia River near the Oregon city called The Dalles. In 1957 a sample of about forty stunning ancient rock art images destined to be swallowed up by the rising waters of the impounded Columbia River were jackhammered out of their homes in the cliffs and moved into storage. Luckily for the archaeological tourist, the art was brought together and placed along a short trail, which is open to the public. That trail is only a prelude to the ultimate Washington State rock art experience, a guided tour to an absolutely stunning petroglyph named Tsagaglalal, "She Who Watches."

What You Will See

Admittedly, viewing the relocated petroglyphs at Horsethief Lake isn't the perfect stop on an archaeological odyssey. Nevertheless, the art itself is so compelling and so different than anything I had seen in the Southwest, it was certainly worthwhile to have a look. About forty images were salvaged during the construction of The Dalles Dam along the Columbia River. It was readily apparent that the impounded waters of what became Lake Celilo would, among other things, inundate the canyon local Indians referred to as *Tamani Pesh-Wa*, "Written on the Rock." Those forty images have been aligned in a parade of monoliths along the Tamani Pesh-Wa Trail, immediately adjacent to the parking area at

Figure 118. Much of the art you'll see at Horsethief Lake in southern Washington State was saved by its removal when the Columbia River was dammed for hydroelectricity. I love this little critter. I think it's a wildcat.

the end of Horsethief Lake Park Road. Along the very short, paved trail (it's wheelchair accessible), you'll see a gorgeous array of various animals pecked and incised into basalt (volcanic rock) plinths: There are a number of different kinds of birds, including a handful that look like adorable, squat little owls; a bunch of bighorn sheep; a few antlered deer or elk; some anthropomorphs; and an image lying on its side with a big crack down the middle that looks, at least to me, like a small wildcat with round eyes, erect ears, whiskers, and a beard (Figure 118). I'm not sure the artist intended it to be a cat—for example, a bobcat or mountain lion—but whatever his or her intention, it's really quite striking.

Once you've examined these salvaged examples, the ranger-led tour takes you to the highlight of the trek. The trail is pretty easy and only about 0.5 mile each way. Altogether, you'll be back at your car in about 90 minutes. The pièce de résistance of the guided hike is *Tsagaglalal*, or "She Who Watches" (Figure 119). And she really does look as though she's watching over the lake. But the waters of the modern lake hide the true focus of Tsagaglalal's gaze. Where the lake now stands, even in recent memory once stood the Indian village of Wixsham. In the legend told by those who lived in the village, Tsagaglalal was the chief. One day when she was speaking to Coyote, a powerful and tricky spirit, he asked how she was planning to care for her people after she was gone. Tsagaglalal made a deal with Coyote, and he turned her into an eternal image in stone, enabling her to watch over, care for, and protect the people of her village forever. Ironically, Tsagaglalal now watches over not her village and her people but a giant hydroelectric project built by people from another place and another time.

Figure 119. True to her name, Tsagaglalal continues to watch over her dominion. And she's quite beautiful.

The image itself is pecked into a basalt boulder, with red paint added to the mix. Tsagaglalal, therefore, is a rare combination of petroglyph and pictograph. She has erect ears, enormous eyes demarcated by a series of concentric circles, and a wide mouth. The style of She Who Watches is very similar to that seen throughout the Northwest coast of North America. In three dimensions, She Who Watches would not look out of place at the top of a totem pole. The image probably dates to not much more than 300 years ago.

Why Is Horsethief Lake Important?

As is the case for all the art sites included in my fifty-site odyssey, the importance of Horsethief Lake is in a way self-evident. It's just beautiful, and everyone should visit the place to appreciate that beauty. Another reason this site is important is that without the encouragement and even insistence of local Indian tribes, themselves the descendants of those who produced the art, we might not be able to see very much of it. I mentioned previously that forty of the most impressive (but by no means all) of the art images threatened with inundation by the creation of Lake Celilo were salvaged in 1957 by being removed from their original locations, jackhammered out of the basalt cliffs into which their creators incised and pecked them. They were moved to a warehouse and left there for more than forty-five years, hidden from sight, removed from memory. But at the urging of local Indian tribes, including the

Confederated Tribes and Bands of the Yakama Nation, the Confederated Tribes of the Warm Springs Reservation of Oregon, the Confederated Tribes of the Umatilla Indian Reservation, and the Nez Perce Tribe, the art was placed in a public park only about a mile from where it had been located by the original artists. The Indians who to this day conduct religious ceremonies at the site felt an obligation to share the art "for the benefit of all people as a tribute to all living and nonliving things." That's pretty damn cool.

Additional Note

If you want to see She Who Watches, and you definitely should, you need to call ahead for a reservation on a ranger-guided tour. The number to call is (509) 439-9032. The tours are limited to twenty-five people, and it's advisable to make a reservation two to three weeks in advance.

Site Type: Pictographs, petroglyphs
Wow Factor: *** All the rock art is impressive, and *Tsagaglalal* is breathtaking.
Museum: None
Ease of Road Access: *****
Ease of Hike: ****
Natural Beauty of Surroundings: ****
Kid Friendly: ***
Food: Bring your own.
How to Get There: On the Washington side of Lake Celilo, get onto the Columbia Gorge Scenic Byway (WA 14). Turn onto the access road to Horsethief Lake State Park. Take that access road to a parking area before you cross over the railroad tracks—and definitely before you drive into the lake.
Hours of Operation: The relocated rock art can be seen 9 a.m. to 5 p.m., seven days a week, April to October. Tours to see She Who Watches are available on Friday and Saturday, April through October, at 10 a.m.
Cost: No fee for the ranger-guided tour of She Who Watches. See website for admission to the park for boating, camping, and hiking.
Best Season to Visit: April through October
Website: www.lewisandclarktrail.com/section4/orcities/thedalles/horsethief/
Designation: State park

Site 49 Bighorn Medicine Wheel

Bighorn National Forest, Wyoming

Journal Entry

August 22, 2014

The weather was awful, and by that I mean perfect.

On the previous day we had driven from Billings, Montana, to the Little Bighorn Battlefield National Monument in Crow Agency to see the memorial to the US soldiers, Indian warriors, and, as it turns out, horses who died in battle on those two terrible days of June 25 and 26, 1876. It is an amazing and evocative memorial, and clearly deserves to be included in another book focused on the fifty historical sites every American should see. After spending a day at the memorial, we drove south to Sheridan, Wyoming, to spend the night. Next, on the morning of August 22, we drove west 70 miles into the Bighorn National Forest, climbing to an elevation of about 9,600 feet until we came to the well-marked turnoff for the Bighorn Medicine Wheel.

During the 90-minute drive, we repeatedly drove into and then back out of the clouds as the road ascended into the heart of the Bighorn Mountains. The mist-shrouded mountainscape was incredible, beautiful, and also eerie. When we finally arrived at the parking area for the Medicine Wheel Trail, it was apparent that the clouds were not going to dissipate, at least not in any significant way; but the mood created seemed completely appropriate. Walking uphill 1.5 miles in the cold and thick mist to the medicine wheel, we caught glimpses of the surrounding peaks blanketed in thick fog and cloud banks. All was not gloomy, however. Along the way we laughed at the fat, furry, and playful marmots, critters that look a bit like groundhogs, scurrying among the rocks. Their cuteness was trumped by that of the tiny, impossibly adorable pikas, which look sort of like a cross between a hamster and a rabbit, but lacking the big ears. (Legend has it that Pikachu in the Pokémon universe is modeled on these little and quite real critters.) The animals were very active because, though it was only late August, they were already collecting food for the coming winter snows.

I cannot adequately describe the feelings engendered as we walked at 9,600 feet amid the clouds, pelted by cold drizzle in August, and then finally encountered the amazing, ancient monument that has served as a pilgrimage destination for local Native Americans for hundreds of years. I have been to Stonehenge in bright sunshine, and I have been there on a cloudy, rainy day. I got better photos on the sunny day, for sure, but the hair on the back of my neck rose only on the gloomy day. I had a similar feeling when standing adjacent to the Bighorn Medicine Wheel as the pale mist slowly skittered among the stone cobbles that make up the monument, providing only brief glimpses of the form of the site. It just felt right, as though this was how it was meant to be seen.

What You Will See

The Bighorn Medicine Wheel is the best preserved of a category of sites located throughout the northern plains of the United States and Canada. All together, there are about seventy existing medicine wheels, most of them in Alberta. The form of these sites is based on a common plan: stone cobbles laid out in a large circle on a flat surface, a separate pile of stones creating a hub in the center of the circle, and linear arrangements of stones radiating out from that central hub, extending out to the edge of the circle (Figure 120). These monuments are called "wheels" because they look like giant, recumbent, spoked wagon wheels.

Figure 120. Make your own pilgrimage to the Big Horn Medicine Wheel, located in the Big Horn Mountains of northern Wyoming.

The Bighorn Medicine Wheel likely was created between about 800 and 300 years ago and is still being used by Native Americans as a sacred pilgrimage destination. It is sprawling, with a diameter of about 75 feet. Along with its central cairn of stones, there are twenty-eight lines, or "spokes." That number likely is significant, likely reflecting the number of days in a lunar cycle. Additionally, in the Bighorn example there are four more stone piles located along the outside of the stone circle. The place is quiet, the air is thin (at least to this sea-level dweller; the highest point in my state of Connecticut is barely 2,300 feet), and the landscape is rugged and magnificently alien. The surroundings, along with limited visibility in the mist, made it impossible not to contemplate the meaning of the place. It seems certain that it was intentionally placed in this landscape to elicit in those who visited it at as a sacred place many of the same feelings of awe and mystery engendered in the modern visitor.

The monument itself is surrounded by a fence consisting of thick wooden log posts and heavy rope. Many visitors, continuing what may be an ancient tradition, leave offerings tied to the rope. Part of the reason for the fence is to keep people from walking onto and possibly disturbing the monument. Because the wheel is large, a wide-angle lens is required to capture the entire monument in a single photo. GoPros have very wide-angle lenses and, mounted on a selfie-stick and then raised high above your head, are a terrific choice for photographing the medicine wheel.

Native Americans, following their historical traditions, are able to enter the monument for worship. When this takes place, non-Indian visitors are asked to respect those traditions and wait to take photographs until the ceremonies are complete. Imagine tourists entering into your place of worship and taking pictures of you during your ceremonies. That would be rude.

Why Is the Bighorn Medicine Wheel Important?

It is fascinating to consider that people all over the world, in their myriad, distinct, and unrelated cultures, incorporated circular features into their sacred architecture. There are literally hundreds of stone circles (consisting of upright stones) all over Europe, for example, dating back more than 4,000 years ago. Stonehenge, the best known, is in many ways unique, but it's still fundamentally a circle of stones. It is reasonable to suggest that a circular structure built on a large scale may have been intended to represent a model of the horizon and, in turn, the world. At Stonehenge it seems pretty clear that stones were positioned to mark significant points on the horizon; for example, the place where the sun rises on the summer solstice. The spokes and cairns of the Bighorn Medicine Wheel might have served a similar purpose, marking key seasonal locations of the sun's and the moon's celestial voyages across the horizon.

For local Native Americans, the Medicine Wheel has long been a place where people go for vision quests—a sacred destination where, perhaps in isolation, a person contemplates the sacred, seeks out the divine, and reaches out to touch the face of his or her god. If you visit the Bighorn Medicine Wheel, at the very least you'll gain a firsthand appreciation for such a quest. The raw beauty of the place, the overwhelming majesty of the landscape, and the remarkable stone monument situated in its midst; well, it all makes sense that this would be a place to go to contemplate your place in the universe.

Additional Note

Realistically, the site is accessible only in summer, and even then you need to check before attempting a visit. At an elevation close to 10,000 feet, weather can be pretty vicious. It snows a lot in the area, so much so that the access road, US 14 Alt., closes down completely for long stretches. We were there in August, and a ranger told us there was snow on the ground as late as June! Figure July and August are the best times to go, but always check whether the roads are passable before attempting to visit the medicine wheel.

Site Type: Geoglyph

Wow Factor **** The medicine wheel itself is remarkable, and it still being used by Native Americans. It is a living place, not an abandoned ruin.

Museum: None

Ease of Road Access: ****

Ease of Hike: ** The hike from the trailhead to the medicine wheel is 1.5 miles, pretty much uphill all the way. That can be a tough slog at 9,600 feet if you're unaccustomed to that altitude. At least the 1.5-mile hike back to the parking lot is downhill.

Natural Beauty of Surroundings *****

Kid Friendly: **** Even if your kids aren't that interested in the medicine wheel, the adorable marmots and the even more adorable pikas that frolic along the trail will get their attention.

Food: Bring your own.

How to Get There: From Lovell (heading east) or Sheridan (heading west), hop onto US 14 Alt. and continue until you reach the intersection with WY 12. The intersection is in about 67 miles on the north (right) side if you're approaching from Sheridan and about 32 miles on the north (left) side if you're approaching from Lovell. There's a sign at the intersection directing you to the medicine wheel. Turn onto WY 12; it will take you directly to the parking lot, about 3 miles after you make the turn, where you will find a little ranger station and toilets. There should be a ranger on site to answer any questions you might have about the place.

Hours of Operation: When the site is accessible (see the "Additional Note" for this entry), it is open dawn to dusk.

Cost: Free

Best Season to Visit: Basically, August

Website: http://solar-center.stanford.edu/AO/bighorn.html

Designation: National Forest

Site 50 Dinwoody Lake Petroglyphs

Crowheart, Wyoming

Journal Entry

August 23, 2014

Most art museums organize their exhibits both chronologically and stylistically. For example, in any given museum you may find a hall that features medieval paintings, another focused on the work of surrealists, and yet another exhibiting the paintings of abstract artists. If you're like me, while you may not be an art historian or all that familiar with the various categories or subcategories of art, you clearly recognize the differences in the styles of, say, Renaissance painters like Raphael or Michelangelo; the crazy-cool, bizarre imagery of surrealists like Salvador Dali or René Magritte; and the rigid geometry of abstract artists like Mondrian.

We accept and even expect and celebrate the enormous diversity of Western art. Why should American Indian art be any different? It isn't. The rock art already featured in this book exhibits some of that diversity: the Barrier Canyon pictographs in **Site 40, Horseshoe Canyon** and **Site 45, Sego Canyon;** the Fremont-style petroglyphs in **Site 44, Nine Mile Canyon;** the Jornada Mogollon imagery seen at **Site 38, Three Rivers.** Here we will visit the unique art of the Dinwoody style seen at a number of sites in Wyoming, as typified by the place that lends its name to that style: Dinwoody Lake, near the town of Crowheart. The art I saw at Dinwoody (and another cluster located in Thermopolis, Wyoming, at Legend State Park) was unlike anything else I visited in my fifty-site odyssey. It is unique and beautiful.

What You Will See

Dinwoody Lake isn't the biggest site in my fifty-site odyssey, and the number of individual elements in the art panel isn't the largest. But the art is really quite stunning. When you reach what is essentially the terminus of West Dinwoody Lake Road and park in the cul-de-sac, just look up along the red-rock cliff to the west (Figure 121). There you will see an array of evocative images, some of which appear to be birds with outspread wings. The shape of the birds and, perhaps especially, the wide eyes suggest that the birds are owls. There are a number of images of upright, humanlike creatures with outstretched arms. Some of the creatures look like insects. All the images have richly detailed etching in their bodies, lots of horizontal and vertical lines. One of my favorites at Dinwoody Lake is a rectangular image with geometric patterns and apparent fringe at all four corners. It looks like a blanket or rug.

Why Dinwoody Lake Is Important

I think one of the things that makes the Dinwoody art important, and one of the reasons I have included it in my fifty-site odyssey, is that it reflects the glorious diversity of Native American artists while, at the same time, showing the vast geographic spread of North American rock art. Using rock as a canvas onto which artists depicted plants and animals, spirits and gods, and realistic images of their

Figure 121. Dinwoody-style rock art is exemplified here at Dinwoody Lakes in central Wyoming.

surroundings, as well as phantasmagorical, almost hallucinatory images whose meaning we can only guess at, situates those artists firmly in the history of human creativity. Ancient America was populated by their own, and now unfortunately anonymous, Rembrandts and Picassos, Dalis, Kadinskys, and Rockwells. Though we will never know their names, we can revel in their art and in so doing afford them a kind of immortality.

Additional Note

The access road to the art—West Dinwoody Lake Road—is dirt, but like many encountered on our odyssey it's passable as long as it hasn't rained recently. After you turn onto it from US 26, you will reach the northern margin of the lake in a little less than 3 miles. At 4.3 miles from US 26, the road curves around to the right (west) when you have reached the end of the lake's main body. Keep on that same road and you'll see another body of water, Upper Dinwoody Lake. At a little more than 6 miles from US 26, close to the northwestern margin of Upper Dinwoody Lake, the road pretty much peters out and part of it curves back around into a cul-de-sac and parking area. Park here and look up at the cliff. Enjoy the art!

Site Type: Petroglyphs

Wow Factor: *** The art is beautiful.

Museum: None

Ease of Road Access: *** West Dinwoody Lake Road isn't particularly well maintained, but it is flat. A high-clearance vehicle is a good idea.

Ease of Hike: ***** There's really no hiking involved.

Natural Beauty of Surroundings: **** The lake is beautiful. We saw pronghorn antelope grazing nearby.

Kid Friendly: ***

Food: Bring your own.

How to Get There: The Dinwoody Lake petroglyphs are located on Wind River Indian Reservation lands, about 2 hours from Yellowstone National Park or 3.5 hours from Cody, Wyoming. Begin on US 26, an east–west highway that runs from Dubois to Crowheart in the middle of the state. From US 26 turn south onto West Dinwoody Lake Road. That dirt road will take you to the rock art.

Hours of Operation: There are no specific hours for Dinwoody Lake, but use common sense and go there during daylight hours. Arrive after sunrise; leave before sunset.

Cost: Free

Best Season to Visit: Any time other than winter is good.

Website: www.tripadvisor.com/ShowTopic-g28973-i480-k7050526-Dubois_and_dinwoody_petroglyph_locations-Wyoming.html

Designation: Wind River Indian Reservation

If You Want to Know More

How Archaeology Gets Done

There are plenty of useful and short introductory guides to how archaeologists study the past. A few of the best are:

Ashmore, Wendy & Robert Sharer. 2013. *Discovering Our Past: A Brief Introduction*. New York: McGraw-Hill.

Bahn, Paul. 2012. *Archaeology: A Very Short Introduction*. New York: Oxford University Press.

Fagan, Brian. 2016. *Archaeology: A Brief Introduction*. London: Routledge. [Brian is a prolific writer, and his textbooks have deservedly been standards in archaeology courses for many years.]

First Peoples

New evidence related to the earliest human settlement of the Americas is published so frequently, it is extremely difficult for book publishers to keep up. A book published today will likely be out of date very quickly, especially regarding advances made in DNA recovery and analysis. Nevertheless, there are several good reads on the subject. For general readers, though several years old now, I still highly recommend David Meltzer's book on the subject. He is a wonderful writer and a thoughtful researcher.

Adovasio, J. M. & Jake Page. 2009. *The First Americans: In Pursuit of Archaeology's Greatest Mystery*. New York: Modern Library. [James Adovasio was the director of excavations at **Site 1, Meadowcroft Rockshelter**.]

Dillehay, Thomas D. 2008. *The Settlement of the Americas: A New Prehistory*. New York: Basic Books.

Graf, Kelly E., Caroline V. Ketron & Michael R. Waters (eds.). 2014. *Paleoamerican Odyssey*. College Station, Texas: Texas A&M University Press.

Meltzer, David J. 2009. *First Peoples in a New World: Colonizing Ice Age America*. University of California Press.

If you want to learn about the latest discoveries related to the First Peoples, your best bet is to go online and search the Science News website: www.sciencenews.org.

The Mound Builders

The best place to read about the myth of the mound builders is Robert Silverberg's book:

Silverberg, Robert. 1989. *The Mound Builders*. Athens, Ohio: Ohio University Press.

An early publication of the Smithsonian Institution has spectacular nineteenth-century illustrations of what the mounds looked like:

Squire, E. G., and E. H. Davis. 1848. *Ancient Monuments of the Mississippi Valley: Comprising the Results of Extensive Original Surveys*. Smithsonian Contributions to Knowledge, Vol. 1. New York: AMS Press. (Reprinted in 1973 for the Peabody Museum of Archaeology and Ethnology, Harvard University.)

For a great read with fantastic photos and illustrations, I highly recommend Brad Lepper's book (listed below). Its focus is ancient Ohio peoples, with their remarkable complement of burial, enclosure, and effigy mounds.

Lepper, Bradley T. 2004. *Ohio Archaeology: An Illustrated Chronicle of Ohio's Ancient American Indian Culture*. Wilmington, Ohio: Orange Frazer Press.

There are a number of terrific books that focus on the platform mound builders along with mound builder villages of the Midwest and Southeast, some highlighting individual sites in my list of fifty:

Birmingham, Robert A. & Lynne G. Goldstein. 2005. *Aztalan: Mysteries of an Ancient Indian Town.* Madison, Wisconsin: Wisconsin Historical Society. **[Site 22]**

Gibson, J. L. 2001. *The Ancient Mounds of Poverty Point: Place of Rings.* Gainesville, Florida: University of Florida Press. **[Site 11]**

Milner, George. 2004. *The Moundbuilders: Ancient Peoples of Eastern North America.* London: Thames and Hudson.

Welch, Paul D. 1991. *Moundville's Economy.* Tuscaloosa, Alabama. University of Alabama Press. **[Site 2]**

And then there's Cahokia **[Site 9]**:

Iseminger, William. 2010. *Cahokia Mounds: America's First City.* Charleston, South Carolina: The History Press. [If you read one or two books about Cahokia, this should be one of them.]

Pauketat, Timothy R. 1994. *The Ascent of Chiefs: Cahokia and Mississippian Politics in Native America.* Tuscaloosa, Alabama: University of Alabama Press.

————. 2009. *Cahokia: Ancient America's Great City on the Mississippi.* New York: Viking. [If you read one or two books about Cahokia, this should be one of them.]

Pauketat, Timothy R., T. E. Emerson & Susan Alt (eds.). 2015. *Medieval Mississippians: The Cahokian World.* Santa Fe: School for Advanced Research.

Bill Iseminger is an archaeologist and the assistant site manager of the Cahokia Mounds State Historic Site. Tim Pauketat is a professor in the Department of Anthropology, University of Illinois, Champaign-Urbana. Both have devoted their careers to the study and preservation of Cahokia, and both are terrific writers.

The Cliff Dwellings and Great Houses of the American Southwest

Frazier, Kendrick. 1999. *People of Chaco: A Canyon and Its Culture.* New York: W. W. Norton and Company. **[Site 31]**

Noble, David Grant. 1991. *Ancient Ruins of the Southwest.* Flagstaff, Arizona: Northland Publishing.

Plog, Stephen. 1997. *Ancient Peoples of the American Southwest.* London: Thames and Hudson.

Reid, Jefferson & Stephanie Whittlesey. 1997. *The Archaeology of Ancient Arizona.* Tucson, Arizona: University of Arizona Press.

One of the best writers about exploring the Southwest is the prolific David Roberts. He writes with enormous passion about his visits to various archaeological sites in a couple of wonderful books I recommend highly:

Roberts, David. 1996. *In Search of the Old Ones: Exploring the Anasazi World of the Southwest.* New York: Simon and Schuster.

————. 2015. *The Lost Worlds of the Old Ones.* New York: W. W. Norton.

Rock Art

There are lots of books about American rock art. The absolute standard is Polly Schaafsma's *Indian Rock Art of the Southwest.* After that, there are lots of detailed regional guides. A few of the best are:

Cole, Sally J. 2009. *Legacy on Stone: Rock Art of the Colorado Plateau and Four Corners Region.* Boulder: Johnson Books.

Grant, Campbell, James W. Baird & J. Kenneth Pringle. 1968. *Rock Drawings of the Coso Range.* Ridgecrest, California: Maturango Museum. [**Site 34, Little Petroglyph Canyon**]

Micnhimer, D. Russel & LeeAnn Johnston. 2010. *Where to See Rock Art: Washington, Oregon, Idaho.* Prineville, Oregon: Pendulum Press. [**Site 48**]

Schaafsma, Polly. 1971. *The Rock Art of Utah.* Salt Lake City: University of Utah Press.

Spangler, Jerry D. 2013. *Nine Mile Canyon: The Archaeological History of an American Treasure.* Salt Lake City: The University of Utah Press. [**Site 44**]

Spangler, Jerry D. & Donna K. Spangler. 2003. *Horned Snakes and Axle Grease: A Roadside Guide to the Archaeology and History of Nine Mile Canyon.* Salt Lake City: Uinta Publishing. [**Site 44**; this is an extremely detailed, mile-by-mile tour of **Nine Mile Canyon**.]

Whitley, David S. 1996. *A Guide to Rock Art Sites: Southern California and Southern Nevada.* Missoula, Montana: Mountain Press Publishing.

To read more about **Site 40, Horseshoe Canyon,** the National Park Service provides an online book with a number of articles by archaeologists. You can access it here: www.nps.gov/cany/planyour visit/upload/HorseshoeBook.pdf.

Alternative Archaeology

The best book to get an archaeologist's perspective on alternative, out-there archaeology is *Frauds, Myths, and Mysteries: Science and Pseudoscience in Archaeology.* That was written by, now, what is his name . . . oh, yeah . . . Kenneth L. Feder. That would be me. I know what you're thinking: *Man; he is shamelessly plugging another one of his books here.* That's entirely untrue. I am very much ashamed.

Feder, Kenneth L. 2014. *Frauds, Myths, and Mysteries: Science and Pseudoscience in Archaeology,* 8th edition. New York: McGraw-Hill.

Additional Sites

Arizona

- **Honanki Heritage Site** (https://en.wikipedia.org/wiki/Honanki). Small cliff dwelling with rock art easily accessible from Sedona.

- **Palatki Heritage Site** (https://en.wikipedia.org/wiki/Palatki_Heritage_Site). Small cliff dwelling with rock art easily accessible from Sedona. Nearby are some truly beautiful pictographs, ensconced in a cave near an abandoned homestead.

- **Pueblo Grande Museum** (www.pueblogrande.org). Great House and evidence of ancient irrigation, located in downtown Phoenix. Great on-site museum.

- **Tonto National Monument** (www.nps.gov/Tont/index.htm). Dramatic cliff dwellings.

- **Tuzigoot National Monument** (www.nps.gov/tuzi/index.htm). Ancient pueblo dramatically situated atop a hill.

- **V-Bar-V Petroglyph Heritage Site** (www.verdevalleyarchaeology.org/VBarV). A short hike brings you to a small panel of some very impressive petroglyphs.

California

- **Inscription Canyon/Black Canyon** (www.blm.gov/ca/st/en/fo/barstow/petroglyph1.html). Great rock art, but you'll need a four-wheel-drive vehicle to access it.

- **Volcanic Tablelands** (www.thesierraweb.com/generalinfo/petroglyphs.cfm). Several hiking trails to rock art panels: Fish Slough, Chalfant, Chidago, and Red Canyon.

Indiana

- **Kincaid Mounds** (www.kincaidmounds.com). Well-preserved complex of platform mounds viewable from a distance.

Iowa

- **Effigy Mounds National Monument** (www.nps.gov/efmo/index.htm). Earth mounds in the shape of birds and bears. Lots of bears. No viewing towers, so the patterns are difficult to see.

Minnesota

- **Indian Mounds Park** (www.stpaul.gov/indian-mounds-regional-park). Well-preserved burial mounds in a municipal park, located on the bluffs near St. Paul.
- **Jeffers Petroglyphs** (http://jefferspetroglyphs.com). Thousands of images of animals, humanlike images, and atlatls etched into hard quartzite. Ask the site manager to give you a tour.

Mississippi

- **Emerald Mound Site** (www.nps.gov/nr/travel/mounds/eme.htm). Massive mound that effectively reconfigured the landscape, producing a monumental platform on the top of which native people constructed platform mounds and houses.
- **Natchez Trace Parkway** (www.nps.gov/natr/index.htm). Several small but impressive mound sites (Boyd, Bynum, Owl Creek, Pharr, Bear) are open to the public scattered along the 444-mile historical highway.
- **Winterville Mounds** (https://en.wikipedia.org/wiki/Winterville_Site). Impressive site with a number of platform mounds.

Nebraska

- **Hudson-Meng Education and Research Center** (www.fossilfreeway.net/hudson.php). Large accumulation of in-place bison bones, with a shelter built over the site. The animals were killed by human hunters, perhaps 10,000 years ago.

Nevada

- **Valley of Fire State Park** (http://parks.nv.gov/parks/valley-of-fire-state-park/). Impressive petroglyph panels including Atlatl Rock, with lots of examples of images of spear throwers.

New Mexico

- **Gila Cliff Dwellings National Monument** (www.nps.gov/gicl/index.htm). Interesting cliff dwellings almost entirely within a couple of caves.

North Dakota

- **Knife River Indian Villages National Historical Site** (www.nps.gov/knri/index.htm). Visible remnants of an Indian village occupied into the nineteenth century and painted by the artist George Catlin.

Ohio

- **Junction Group** (www.earthworksconservancy.org/what-is-the-junction-group/). Though no longer visible, remote sensing has enabled these impressive mound enclosures to be reimagined in cut grass.

- **Leo Petroglyphs State Memorial** (http://leopetroglyph.com). Nice set of unique petroglyphs protected by a wooden shelter.
- **Seip Earthworks** (www.nps.gov/hocu/learn/historyculture/seip-earthworks.htm). Impressive mortuary complex. Some of the enclosure wall has been preserved, as has the primary burial mound, an impressive earthwork with an oval footprint.

Oklahoma

- **Spiro Mounds** (www.okhistory.org/sites/spiromounds.php). Large mound site. On-site museum with lots of replicas (oh, well) of very impressive shell artifacts excavated at the site.

Tennessee

- **Chucallisa Indian Village** (www.memphis.edu/chucalissa/). Mound and plaza complex. On-site C. H. Nash Museum devoted to the site.

Texas

- **Hueco Tanks State Park and Historic Site** (http://tpwd.texas.gov/state-parks/hueco-tanks/activities). Unique and beautiful pictographs. Contact the site for a guided tour of the most impressive examples of the art.

Utah

- **Capitol Reef National Park** (www.nps.gov/care/index.htm). There are some very impressive petroglyphs of bighorn sheep along the main road through the monument.
- **Edge of the Cedars State Park** (stateparks.utah.gov/parks/edge-of-the-cedars/). Kiva you can enter. Preserved and very beautiful kiva murals in the fantastic on-site museum.

Vermont

- **Bellows Falls Petroglyphs** (https://en.wikipedia.org/wiki/Bellows_Falls_Petroglyph_Site). Phantasmagorical rock art of ghostly faces tucked alongside the Connecticut River.

Wyoming

- **Legend Rock State Petroglyph Site** (http://wyoparks.state.wy.us/Site/SiteInfo.aspx?siteID=34). Short trail along a low rock exposure with dozens of examples of impressive Dinwoody-style petroglyphs like those at Dinwoody Lake.

Index

Note: Page references for figures are italicized; color photos are referenced by figure number.